MICROSCOPY OF TRANSITING PLANETS SIMPLIFIED VOLUME-5

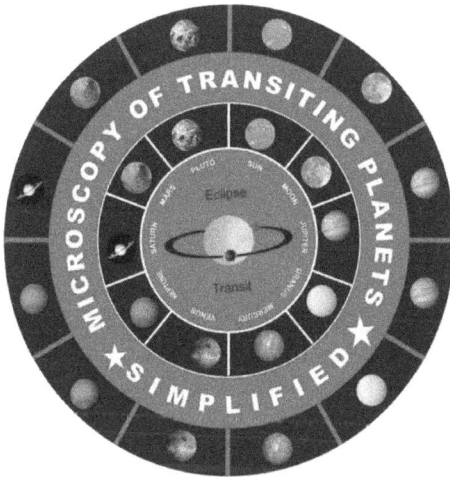

Baldev Bhatia

Become
Shakespeare
.com

First published in 2015 by

BecomeShakespeare.com
Wordit Content Design & Editing Services Pvt Ltd
Newbridge Business Centre, C38/39,
Parinee Crescenzo Building, G Block,
Bandra Kurla Complex, Bandra East,
Mumbai 400 051, India
T: +91 8080226699

ISBN 978-93- 83952-47-2

With the blessing of GOD GANESHA

WITH THE BLESSISNG OF LORD SHIVA

OMKAR

WITH THE BLESSINGS OF GOD SHIVA AND GODESS PARVATI

"OM NAMAH SHIVAY"

WITH THE BLESSING OF MAA SARASWATI

MICROSCOPY OF
TRANSITING PLANETS
SIMPLIFIED
VOLUME-5

ABOUT THE BOOK

In Astrology, the planetary transits are important to understand the effects of planets on an individual at a given moment. Transiting of a planet means movement of that planet from one sign to another, and from one constellation to another. When it enters or makes a connection with any zodiac sign it shows some effects which can be either good or bad.

This book then goes to reveal, ascertaining the real facts of life and the destiny as to what is stored for each and every reader in his or her future. Various chapters have been covered and maximum emphasis have been paid to cover the subjects pertaining to the significance of different houses in one's chart; different Zodiac signs, planets and their placements in different houses and signs and the effect and influence of the Transiting Planets on them.

The book has all the ingredients to bring to the millions of readers the 'real knowledge' of the Transiting Planets by letting them know more about themselves in detail through their Zodiac Signs and the effect and influence of the Transiting Planets on them. This book also intends to guide the readers to achieve their personal goals with ease that would assist them to overcome all the problems, crises, speed breakers and the unforeseen negatives forces, in their lives, as not to get worried or disheartened or depressed in their lives if the influence of the Transiting Planets is weak, dis guesting depressing, unfavourable and disappointing.

The manuscript also guides all People, who are keen and interested; to keep a Transit Calendar that shows the transit of planets in a given year. Since each planet moves at its respective pace which is different from others, so its time of transit is also different from others.

Through this marvellous scripture one can understand that during the transits of planets, it is generally best to first look at the outer planet (slower-moving) transits and cycles in order, to get an overview, and a real context before refining the predictions with inner planet cycles and transits.

Outer planet transits affect us in large chunks they can be active before the transit is exact by aspect, but we have seen the following: Many times an outer planet transits our natal point once by direct motion, moves forward and then retrogrades back over that point, only to turn direct again and pass that same natal point for the final time in that cycle.

This book goes to emphasise that if the influence is good, it brings good or positive changes or events in life. But negative influence gives undesired results. One needs to understand that no matter what aspect a transiting planet makes to natal planets, if the birth charts does not support the same aspect or similar aspect, then the energy imposed by the transiting planet is lessened.

It is hoped that this book would work and guide the readers to achieve their personal goals and would assist them to overcome all the crises, speed breakers and the unforeseen negatives forces, in their lives, and which would assist them in achieving their targets with a aim to reach to the destined goal of their financial prosperity, maximum happiness and progress in life.

By scripting this book the author has put his entire life experience in promoting Astrology in various fields. He has done so in order to serve millions of curious readers of this mystic science with a good intension of imparting them the basic knowledge of Transiting Planets in Astrology through this marvellous scripture.

This book "Microscopy of Transiting Planets." is just one of the many fruits of his passion and he describes it as a "Unique Guide to Happy Living" even if the effect and influence of the Transiting Planets is week, depression and negative. The book encourages and empowers its readers to be bold, brave and strong and to take control over their lives by letting go of the negativity in them even if the effect of this Transiting Planets becomes depressing and unfavourable.

This book guides his readers to ward off the negativity in them and also, asserts, its readers to be happy, successful and prosperous as many people have been deprived off happiness because of negativity prevailing in them,

" Bhatia says, "This book will help them to strengthen their will power and generate confidence in them which they could have lost in today's hectic world." Microscopy of Transiting Planets offers an informative glimpse into the fascinating world of Astrology and practical ways of utilizing its principles in one's journey towards happiness of life.

The author after meeting several thousand people, who have suffered negativity in their personal lives and those who have lead miserable lives, totally being depressed and dejected has finally come to the conclusion of penning down this marvellous scripture with the main aim, purpose, and intension of writing this manuscript is to impart the basic knowledge of how to become bold, courageous, and how to throw away the negative forces in them. His manuscripts reveal a whole lot of information when one is in search for the truths of a positive attitude and a happy peaceful and prosperous life.

BALDEV BHATIA
AUTHOR

MICROSCOPY OF
TRANSITING PLANETS
SIMPLIFIED
VOLUME-5

ABOUT THE AUTHOR

Astrology has stood the test of times ever since it revealed the Mystery and the Mastery of the ancient wisdom of forecasting the influence of the stars on human bodies.

The author Baldev Bhatia a renowned and world famous Astrologer has penned several simple books on Astrology-this mysterious subject that reveals the true perception of knowing oneself through the art of prediction.
Professionally the author has put his entire life experience in promoting Astrology in various fields with a view to serve the millions of curious readers of this mystic science with the intension of imparting them the real knowledge of Astrology through various marvellous scriptures.

The Astrologer has been associated with Astrology for the past 45 years and has been practicing Astrology in various forms. The Author-cum Astrologer has been in touch with general public throughout his life and has been practicing phycology and pubic healing. His intension is to guide his readers to achieve their personal goals with ease that would assist them to overcome all the problems, crises, speed breakers and the unforeseen negatives forces, in their lives so as not to get disheartened or depressed in their lives and finally lead a happy life and peaceful life, after going through this manuscript of "Microscopy of Transiting Planets"

More over Mr. Baldev Bhatia the Author is an established writer himself with a sound reputation of being a good

Astrologer has put his valuable life experience in promoting positivity among his clients. The author also shares with millions of curious readers the 'real knowledge' by letting them know more about themselves in detail and also about their in born positive qualities, possessed by them and guides them to ward off the negativity in them, by getting to know as how to lead an happy and powerful life., without caring for the worries troubling them, the negative forces influencing them, which needs to be discarded forever, for a positive and happy living if the influence of the Transiting Planets happens to be unfavourable, negative and disheartening.

The main object of writing this manuscript is to impart the basic knowledge of how to become positive, bold, strong, courageous, and how to throw away the negative forces and become a happy person in life even though, if the effect of the Transiting Planet happens to be negative disheartening and depressing.

The author also shares the valuable experience of his life with his readers through his valuable and helpful book. His published books "Microscopy of Astrology", Microscopy of Numerology", Microscopy of Remedies, Microscopy of Happy Living guide his readers to achieve their personal goals with ease and assists them to overcome all the problems, crises, and the unforeseen negatives forces, in their lives gracefully which guides them not get disheartened or depressed at any stage of life irrespective of all the odds and negative forces troubling them.

His readers have gained good experience going through his useful and purposeful books. His books have made his readers to feel secure, sound and have also encouraged them to face their destiny with immense strength and have also given them the power to face the challenges of this universe with utter confidence zeal and power.

The author Baldev Bhatia leads way to happiness, success, positivity and advices his people suffering from depression and negativity in their personal lives to wake up and lead a positive and happy life and to understand, properly the effect and influence of these transiting planets.

After meeting hundreds and hundreds of depressed dejected disappointed and unhappy people from all over the world and people from all walks of life and he being a highly experienced astrologer and consultant in Astrology and Numerology felt it necessary to write books on Happiness, Love, Peace which could guides his readers to ward of their depression, dejection, hatred and negativity in their lives. His books have also revealed to his readers to attain positive- ness in their lives so that they could easily achieve their path of glory and reach to be a positive and happy person and also be a brave strong and courageous human being.

His books have given gracefully accepted by the people worldwide. His books have helped the masses to achieve and lead a life full of positivity, boldness, strength, courage happiness and have generated confidence in depressed and dejected people. His books have helped his clients and readers to lead a good, peaceful and happy life.

His books have been very different as they guide and help the readers to strengthen their will power and confidence which the readers have lost in today's world. In order to encourage his readers and to help them, in all walks of life the esteem Author finally decided to manuscript the following books in the interest and happiness of the universal world.

1. Microscopy of Astrology
2. Microscopy of Numerology
3. Microscopy of Remedies
4. Microscopy of Happy Living
   All published by Partridge India Pvt Ltd
   (A Penguin Publishing Company)
5. Microscopy of Transiting Planets Vol-1
   Published by Notion Press Pvt Ltd
6. Microscopy of Transiting Planets
   Vol-3 and Vol-4
7. Microscopy of Transiting Planets
   Vol-5 is under process

He finally wishes his readers all the success happiness and prosperity. He always praises God and prayers Him with the following words.

"May the Heavens Shower Peace Prosperity and
Happiness to All"

"GOD BLESS YOU"
"THANKS FOR READING "

BALDEV BHATIA
AUTHOR

MICROSCOPY OF TRANSITING PLANETS SIMPLIFIED VOLUME-5

INTRODUCTION

Astrology has stood the test of time ever since it revealed the mystery and the mastery of the ancient wisdom of forecasting the influence of the stars on human bodies.

The time in which someone has been born, refers to their characteristics; appearance; personality; profession, career; business, finances, their match with other Zodiac signs; romance, marriage, weakness and finally their health and disease.

This book then goes to reveal, ascertaining the real facts of life and the destiny as to what is stored for each and every reader in his or her future. Various chapters have been covered and maximum emphasis have been paid to cover the subjects pertaining to the significance of transiting planets in different houses in one's chart; different Zodiac signs, planets and their placements in different houses and signs.

Natal Planetary Aspects
This influence represents growth and expansiveness. You are more aware of moral issues, and have a desire to improve and learn. Optimism and confidence are basic elements in the energy of this transit. Natal interplanetary links and relationships between the Planets and are calculated by precise degree measurements.

Now we need to find out if your aspects are exact, close or wide by examining the degrees of the planets in transit.

Aspects to the natal Sun, Moon and the and the ruler of your Rising Sign are important and influential aspects are to be considered to the Trines, Squares, Oppositions and Conjunctions of their links and aspects. Aspects that are exact are more influential than those that are wide. We need also to know the Elements which show the method of expression of these planets using.

General Guidelines and Overview of Conjunctions Oppositions Squares Trines
They are used for Natal or Transiting Aspects are to be used only as a general guide to understand their interpretative influence. This could be a period in which you realize a long-term goal. Your enthusiasm is boundless, and you are inclined to take the high road in your dealings with others.
Minor aspect of Planets is of:

Sun, Moon, Mercury, Venus and Mars

SUN
When Sun Conjuncts other planets: This denotes Accentuates initiative & will power to work with other Planets involved. When Sun Opposes: This indicates Conflicts of direction & will to Planets, Sign and House involved. When Sun Squares: This shows Difficulty and frustration in using will with other Planet and House involved. When Sun Trines: This is the sign of Easy creative self-expression between the Sun and other Planet and House which can be often seen.

MOON
When Moon Conjuncts: This is the indication of Heightened emotional responses influence other Planet, Sign and House. When Moon Opposes: Emotionally difficult situations influencing Planet and House opposed.

When Moon Squares: This gives response of Challenges of emotional frustration and incidents to Planet and House involved. When Moon Trines: This leads to strength of Emotional balance with other Planets influence.

MERCURY
When Mercury Conjuncts: This creates Mental abilities are enhanced and heightened in connection with other Planets. When Mercury Opposes: This is the indication of Difficulty in communicating with others and matters relating to Planet and House involved. When Mercury Squares: This leads to Argumentative and blocked in matters relating to the Planet and House involved. When Mercury Trines: This shows the signs of Inspired and harmonious abilities influence other Planet and House.

VENUS When Venus Conjuncts: This creates Ease and harmony in expression; works well with other Planet and House influence. When Venus Opposes: This is the Areas of House, Sign and Planet concerned are Out of Sync and receiving inharmonious influence. When Venus Squares: Indication of that There is unfulfilled and blocked emotion transmitted to energy of the Planet and House concerned. When Venus Trines: Good and beneficial accepts of Benefits of harmony, ease, grace and artistic expression influence relationships between planets

MARS
When Mars Conjuncts other planets: it is Courageous indication Energizing & passionate influence to Planet involved. When Mars Opposes: it leads to Rash and aggressive opposition to Planet concerned. When Mars Squares: Having thwarted actions and misdirected energy to Planet and House concerned. When Mars Trines: Possessing Strong passionate energy source working well with Planet and House concerned.

Major aspect of Planets is of:
Jupiter Saturn Uranus, Neptune and Pluto

Jupiter
When Jupiter Conjuncts other planets: Encourages
Enhancement and boost of optimism to Planet involved.
When Jupiter Opposes: It shows and Relates to difficulties
in estimating actual abilities of Planet and House
concerned. When Jupiter Squares: It creates and indicates
the challenges ability to utilize expansive energy between
Planets. When Jupiter Trines: It showers and indicates
Additional optimistic expansive resource for Planet and
House involved.

Saturn
When Saturn Conjuncts other planets: It depends on the
other Planets. This is an indication that This Planet receives
its structure well and inhibits its expression. When Saturn
Opposes: Isolates, shuns and restricts energy of other
Planets. When Saturn Squares: Frustration and difficult
circumstance to overcome in connection with Planet and
House involved. When Saturn Trines: Concise abilities and
Good Fortune enhance planet placement and House.

Uranus
When Uranus Conjuncts other planets: Dynamic
enhancement which may or may not work well with
involved Planet. When Uranus Opposes: It shows
demanding erratic energy directed towards Planet and
House involved. When Uranus Squares: It indicates
Impulsive influence directed towards Planet, House and
Sign. When Uranus Trines: it leads to Originality and
excitement energizes Planet and House involved

Neptune

When Neptune Conjuncts other planets: This gives The Intuitive and unconscious subtle influence units with Planet are its outcome. When Neptune Opposes: This is Enlightening or Disillusioning. Confusion and unreliability influence to other Planet involved. When Neptune Squares:

This leads to The Disorienting vague and the unclear direction concerning other planet are involved. When Neptune Trines: It shows Inspirational and creative influence.

Pluto

When Pluto Conjuncts other planets: It's Penetrating and concentrating abilities to boost and revive other Planets energy. When Pluto Opposes: Dominating and alienating relationships between Planets occur. When Pluto Squares: It's Dictatorial, overbearing influence in relationship to other Planet or House take place. When Pluto Trines: Powerful Will to use creatively in connection with other Planet.

A thought of penning down the wonders of the mystic science of Astrology has lured the astrologer and now published author Baldev Bhatia to bring to the millions of readers the 'real knowledge' by letting them know more about themselves in detail through their Zodiac Signs, the effect and influence of the transiting planets on them reveals a whole lot of information when one is in search for the truths as foretold by the stars.

Dated: February 15th 2015

SD/-
Baldev Bhatia
Author

MICROSCOPY OF TRANSITING PLANETS SIMPLIFIED VOLUME-5

PREFACE

ASPECTS TO NATAL PLANETS

In Astrology, the planetary transits are important to understand the main effects of planets on an individual at a given moment in his chart. Transiting of a planet denotes the movement of that planet from one sign to another and from one constellation to another. When it enters or makes a connection with any of the zodiac sign it shows some effects which can be either good or bad and influences its governing bodies.

We ought to know that if the influence is good, it brings good or positive changes or events in life. But negative influence gives undesired results. People, who are interested, keep a transit calendar that shows the transit of planets in a given year. Since each planet moves at its respective pace which is different from others, so its time of transit is also different from others.

We need to understand that when a planet become combust and retrograde which are indicated in the transit calendar. All seven planets (Sun, Moon, Mars, Mercury, Jupiter, Venus, and Saturn) and two nodes (of Dragon's Head and Dragon's Tail) have different movement and time of transits on twelve zodiac signs.

It shows generally the planetary transits of Dragon's Head and Dragon's Tail along Jupiter and Saturn have long lasting effects. Transits of planets like moon and mercury bring quick changes. Transit of planets and their effects are always studied with reference to the natal chart of a person. The fixed stars are what make up the constellations or signs. The transiting planets in a chart are where the planets are currently in the sky. As they form aspects to the natal planets in a chart they trigger events in an individual's life.

It is commonly understandable that while the transits of the two slow moving and powerful planets Saturn & Jupiter are very important as they have a long duration effects, the transits effects of the other planets cannot be ignored especially for the short duration effects.

Jupiter takes almost twelve years to come full circle. Therefore, every three years or so, Jupiter will transit conjunct, square, or opposite a natal point. When that natal point is an intensely personal planet or point such as the Sun, Moon, Ascendant, Mercury, Venus, or Mars we feel its effects in a similarly personal way.

Jupiter transits perhaps receive more positive press than they deserve, as those of us who have waited for Jupiter to transit conjunct our Sun can come to test, because if we wait for Jupiter to bestow us with wonderful gifts, we are sure to be disappointed if we do not get them. What Jupiter does do is infuse us with the license to dream, to hope, and to feel good about ourselves.

The planet Jupiter's influence acts to expand the desire to experience something new, for acknowledging more freedom to explore new possibilities and enlarge our confidence, level of joy is increased in these areas of life, and we feel motivated to improve or gain in these areas of life. These are times in our lives when we feel a little more free and confident, and when we are not as aware of restraints. Problems arise when we overdo, and are so confident that we ignore reality and don't think of consequences. However, just as we need Saturn to remind us that we need to buckle down, we also need Jupiter to remind us that we won't get very far if we don't believe in ourselves.

Jupiter acts to expand and it gives us hope and enthusiasm. Serious matters may grab our attention now, or circumstances are such that we are required to show more competency and responsibility. Jupiter is the planet of possibilities and it offers us promises. Whether these promises are realistic is something to consider seriously. However, Jupiter is a jovial influence, and we all need that kind of energy from time to time.

When Jupiter transits a natal planet, it gives that part of our personality a boost, reminding us that we may have been underestimating our capabilities. It invites us to have some faith in ourselves and our abilities. Through this marvellous scripture the author intends to guide the readers to achieve their personal goals with ease that would assist them to overcome all the Problems, Crises, Speed Breakers and the unforeseen Negatives Forces, in their lives as not to get worried or disheartened or depressed in their lives if the influence of the transiting planets is weak or depressed and unfavourable.

By scripting this book the author has put his entire life experience in promoting Astrology in various fields. He has done so in order to serve millions of curious readers of this mystic science with a good intension of imparting them the real knowledge of Astrology through this marvellous scripture. The astrologer has been associated with Astrology for the past 45 years and has been practicing Astrology in various forms. His predictions have been very useful, purposeful, and a pin point to the service of mankind. He wishes success for all his readers.

The author Mr. Baldev Bhatia, expresses his sincere thanks to Ms. Alpa Shah Director, Travel Company of UK, Ms. Vimla Gidwani Lendway owner of a travel company of Las Vegas USA, Mrs. Rita Vaswani Banker of reputed bank of Las Vegas USA for helping and encouraging him to pen down this book in the interest and lovers of astrology. The author is also grateful and thankful to for publishing his book.

SD/-
BALDEV BHATIA
AUTHOR

Dated: February 15th 2015

MICROSCOPY OF
TRANSITING PLANETS
SIMPLIFIED
VOLUME-5

INDEX

MICROSCOPY OF TRANSITING PLANETS SIMPLIFIED VOLUME-5

CHAPTER ONE

Transit results of Sun from natal Moon

Transit of Planet Sun from First house of Moon Sign

Watch your tongue at your workplace and don't be stubborn. This is a positive time when you express your deepest feelings openly and intensely. There will be difficulties at your workplace and a temporary change in place is possible. You must be extra careful about your dealings and sayings as you may get a bad reputation at the workplace. You need to put in a lot of extra efforts to complete your tasks as things will not move smoothly. Money will not come on time.

Your dreams and ideals may conspire to ignore and push aside the need in you for real inner growth and transformation. Control your temper and irritability as it is a period of disagreements and clashes with your spouse and may affect your married life. Avoid disputes and showdowns with family members and friends and make sure you good rest to minimise irritability and mental tension. Peace and harmony will be at a premium this month.

You are emotionally charged now. You should be aware that your current state of mind can, in an indirect way, determine much about how you will be feeling in the month ahead. You will be tired and irritable. Your health would need extra attention and you will be susceptible to stomach problems, irritability and infection in the eyes. Heart and BP patients should take extra care. It is an accident prone time and hence you should avoid physically risky activities. You may undertake unnecessary travels and may not get the desired result.

Transit of Planet Sun from Second house of Moon Sign

There could be loss in business and in your professional field. Your projects and endeavours may not bring in the desired result. Relations with your superiors will be spoiled. Money will be at a premium as this is a period of financial tightness. Profits and wealth will have adverse effects especially for people in the trading and finance related business. You will overcome problems easily and work will bear fruit. Do not take or give loans. Control your irritability and your tongue. Relations with your spouse's family will be sour and this may cause friction between you and your partner.

You would need to hold on to your courage and confidence as these may also be shaken due to these hurdles at work. Your social life will also take a back seat. Conjugal harmony will also be adverse. Overall relations with your family members will not be good. Lack of concentration, suspicion and unnecessary fears of being cheated and general unhappiness will give you anxiety and mental tensions. Headaches and eye troubles are what you have to watch out for. Not a good time for travel. If travel is unavoidable, take extra care of your money and belongings as chances of loss or theft are possible.

Transit of Planet Sun from Third house of Moon Sign

General good feeling and a sense of support and harmony make this a happy time. This transit of the Sun brings a positive boost in your professional life. Your higher authorities will be favourable. You will make progress in your profession with an increased recognition and praise from your employers or authorities. Your enemies and competitors will take a back seat. If you want to appeal for a promotion or increment this is the time. Money flow will be good and will come easily when needed.

This could be regarded as a socially good time as well, as you would be able to command more respect and honour in the society. It is a very good month to enjoy life as you will be free of professional and financial worries. This is a time of peace and harmony. There will be enjoyment with family and friends and you will be popular and respected. You may get a position of importance or honour. Relations with spouse and children will be good. Mental peace and physical fitness will ensure sound health and you will be cheerful and enthusiastic this month. Travels will be good, comfortable and will bear fruits.

Transit of Planet Sun from Fourth house of Moon Sign

This transit offers you increased clarity derived from a feeling that what you want and what you need are in harmony. Your image and status will take a beating at the workplace. You must avoid arguments with your seniors and co-workers during this time. Work pressure will be high and stressful and this will affect your work adversely. Monetarily it is a period of fluctuating finances and make sure you save for the rainy day. Avoid real estate dealings.

Your projects and endeavours may not bring in the desired result. You may even face difficulty in completing your previous tasks on time. Domestic comforts will be at a premium this month. Married life during this month will lack mutual understanding and rapport. Relations with your mother will also suffer. Social life will be sluggish. From health point of view you will be mentally disturbed and you need to watch out for chest and breathing disorders. Journeys will not bear fruits and you will face obstacles. If you travel be prepared for lack of comforts and lack of good food.

Transit of Planet Sun from Fifth House of Moon Sign

There may be some false charges against you. Avoid any tricky situation during this time. Keep away from corruption and malpractices as you may end up with the judiciary. You will feel tired and mentally depressed. This brings in mixed results for you. Your superiors will not be happy with your work and you may face some insult or dishonour. Your enemies and competitors will have the upper hand and will create obstacles in your path. A disturbing time at work and there will be a decline in mental peace. Avoid arguments with your seniors.

Avoid any kind of arguments with your siblings. Handle your friends and acquaintances carefully to avoid being forsaken by them. Relations with family members, especially with your children, will be somewhat sour and will cause mental anxiety. Socially it is a period of loss of respect and goodwill. Respect and dignity will be at a premium this month for you. Unnecessary fears and anguish will have their effect on you. You will be restlessness and unstable in your tempera-ment. Heart patients should be extra careful about their health. Take extra care of your children's health. Journeys will tiresome and unhappy.

Transit of Planet Sun from Sixth House of Moon Sign

This transit suggests you now have a stronger sense of who you are and the principles you represent. The realization of a long-term goal may come now. You will overcome obstacles easily and will get victory over your enemies and competitors. You will complete the unfinished projects and will initiate new projects and will gain the appreciation from your superiors. Financially a very good month and you will gain through investments and speculation. This is a very happy and fruitful period for you and your family.

This brings along considerable good times along. Financially this period is expected to be very good. Your relations with your spouse and family members will be very good. Socially you will enjoy a more respectable position. There will be merrymaking, good food and sweets at home during this time and you will have a great time with spouse and children. Relations with spouse and family will be happy and enjoyable. Peace and harmony will prevail at home. With success and happiness all round, your mental and physical health will be very good. Free from stress and anxiety you will enjoy life this month. Journeys will yield the desired results and you will enjoy your travels.

Transit of Planet Sun from Seventh House of Moon Sign

You also tend to get involved in unnecessary litigations during this time. Keep away from all kinds of litigations to avoid humiliation and defamation. There will be opposition and clashes with your superiors at the workplace and this may result in disgrace and humiliation. The progress of work will be slow and there may be some setbacks in your professional. Your opponents will be stronger and will cause you worries. Avoid quarrels. The relationship with your spouse will also be bad and try your best to avoid clashes.

At home, you would have to make that extra effort to keep the atmosphere conducive for peaceful living. Friends and neighbours will not be receptive this month. Even in personal life you may face some humiliation. The level of enthusiasm will be low and you may suffer from fevers, fatigue, cuts and wounds this month. Take extra care and attention with your diet as you will be prone to indigestion, food poisoning and allergies. The health of your wife and children will also be delicate. Travel: This period is not good for travel as travels will only cause fatigue and troubles and will not be fruitful.

Transit of Planet Sun from Eighth House of Moon Sign

Emotions that you may have never been in touch with, particularly of a darker, obsessive, or primal quality, come bursting forth. At your work place you may be forced to take up undertakings beneath your current level and dignity. Your superiors and competitors will be against you. Avoid getting involved in any kind of arguments or quarrels with your enemies as you will be the loser. Make sure to avoid unnecessary expenses and risky investments as it is a period of losses.

At home, you would have to make that extra effort to keep the atmosphere conducive for peaceful living. Relations with friends and relatives will also be not cordial and social life will be dull. It is a bad month for health also. You may develop intestinal and stomach disorder, piles and blood. Unnecessary fear of death and suicidal thoughts will cause worry and anxiety. Drive carefully and watch your step on the stairs as it is a period of accidents. Avoid sports and all activities that involve physical risks. Avoid travels this month as they will cause worries and injuries.

Transit of Planet Sun from Ninth House of Moon Sign

You express great intensity and passion in the way you appear and express yourself to others. Your bosses and employers will not be happy with your work and you will face blame and you face some humiliation. There may be some false charges against you. Avoid any tricky situation during this time. Financially this is a bad period for you. Avoid speculation as it will cause losses. It will be difficult for you to recover pending dues hence avoid unnecessary expenses and wasteful spending.

Your motives come to the surface and relationships become deeper and more meaningful. There will be some confrontation with you father or teachers or guru. You will be unnecessarily blamed and there will be lack of mental peace. There will be misunderstandings and clash of opinion with your spouse and family members. However, it is a good period for pujas, charity and religious activities, as these activities will be successful. Avoid taxing yourself physically as you will be prone to pains in the hips, knees and spine. You will feel tired and mentally depressed. Travel is on the cards but do not overstrain.

Transit of Planet Sun from Tenth House of Moon Sign

This is a period when ego-gratifying circumstances are highlighted. You receive some sort of boost to your ego and confidence, perhaps through some form of recognition. This period Sun will be very favourable and will give you excellent results. The progress of work will be excellent and your seniors will appreciate and honour your efforts. A promotion, increment or better opportunities are on the cards this month.

There will be progress and success in all your endeavours. Financially too it is a very fruitful period and you can expect gains from unexpected quarters. There will be respect and honour from your circle of friends and relatives. It is a very good time to acquire gold, jewellery, land and conveyances. You will enjoy a good social life and will make new fruitful acquaintances especially with the opposite sex. Your health will be excellent during this month. Travels will give you desired results and happiness.

Transit of Planet Sun from Eleventh House of Moon Sign

A sense of value and valuing that may find you lavishing affection on those near you. You might feel love or value for an older person. This is a pleasing influence for harmonious contact with others and for prosperity in general. You will raise your standard at the work place and get unexpected benefits from your bosses.

This transit of the Sun is an excellent one for monetary gains. Hence if you want to approach your boss for an increment or a promotion this is a very favourable month. Money will come on time and investments will yield excellent results and you will enjoy an improved economic and social status.

You are likely to feel energetically supported by others and by life's circumstances. This is a very happy and fruitful period for you and your family. There will be merrymaking, good food and sweets at home during this time and you will have a great time with spouse and children. You will enjoy a good prestige and respect in your neighbourhood. It is a very good month to party and enjoy life. Health will be sound without any troubles. Travels, both professional and personal, will be successful and enjoyable.

Transit of Planet Sun from Twelfth House of Moon Sign

Unnecessary fears and anguish will have their effect on you. An important relationship, perhaps an older person or someone in authority, may come into focus today. You will have a tough time with your bosses. Your efforts and hard work will not give you the desired result at this time. Your work will not be appreciated and you may be given less responsibilities or less pay. Be extra careful with your finances during this period and avoid impulsive buying and waste. Avoid all risky investments as this is a period of losses. This period will also give you a rough weather at home. Avoid arguments with spouse and friends. Conjugal life will not be happy.

There could be some tension or sense of opposition requiring compromise or negotiation on your part. Lack of sleep and irritability will affect peace and harmony at home. Social life will be dull. Take care of your health and especially sleep well and rest. Watch out for fevers, stomach troubles and eye troubles. There may be a few long trips but don't expect good results.

MICROSCOPY OF TRANSITING PLANETS SIMPLIFIED VOLUME-5

CHAPTER TWO

SUN TRANSITS URANUS NEPTUNE PLUTO

Sun conjunct Uranus

The day can bring the unexpected or find you in a very unusual mood. It may be that you may feel like getting away from the routine and just doing something different. New insights or break throughs are possible with authorities or someone older. A new change is about to begin and you are more inclined to accept and appreciate all that is new, unusual, and of higher grade. You have an opportunity to shine for what makes you unique.

This transit gives a brighter light for matters concerning the media, computers, and metaphysical subjects. A need for change is indicated. There is a need to be creative and unique in your expression of self. This is usually a time to join with groups and to become a group leader. It's also an easy time to make new friends. This can be a time when others notice a sparkle in your eye and find you specially clever and witty.

Sun sextile Uranus

You may want to break that routine and try something new. You need to take a little trip, or get outside today You may discover insights into day-to-day problems that will be of great value later. There's a noticeable sparkle in your eye now, and others seem to appreciate your quirks and idiosyncrasies. Perhaps it's your willingness to adapt to new circumstances, ideas, and unfamiliar situations that gets you just the right attention. It's a good time to have the company of organizations and groups and to attend meetings or social events. You can find creative solutions to problems now. You are seeking out brightness for your life now, and you simply won't stand for anything routine and common in place.

Sun square Uranus

This transit could offer you the drive to do something new, but avoid making hasty, major decisions for the time being. You can't expect much of anything when the transiting Sun squares. You may feel that your originality and independence are stifled or just not available to you. Disrupted routines and plans figure now, which help to stimulate the adoption of new approaches. You feel the need for action, but if you don't know where you're headed, you might take the wrong turn. Unexpected changes in plans or events can test your patience, and you might feel a bit out of control.

Sun trine Uranus

This is a time when tensions with others can come from a lack of self-confidence or a sudden awareness of unfulfilled wishes and goals. This is a dynamic and exciting period, one in which taking advantage of unusual or unconventional opportunities may reap rewards. Flexibility is the key to success at this time, and pleasant changes are in store. You may want to break that routine and try something new or different right now. You may discover insights into day-to-day problems that will be of great value later. You could make some creative changes and discoveries, experiment with new possibilities, or invent a new way of doing things.

Sun opposite Uranus

Your wants are somewhat unstable and changeable someone may oppose you and frustrate your sense today. You may feel squelched or thwarted in a relationship, be it romantic, a friendship, or job related. New ideas and insights may be slow to come just now. Your wants are somewhat unstable and changeable, however, and you can send off some real mixed signals. Sudden changes of plans can happen now, and you might react impatiently.

Sun conjunct Neptune

You can benefit now from a more confident manner and increased certainty about your goals in life. New attachments or projects may be formed now. You are extremely sensitive to the moods and undercurrents around you during this transit. You may feel very dreamy and imaginative. You could find yourself ignoring the practical in favour of considering your more eternal prospects for the moment. You make judgments intuitively and instinctually. You may have a hard time defining your actions and your goals, perhaps temporarily losing sight of reality and reason. This is a time of flexible morals, increased spiritual awareness, imagination, and inspiration.

Sun sextile Neptune

You might find yourself inspired during this transit. This is a good time for self-improvement programs or efforts. Instinctual judgment is enhanced under this influence and charitable acts now will serve to lift your spirits like no drug can. These days don't come too often, so don't ignore this opportunity to let your imagination loose. Perhaps a good book or movie will take on that more-than-real dimension. Consider the stars. You're at the right place at the right time, probably because your hunches are more likely to be.. Pay attention to the dreams and insights that come into your life now.

Sun square Neptune

Arrogant, boastful, wasteful, or extravagant behaviour could figure now. Channelled well, however, this energy can represent creative power. Minor disappointments or just plain fatigue might hit you like a ton of bricks today. Don't ask for anything, such as help. You may feel separated and this may be a discouraging day when things don't quite seem to go your way, or when you feel a bit drained. Take a break and don't start any serious new project today. Instead, find time to help someone. It could lift your spirits, and you won't fall into the easy tendency to feel sorry for yourself that this aspect often brings. Concentrating on artistic or spiritual pursuits is better than focusing on things that require straightforward, factual thinking. Avoid such things as scheduling surgery, important appointments, job interviews, new projects.

Sun trine Neptune

This is a good time for self-improvement. Let yourself dream today. These days don't come too often, so don't ignore this opportunity to let your imagination loose. You may be feeling inspired, and charitable acts now will serve to lift your spirits like no drug can. Instinctual judgment is enhanced under this influence. You might solve a mystery be rewarded for a past deed now.

Sun opposite Neptune

You may find yourself going head-to-head with someone over matters of honesty and integrity. Many may oppose or challenge your own life dreams question the motives of authorities. It's easy to get lost in fantasy. Your willpower is low as you tend to stray from your goals and temporarily lose focus. It's difficult to stick to goals, during confusing, disturbance misconceptions. This is not a good time so plan accordingly.

Sun conjunct Pluto

You would gain more control over your life which motivates you to greater heights. This could be an action-filled day when time seems to slow down as you encounter some of your more sensitive areas. You are strong-willed and focused under this influence. You are in the position to gain some personal power search out for opportunities.

Sun sextile Pluto

You want to do and what you think you should do. You are more excitable than usual, and less inclined to make rational, thought-out decisions. Real sight into your own inner workings could surface today, and you may be in the mood for deep and penetrating conversations or thoughts. Opportunities to find or renew something you had lost. You have the energy and drive to accomplish things today. This is a good day for new business, and accounting.

Sun square Pluto

It may not be possible for you to penetrate to anything remotely meaningful or moving. You can't seem to get beneath the surface. The need to make changes in your life that will further your psychological development arise. Impatience with rules and compulsiveness are shadow energies of this transit. A tendency to want to control your life through some form of manipulation is strong during this influence, but is best avoided for good results. A very lucky period for making plans or decisions and finding your way through just about any problem you may discover. You feel successful and able to cope.

Sun trine Pluto

You are more willing to take a risk or two, and you are motivated by a desire to impress others. Enthusiasm runs high, and cooperation comes easily. You may be in the mood for deep and penetrating conversations or thoughts. You are **able to get** to the bottom of things. You are more decisive than usual, and your ability to concentrate what you set out to do. This is a very positive aspect for starting a money-making endeavour or a new project. You stand to gain some personal power or influence. You might uncover information or material items that help further your goals.

Sun opposite Pluto

There could be some devious goings-on behind the scenes as well. Tension of political nature may be present. Your own inner need for change and growth may be threatened. The Sun in dynamic aspect to Pluto suggests wilfulness and dealing with issues of power and competition. You may feel on edge, volatile, or even threatened. A tendency to control your life through some form of manipulation is strong during this influence, but should be avoided for best results.

MICROSCOPY OF
TRANSITING PLANETS
SIMPLIFIED
VOLUME-5

CHAPTER THREE

TRANSITING PLANET SUN

Overview:

The transiting planets in a chart are where the planets are currently in the sky. As they form aspects to the natal planets in a chart they trigger events in an individual's life. The Sun's transits to planets and points in the natal chart are relatively brief influences, lasting approximately a day. The Sun acts to spotlight and illuminate the issues and conditions surrounding a natal planet or point.

Sun conjunct Sun

Projects begun today have a good chance in turning out well. Good for approaching those in power. It's time to celebrate as a new solar cycle begins. Pay close attention to your overall mood as well as to any insights you have now. Concentrate on what you want from your life, and where you want your life to head. How you handle today impacts the kind of year you have ahead of you. This is the actual date and time of your Solar Return. You may wish to do something special at this hour.

Sun sextile Sun

You will overcome obstacles easily and will get victory over your enemies and competitors. This is a good period for dealing with others in general, but particularly on professional levels or with those in charge. Ideas and interaction with authority figures or older people may be in the fore. Working with rather than against the flow should be easy to do. Self-expression flows smoothly without social faux-pas or hiccups. Increased vitality and self-confidence come from a sense of peace on both body and spirit levels.

Sun square Sun

You will complete the unfinished projects and will initiate new projects and will gain the appreciation from your superiors. You may find it very easy to overdo or work at cross purposes to yourself just now. This can result in a frustrating and stressful day. There is a sense of testing the limits. You might find you have to push a little harder during this transit than you normally would. Obstacles in your path tend to arrive now, although you are capable of turning them into positive energy. Challenges you face now are actually quite revealing if you look at them as learning experiences.

Sun trine Sun

Your enemies and competitors will not be able to have the upper hand and will create obstacles in your path. This is a period when ego-gratifying circumstances are highlighted. You receive some sort of boost to your ego and confidence, perhaps through some form of recognition, however big or small. You are likely to feel energetically supported by others and by life's circumstances. Battles of will could occur now. Don't stress or strain--pushing your agenda on others is unlikely to do anything except cause friction.

Sun opposite Sun

Unnecessary fears and anguish will have their effect on you. An important relationship, perhaps an older person or someone in authority, may come into focus today. There could be some tension or sense of opposition requiring compromise or negotiation on your part. This is a time when tensions with others can come from a lack of self-confidence or a sudden awareness of unfulfilled wishes and goals. You are unlikely to feel on top of your game now, so don't push matters. Instead, take time for rest and relaxation.

Sun conjunct Moon

Relations with your spouse's family will be sour and this may cause friction between you and your partner. Emotions are up, and you may even find yourself pondering a bit on the meaning of life. You feel at one with your situation. You can benefit now from a more confident manner and increased certainty about your goals in life. New attachments or projects may be formed now. The only cautions are to try to avoid making decisions that are based on your emotions of the moment, and to avoid taking everything too personally.

Sun sextile Moon

Lack of concentration, suspicion and unnecessary fears of being cheated and general unhappiness will give you anxiety and mental tensions. In particular, you will do well in activities that include children, younger people, and your home and surroundings. You could feel real support and harmony at this time for circumstances and those around you. You are currently able to handle opportunities well by focusing your energy on constructive activities and goals. This is a time of conscious striving knowing what you want and working towards getting it. Your vitality gets a little boost and your recuperative powers are better than normal. Relations with others tend to flow smoothly now.

Sun square Moon

This transit of the Sun brings a positive boost in your professional life. You may not have a sense of circumstances working against you or feel a lack of support and love from those around you. You could clash with younger people or old habits. This is a brief period in which emotional frustrations or setbacks are more like to occur. Relationship problems that arise now likely have their roots in emotional unrest and some confusion between what you want to do and what you think you should do.

You will overcome problems easily and work will bear fruit. Your enemies and competitors will take a back seat. You are more excitable than usual, and less inclined to make rational, thought-out decisions. Whims could take hold. If you are having problems on the domestic front, they are magnified now. Do your best not to force changes in your life. Circumstances and others tend to be less supportive than usual, and you might find you have to push yourself harder to achieve the same results you would on other days of the month.

Your image and status will take a beating at the workplace. You must avoid arguments with your seniors and co-workers during this time. This is not an ideal time for new enterprises or undertakings. Inner restlessness may take you out of your typical routine. Relationships with others may be strained for the time being. This is a good time to uncover issues of emotional unrest that have been bubbling under the surface, and to take steps to take better care of your emotional needs.

Sun trine Moon

Though work pressure will be high and stressful and this may affect your work adversely. Monetarily it is a period of fluctuating finances and make sure you save for the rainy day. This is a time when you handle opportunities that come your way very well. The possibility of some form of recognition or validation for what you do may come during this brief but effective period. Favourable trends in your domestic or professional affairs may be noticeable. A positive frame of mind does wonders now. Familiarity and comfort are dominant motivators for you during this period. It's a good time to mend relationship problems and to surround yourself with people.

Sun opposite Moon

Your enemies and competitors will have the upper hand and will create obstacles in your path. Avoid arguments with your seniors. An important relationship, perhaps a younger person or someone in your near environment, may come into focus today. There could be an emotional overtone to all of this that may require understanding and flexibility on your part. You take things more personally now, and issues that have been stewing beneath the surface reveal themselves now. On the other opposite side, your relationships with others could be strained. You could be feeling less vigorous than usual or more stressed. You might find that you attract challenging situations simply because you are overreacting emotionally.

Sun conjunct Mercury

Your work will bear very good results. You will overcome obstacles easily and will get victory over your enemies and competitors. You may feel like talking a bit more than usual, exploring new ideas or getting happily lost in a conversation. There will be an urge to communicate. Also, perhaps a short trip or a special phone call is in order. You are especially sharp, communicative, and open at this time, as your wants are aligned with your thoughts. It's a favourable time for solving problems. For the most part, you are on the ball.

You will complete the unfinished projects and will initiate new projects and will gain the appreciation from your superior. Circumstances are such that you need to adapt, adjust, communicate, or travel. Transportation and movement, in general, are issues now. Because it's easy to rationalize your behaviour, it's a favourable time to work on improving your skills. You tend to say what you think now. Keep in mind that what you say or write now has impact, for better or for worse.

Sun sextile Mercury

There will be opposition and clashes with your superiors at the workplace and this may result in disgrace and humiliation. New ways to communicate or an easy manner will make conversations and interactions go well today. You may find yourself more talkative and facile than otherwise. A dialogue with an older person may take place. During this transit, you find it easier than usual to rationalize your own behaviour and that of others. It's an excellent period for improving your skills and for opening up discussions on topics that you normally might sidestep. Dealing with details may be necessary now, but also quite easy to do.

Sun square Mercury

At your work place you may be forced to take up undertakings beneath your current level and dignity. Don't be surprised if you are not in top mental gear today. You could find yourself struggling to communicate or being easily misunderstood. Hard words are possible with an authority figure or an older person. Circumstances are such that you need to adapt and adjust, deal with nagging details, and/or run a number of errands. You may have a hard time concentrating on any one subject. Either you are easily distracted or a whole slew of information and demands are thrown upon you at once. Nervous tension is a potential by-product.

Sun trine Mercury

Your bosses and employers will not be happy with your work and you will face blame and you face some humiliation. New ways to communicate or an easy manner will make conversations and interactions go well today. You may find yourself more talkative and facile than otherwise. Improving your skills also comes naturally and easily. Taking tests, making plans, presenting your work or ideas, and communications of all kinds are favoured. Others tend to value your opinions and ideas under the influence of this transit.

Sun opposite Mercury

There will be misunderstandings and clash of opinion with your spouse and family members. You may find yourself somewhat argumentative today. For instance, you could disagree with ideas or find communication with others difficult or fouled up. You may clash with someone older or in authority over ideas. Words may be exchanged. This could be a time of nervous tension due to overactive or upset schedules. As well, you could feel slighted as a result of others misunderstanding what you communicate or get offended over a difference of opinion.

The progress of work will be excellent and your seniors will appreciate and honour your efforts. Try to avoid a tendency to look at matters with a negative perspective it doesn't help! New ideas or projects initiated now may not come to fruition. A change of mind down the road is likely. Take care in your personal and professional communications--you can too easily misrepresent yourself with what you say or write now.

Sun conjunct Venus

Your relations with your spouse and family members will be very good. Socially you will enjoy a more respectable position. This transit stimulates your love nature. This is a good day for expressing yourself creatively through relationships or other pursuits. You want to be the centre of attention right now, and you are feeling more vulnerable to how others receive you, so you may pay special attention to your charm and appearance or mannerisms. You might make some social contacts that benefit your career or life direction. Watch out for over-spending, as you may feel a greater than average need to please or pamper yourself.

Sun sextile Venus

This transit offers you increased clarity derived from a feeling that what you want and what you need are in harmony. A very nice day, perhaps filled with some renewed appreciation for all that is beautiful and fine. A sense of value and valuing that may find you lavishing affection on those near you. You might feel love or value for an older person. Some social networking is likely to occur now. Pleasurable activities are emphasized, and relationships with others tend to be gratifying and agreeable. It's an excellent period for negotiations and smoothing over of differences.

Sun square Venus

Don't pick out that new car today, because your sense of value may be stressed. You may be unable to appreciate or value people and things now. Your tastes may offend someone older or in authority. Do your best to control yearnings for more than what you have, and search for a creative solution for your inner dissatisfaction. Disagreements that may crop up now tend to be about differences in principles or matters of personal style

Sun trine Venus

A very nice day, perhaps filled with some renewed appreciation for all that is beautiful and fine. A sense of value and valuing that may find you lavishing affection on those near you. You might feel love or value for an older person. This is a pleasing influence for harmonious contact with others and for prosperity in general. Expressing yourself creatively through relationships or other pleasurable pursuits is favoured now. Your personal charm is natural and well-received now, making this a good time to be amongst people.

Sun opposite Venus

You may come face-to-face today with someone who has very different values than you do. You could find yourself cast in an opposing position, and this might require compromise and understanding on your part. You may not appreciate authority now. Ego reactions to feeling underappreciated are quite possible now.

Your gut instincts tend to serve you well now, as they are not undermined by fears or insecurities. This is not the best time for ego stroking on social and romantic levels. You may not appreciate how others are handling your just now. Pushing it won't solve any problems. In fact, lonely or frustrated feelings that might arise now are likely a reflection of your own inner discontent. Getting in touch with what is making you feel down could help you to solve problems now. This is not the best time to ask for what you want.

Sun conjunct Mars

This is the day to start new projects or push forward with those already in motion. You may enjoy a sense of creating your own opportunities. Someone older or in authority may be a motivating force. This is one of your most courageous and animated periods of the year. How you handle the energy at your disposal is the key to the kinds of outcomes you'll experience. You're not going to wait for anyone now. This transit rids you of inhibitions, at least for the time being. This is a time of much enthusiasm.

Your intentions and actions harmonize, which improves your relationships with others and with your own body and spirit. Acting on things you have only entertained on a mental level is probable. With the Sun placing its spotlight on Mars the planet that rules anger, assertion, sexuality, and competitiveness you can learn much about your desire nature and how you handle anger.

Sun sextile Mars

You may not find the support you flowing to you. Some sort of temporary obstacle may appear. You may feel like exercising or getting out and about. Emotions are very present but within control. You are able to creatively solve problems and to instinctively take action when necessary under the influence of this transit. Stress is eased as you feel confident about your abilities and your judgment. You are more able to assert yourself without rubbing people the wrong way just now.

There could be a noticeable discrepancy between the demands of your personal life and what is expected of you at work. You may feel frustrated. You may become aware of a conflict between what you want and what you need. You might find that you stand up for yourself or your principles. You are progress-oriented, and your more passionate nature comes to the fore. It's time to take the initiative, to apply your confidence and energy to something constructive. This is a period in which you are living spiritedly, indulging your desires without going overboard, and acting spontaneously.

Sun square Mars

Frustration, especially in getting things accomplished, may set today's mood. You could fly off the handle with very little provocation, so exercise some control and be ready for a possible emotional overload. You have spring fever now, no matter what the season! You could find yourself driven by a restless desire to do something; but without a well-defined goal, you tend towards impulsive actions and get yourself into needless arguments.

It's easy to put your best face forward and to cooperate with others because you are not conflicted on the inside .Circumstances spur you into action. Your more passionate nature comes to the fore. You could be a little too eager to impress others with an aggressive or inappropriate stance, or you may find yourself competing with others in unhealthy ways. You can easily rub people the wrong way and instigate conflicts.

Sun trine Mars

You may feel like exercising or getting out and about. Emotions are very present but within control. You are living life with spirit just now, and your energy and vitality are strong. The natural confidence that you exude during this transit doesn't come across as offensive. In fact, your enthusiasm is well-received.

It's a good time to take the initiative and to act on things that you've only been thinking about doing. You are drawn to physical activity, and if you are involved in a compctitive event, you are more likely than usual to come out a winner. Effective decision-making is possible now. This transit whets your sexual appetite, increases spontaneity and courage, and helps you to let go of some of your inhibitions.

Sun opposite Mars

You may find yourself at odds with someone today, in particular at the gut or emotional level. Feelings could run strong, and this may require presence of mind and real patience in order to avoid a flare-up. Careless or impulsive behaviour can be a problem under this transit. You could find yourself feeling thwarted, frustrated, or restless.

You may become aware of a conflict between the demands of your personal life and your professional life. You are expressing yourself more genuinely, and you are received well as a result. This is likely due to the fact that you are not in touch with what it is you really want at this time. If you do know what you want, how to go about getting it doesn't come naturally to you right now. A tendency to fly off the handle characterizes this transit, due to inner tension between your will and performance. It's hard to find satisfaction or a sense of peace at this time.

Sun conjunct Jupiter

You will find a way around almost any obstacle and are in control and able to guide yourself with ease. Your sense of inner direction is good and should lead to opportunities. Vitality increases now as your confidence in your effectiveness builds. You feel more generous, optimistic, and sociable under this influence. You might hunger for increased recognition and respect, and, with your generous attitude and concern for others' well-being, you might just get them.

This is a good time to take steps to grow something your business, your significant relationships, and so forth. This transit also favours legal, educational, religious, and cultural endeavours. You seek a larger range of experience. Your actions are benevolent, your attitude is enthusiastic, and your style is dramatic. This transit suggests you now have a stronger sense of who you are and the principles you represent.

Decision-making can be challenging right now, as there is a basic conflict between your instincts and what you feel you should do. The realization of a long-term goal may come now. You may gain honour or distinction in some way. This is an excellent time to begin a self-improvement program. This is not an especially sexual energy you are more inclined to philosophize and seek out bigger and better experiences. You may be particularly generous, and perhaps indiscriminately so.

Sun sextile Jupiter

A very lucky day for making plans or decisions and finding your way through just about any problem you may discover. You feel successful and able to cope. Good advice from a guide or older person may be forthcoming. This transit represents hopefulness, good will, and increased influence. You may be especially sociable, tolerant, and generous. Confidence comes from a stronger sense of who you are and the principles you represent. People in high places can be generous to your cause, and you could receive gifts or rewards.

Sun square Jupiter

Not a great day to make plans or decisions. It could be hard to figure out the right move. You may feel frustrated as to where you are headed in life just now. Someone older or in authority may disapprove of your actions or decisions. You may feel vague restlessness and discontent with life as it is. You want more than what mundane existence offers, but perhaps too much.

You are emotionally charged now. You should be aware that your current state of mind can, in an indirect way, determine much about how you will be feeling in the month ahead. Overestimation and exaggeration are possibilities, either in your own attitude or in the circumstances and people you attract now. Your mood may be elevated, but somewhat unstable as the source of your enthusiasm may not be based on reality.

Take care that you don't throw practical considerations out the window. Avoid promising more than you can deliver, as you are unlikely to be able to follow through on your promises. Arrogant, boastful, wasteful, or extravagant behaviour could figure now. Channelled well, however, this energy can represent creative power.

Sun trine Jupiter

A very lucky day for making plans or decisions and finding your way through just about any problem you may discover. You feel successful and able to cope. Good advice from a guide or older person may be forthcoming. This influence represents growth and expansiveness. You are more aware of moral issues, and have a desire to improve and learn. Optimism and confidence are basic elements in the energy of this transit.

You are more sensitive and responsive than you are typically. You are more willing to take a risk or two, and you are motivated by a desire to impress others. Enthusiasm runs high, and cooperation comes easily. This is generally a good time to schedule new beginnings in business, education, personal relationships, marriage, creative projects, and so forth, all things equal. Sincerity and honesty works best for you now.

A great time to reflect and understand your own situation, just how you feel about yourself. This could be a period in which you realize a long-term goal. Your enthusiasm is boundless, and you are inclined to take the high road in your dealings with others. Health and vitality are strong. An opportunity to take a trip or to embark on an adventure, however big or small, could arise now.

Sun opposite Jupiter

You may feel overworked; alternatively, you might welcome some discipline into your life. You may find opposition from others today to some plan of action or project of yours. You might find yourself struggling with someone older or even with yourself and goals. Conflicting urges with regards to what you think you should do and what you want to do can be frustrating now. There can be a tendency to go overboard and to indulge in extravagances. Watch that you don't overestimate your capabilities now. The desire to experience something new, or the desire for more freedom to explore new possibilities, can amount to restlessness if you don't know what it is you want.

Sun conjunct Saturn

You may well be reminded of your various responsibilities today. A good time to get down to the nitty-gritty and take care of some business you have postponed. Obligations may come to your attention. You feel the constraints of time and you are motivated by the desire to manifest tangible results.

Avoid launching new projects, particularly financial ones, for the time being, as progress may be slow. Instead, work on a new plan for creating order in your life, or on an old project that requires a new commitment. Serious matters may grab your attention now, or circumstances are such that you are required to show your more competent and responsible side. Self-restraint is characteristic of this influence.

Arguments of an emotional kind could be easy to find. Minor forced changes to your routine or habits may upset you now. It is easier for you to get in touch with your feelings and to recognize your inner resources now. Feeling emotionally at odds with others will pass soon enough. Emotional energy is not enough to fuel you for the time being; thus you could feel sapped on a physical level. However, making new commitments to old goals, shouldering responsibilities, and making careful use of your resources could feed your need for structure and order in your life.

Sun sextile Saturn

Today you will be able to tackle tasks that require real discipline or organization. You find yourself in a very practical mood and working with, instead of against, yourself. You may have some serious or contemplative moments. This is perhaps an unglamorous time, but one in which you feel grounded and stable. It's easy to stick to a specific task and make headway. Productivity may be slow, but it's steady.

You may be very eloquent or forceful in speaking or communicating. You may find yourself having emotional differences with someone. Your emotions are stable with this influence. Feelings of contentment and a generally good mood help you to deal with changes effortlessly. You are happily self-reliant now, rather than grudgingly so. You may find yourself in a position of responsibility.

Contact with older, mature, or more experienced people could be significant now. This could mark the start of a big, long-lasting project. Your outlook is serious and realistic.

Sun Square Saturn

You are more inclined towards personal communications, social discourse, and sharing. It may be hard to organize or persevere today. Everything may seem to be falling apart and coming unglued. Don't force things. Be patient and let the chaos blow itself out.

Clashes with authorities or someone older over responsibilities are possible. You could feel blocked by circumstances or by others. It's too easy to feel discouraged, but remember that discouragement is a major time waster, unless it motivates you to get back on your feet.

Connections could be made or enhanced with younger people. You express your feelings in an honest way, and you are likely to be preoccupied with personal matters. Sacrifices may be necessary now. You might have to face failures or inadequacies. As you face obstacles to your goals, you begin to see the tools you have to overcome them. A heavy dose of realism seems forced upon you during this influence, but your efforts to measure up to expectations can ultimately increase your confidence in your ability to be responsible for yourself. This influence is a sombre one.

Sun trine Saturn

Today you will be able to tackle tasks that require real discipline or organization. You find yourself in a very practical mood and working with, instead of against, yourself. You may have some serious or contemplative moments. You feel grounded and stable right now. You are willing to look reality in the eye and to take responsibility for your life. Practical, professional, and business matters come to the fore. Your respect for authority is natural and helps superiors to look upon you favourably. This could be a good time to make a lasting investment if concurrent influences are favourable.

Sun opposite Saturn

Obstacles to self-discipline or to your sense of organization may appear. You could be frustrated by someone in this regard, or external events might pile up and be thrust upon you. Authorities and red tape may stand between you and your goals. Your confidence may be undermined by feelings of doubt, pessimism, or feelings of guilt just now. Encountering obstacles to progress and inhibitions in your own attitude are prominent under this influence.

There will be respect and honour from your circle of friends and relatives. You could be plagued by a feeling of not being good enough. Lack of faith in yourself, in others, and in life itself could put a damper on your initiatives. This is a time when others don't seem to notice your efforts, when progress appears to be minimal if at all, when nobody seems to extend their hand to you.

You will have a tough time with your bosses. Your efforts and hard work will not give you the desired result at this time. Because this is one of your less attractive and magnetic periods of the year, you might want to avoid scheduling personally significant activities, job interviews, or self-promotion efforts during this period.

Although there is a positive side to every aspect, while it's happening, this one doesn't feel very good. A heavy dose of realism seems forced upon you now, but your efforts to measure up to expectations can ultimately increase your confidence in your ability to be responsible for yourself. This influence is a sober one.

Sun conjunct Ascendant

This is a time when you can expect a little boost, some sort of extra support or recognition from those around you. You may feel very focused and even a bit radiant. You could find yourself in the limelight or able to really communicate and get yourself across to others Shine brightly! This transit sometimes brings recognition for a personal achievement. Whether or not this occurs, you radiate strength and have increased personal presence now. Praise may be forthcoming.

Sun sextile Ascendant

You may appear very at ease and loose today. Everything seems to be working together, and you may find yourself expressive and able to communicate well. You possess strong presence and generally feel confident about who you are and how others are receiving you now. Others may praise you or recognize some of your better qualities today. Dealing with superiors is a breeze now, and you could win at a game or competition, if applicable.

Sun square Ascendant

You may lack any real sense of yourself today, or be unable to communicate or convey your ideas. You tend to feel that your personality lacks any vitality. An authority figure could be hard to connect with now. You should watch that you don't come on too strong today and attract conflict with others. Feeling slighted, overlooked, or misunderstood could lead you to seek out attention now. However, the attention that you receive is unlikely to be very positive for the time being. You could have problems relating to superiors, and your vitality may be on the low side.

Sun trine Ascendant

You may appear very at ease and loose today. Everything seems to be working together, and you may find yourself expressive and able to communicate well. You possess strong presence and generally feel confident about who you are and how others are receiving you now. Others may praise you or recognize some of your better qualities today. Dealing with superiors is a breeze now, and you could win at a game or competition, if applicable.

Sun opposite Ascendant

You may experience opposition to the way you present yourself. Someone could challenge your sense of identity. You may not be able to communicate or get yourself across as well as you wish. Expect significant encounters, meeting individuals who are or will be important players, at least for the moment. The focus is on relationship, balance, taking each person's tastes, styles, needs, and personal agendas into account. There may be some friction and adjustments needed. It is your choice whether you want to compromise or go solo, but including the other makes for a fuller picture.

MICROSCOPY OF TRANSITING PLANETS SIMPLIFIED VOLUME-5

CHAPTER FOUR

PLACEMENT OF PLANETS IN DIFFERENT HOUSES

SUN

In the First house. –

Righteous- minded, healthy, bilious, eye-disease, intelligence, good morals, political success, stately appearance, humanitarian instincts, lazy in work, fond of daring deeds, hot constitution, careless of reputation, string will, caprice, generosity, neglect of personal credit or respect, good work, not combative or impetuous and pioneering.

Second house. –

Diseased face, ugly, losses from prosecution good earnings, inclined to waste, bright speech, enquiring, well-educated, scientific, stubborn and peevish temper, and danger in the 25th year, will stammer.

Third house. –

Courageous, liberal, adventurous, famous, intelligent, wealthy, successful and restless.

Fourth house. –

Mental worry, meditative defective organs, success in foreign countries, hatred of relations, keen-minded, sensitive, good reputation, success after middle age, quarrels without causes, weak constitution, introspective, unhappy, philosophical, squanders paternal property.

Fifth house. –

Intelligent, poor, few children, paternal danger, corpulent, danger to father early, unhappy, disturbed in mind, lover of fine arts, and tactful in decision.

Sixth house. –

Defer of customs and castes, good administrative ability, few cousins and few enemies, bold a successful, war-like, licentious, wealthy, gain from enemies, clever in planning, terror to enemies, executive ability, colic troubles.

Seventh house. –

Late marriage and rather troubled, loose morals and irreligious, hatred by the fair sex, fond of traveling, submissive to wife, wealth through female agency, fond of foreign things, discontented, wife's character questionable, subservient to women and risk of dishonor and disgrace through them.

Eighth house. –

Well-read in solar sciences, attracted by sublime phenomena, charitable, godly, lucky and successful, devoted, ordinary health, little patrimony, dutiful sons, a man of action and thought, self-acquired property, many lands, philosophical, glandular disease, lover of poetry and music, successful agriculturist, learned in esoteric and occult subjects, ambitious and enterprising.

Ninth house. – Well read in solar sciences, attracted by sublime phenomena, charitable, godly, lucky and successful, devoted, ordinary health, little patrimony, dutiful sons, a man of action and thought, self-acquired property, many lands, philosophical, glandular disease, lover of poetry and music, successful agriculturist, learned in esoteric and occult subjects, ambitious and enterprising.

Tenth house. –

Bold, courageous, well known, famous, clever in acquiring wealth, superior knack, healthy, learned, adventurous, educated, quick decision, fond of music, founder of institutions, high position, dutiful sons, much personal influence, successful military or political career.

Eleventh house. –

Learned, wealthy, stately and persevering, success without much effort, famous, many enemies, wealth through fair means, good reputation, profound insight, capacity to befriend, many political enemies, man of principles, great sagacity, great success and position.

Twelfth house. –

Sinful, poor, fallen, thieving nature, unsuccessful, adulterous, neglected, long limbs, ceremonial minded and lover of esoteric and occult knowledge, no happiness from children.

MICROSCOPY OF TRANSITING PLANETS SIMPLIFIED VOLUME-5

CHAPTER FIVE

PLACEMENT OF PLANETS

IN DIFFERENT SIGNS

SUN

In Aries. – Active, intelligent, famous, traveller, wealthy, warrior, variable fortune, ambitious, phlegmatic, powerful, marked personality, impulsive, irritable, pioneering, initiative.

Taurus. – Clever, reflective, attracted by perfumes and dealer in them, hated by women, slow to action, musician, self-confident, delicious drinks, happy meals, tactful, original, sociable, intelligent, prominent nose.

Gemini. –Learned, astronomer, scholarly, grammarian, polite, wealthy, critical, assimilative, good conversationalist, shy, reserved, lacking in originality.

Cancer. – Somewhat harsh, indolent, wealthy, unhappy, constipation, sickly, travelling, independent, expert astrologer.

Leo. – Stubborn, fixed views, strong, cruel, independent, organizing capacity and talents for propaganda, humanitarian, frequenting solitary places, generous, famous.

Virgo. – Linguist, poet, mathematician, taste for literature, well read, scholarly, artistic, good memory, reasoning faculty, effeminate body, frank, lucid comprehension, learned in religious lore, reserved, wanting adulation.

Libra. – Manufacture of liquors, popular, tactless, base, drunkard, loose morals, arrogant, wicked, frank, submissive, pompous.

Scorpio. – Adventurous, bold, fearing thieves and robbers, reckless, cruel, stubborn, unprincipled, impulsive, idiotic, indolent, surgical skill, dexterous, military ability.

Sagittarius. – Short-tempered, spoils, reliable, rich, obstinate, respected by all, happy, popular, religious, wealthy, musician.

Capricorn. – Mean-minded, stubborn, ignorant, miserly, unhappy, boring, active, meddlesome, obliging, humorous, witty, affable, prudent, firm.

Aquarius. – Poor, unhappy, unlucky, unsuccessful, medium height, rare faculties, self-esteem.

Pisces. – Pearl merchant, peaceful, wealthy, uneventful, religious, prodigal, loved by women

MICROSCOPY OF TRANSITING PLANETS VOLUME-5

CHAPTER SIX

REMEDIES OF PLANETS

PLANET SUN

Effects and Remedies

The Sun is the father of our solar system, around which all planets resolve. The power of light in the sky, the temperature of the earth, the power of presentation and progress are represented by the sun. His presence means the "day" and absence means the "night". The soul in human body and the power of rendering bodily services to others have also been referred to the Sun - a royal planet of power, authority and finances.

The effects and remedies of Sun in different houses are as below:

Sun in 1st House

Benefice:

(1) The native will be fond of constructing religious buildings and digging of wells for public purposes.

He will have permanent source of livelihood- more from the government. Money earned from honest sources will keep multiplying. He will believe only his eyes, not in ears.

Malefic:

The native's father may die in early childhood. Having sex in the daytime will make the wife constantly ill and have infection of tuberculosis if Venus is placed in the 7th house. Malefic sun in the 1st house and Mars in the 5th house will cause the death of sons, one after the other. Similarly, the malefic Sun in the 1st house and Saturn in the 8th house will cause the death of wives, one after the other. If there is no planet in the 7th house the marriage before 24th year will prove lucky for the native, otherwise the 24th year of the native would prove highly disastrous for him

Remedial Measures:

(1) Marry before 24th year of life.

(2) Don't have sex with wife during the daytime.

(3) Install a hand pump for water in your ancestral house.

(4) Construct small dark room in the left side at the end of your house.

(5) Either of the spouses must stop eating "GUR" i.e. jiggery.

Sun in 2nd house

Benefic:

(1) The native will be self-dependent, skilled in handiwork and would prove highly helpful to parents, maternal uncles, sisters, daughters and in-laws.

(2) The Sun in the 2nd will become more auspicious if the Moon is placed in the 6th house.

(3) Ketu in the 8th house will make the native very truthful.

(4) Rahu in the 9th house makes the native a renowned artist or painter.

(5) Ketu in the 9th house makes him a great technician.

(6) Mars in the 9th house makes him fashionable.

(7) The generous nature of the native would put an end to growing enemies.

Malefic:

(1) The Sun will affect very adversely the things and relatives associated with the planets inimical to the Sun i.e., wife, wealth, widows, cows, taste, mother etc. Disputes regarding wealth property and wife will spoil the native.

(2) Never accept donations if the Moon is placed in the 8th house and the Sun in the 2nd house is not auspicious; otherwise the native will be destroyed altogether.

(3) The Sun in the 2nd house, Mars in the 1st and Moon in the 12th house make the native's condition critical and pathetic in every manner.

(4) Mars in the 8th house makes the native extremely greedy if the Sun in the 2nd house is inauspicious.

Remedial Measures:

(1) Donate coconut, mustard oil and almonds to religious places of worship.

(2) Manage to avoid disputes involving wealth, property and ladies.

(3) Avoid accepting donations, specially rice, silver and milk.

Sun in 3rd House

Benefic:

(1) The native will be rich, self-dependant and having younger brothers.

(2) He will be blessed with divine grace and will earn profits intellectual by pursuits.

(3) He will be interested in astrology and mathematics.

Malefic:

(1) If the Sun is not auspicious in the 3rd house and the Moon is also not auspicious in the horoscope, there will be daylight robbery or theft in the native's house.

(2) If the 9th house is afflicted, the forefathers would have been poor. If the 1st house is afflicted, the neighbours of the native will be destroyed.

Remedial Measures:

(1) Obtain blessings of the mother by keeping her happy.

(2) Serve others with rice or milk.

(3) Practice good conduct and avoid evil deeds.

Sun in 4th House

Benefic:

(1) The native will be wise, kind and a good administrator. He will have constant source of income. He will leave a legacy of great riches for his off springs after death.

(2) If the Moon is with the Sun in the 4th house, the native will earn great profit through certain new researches.

(3) The Mercury in the 10th or 4th house will make such a native a renowned trader.

(4) If Jupiter is also with the Sun in the 4th house, the native will make good profits through gold and silver trade.

Malefic:

(1) The native becomes greedy, inclined to commit theft and likes to harm others. This tendency ultimately produces very bad results.

(2) If the Saturn is placed in the 7th house he becomes victimised by night blindness.

(3) If the Sun is inauspicious in the 7th house and mars is placed in the 10th house, the native's eye will become seriously defective, but his fortunes will not dwindle.

(4) The native will become impotent if the Sun in the 4th is inauspicious and the Moon is placed in the 1st or 2nd house, the Venus is in the 5th and Saturn is in the 7th house.

Remedial Measures:

(1) Distribute alms and food to the needy people.

(2) Do not take up business associated with iron and wood.

(3) Business associated with gold, silver, cloth will give very good results.

Sun in 5th house

Benefic:

(1) The progress and prosperity of family and children will be assured. If the Mars is placed in the 1st or 8th house and Rahu, Ketu, Saturn are placed in 9th and 12th houses, the native will lead king's life.

(2) If in 5th house placed with any planet inimical to sun, the native will be bestowed hour by the government everywhere.

(3) If Jupiter is placed in 9th or 12th house, the enemies will be destroyed, but this position will not be good for children of the native.

Malefic:

(1) If the Sun in the 5th is inauspicious and Jupiter is in 10th, the wife of the native will die and wives in subsequent marriages will also die

(2) If the sun in the 5th house is inauspicious and Saturn is placed in 3rd, sons of the native will die.

Remedial Measure:

(1) Do not delay in having a child.

(2) Build your kitchen in the eastern portion of your house.

(3) Drop a lit the quantity of mustard oil on the ground continuously for 43 days.

Sun in 6th House

Benefic:

(1) Native will be lucky, prone to anger, will have beautiful spouse and will benefit from that government.

(2) If Sun is in the 6th house and Moon, Mars and Jupiter in the 2nd house, following tradition will be beneficial.

(3) If sun is in 6th house and Ketu in 1st or 7th house then the native will have a son and after the 48th year great fortune will follow.

Malefic:

(1) The native's son and maternal family will face bad times. Will also affect native health adversely.

(2) If there is a no planet in the 2nd house, the native will get a government job in the 22nd year of his life.

(3) If Mars is placed in the 10th house the native's sons will die one after the other.

(4) Mercury in the 12th house causes high blood pressure.

Remedial Measures:

(1) Ancestral customs and ritual also should be strictly followed; otherwise the family progress and happiness will be destroyed.

(2) Underground furnaces should not be constructed with in the premises of the house.

(3) After taking dinner blow off the fire of the kitchen stove by sprinkling milk over it.

(4) Always keep Gangajal in the premises of your house.

(5) Offer wheat or Gur to monkeys.

Sun in 7th House

Benefic:

(1) If Jupiter, Mars or Moon are placed in the 2nd house, the native will occupy a ministerial position in the government.

(2) If the Mercury is exalted or Mercury in the 5th or 7th house is expected by Mars, the native will have unending sources of income.

Malefic:

(1) If the Sun is inauspicious in the 7th house and Jupiter, Venus or any malefic planet is placed in the 11th house and Mercury is malefic in any other house, the native will encounter the death of several members of his family together. Obstacles from the government diseases like tuberculosis and asthma will victimise the native.

Incidents of fire, embalmment and other family troubles will madden the native who may go to the extent of becoming a recluse or committing suicide.

(2) Malefic Sun in the 7th and Mars or Saturn in the 2nd or 12th house and Moon in the 1st house cause leprosy or leucoderma.

Remedial Measures:

(1) Lessen the amount of salt intake.

(2) Start any work after taking a little sweet with water.

(3) Offer a little piece of your chapati to the fire of the kitchen before taking your meals.

(4) Serving and rearing up a black cow or a cow without horns but make sure that the cow is not white.

Sun in 8th House

Benefic:

(1) Government favours will accrue from the 22nd year of life.

(2) Here the Sun makes the native truthful, saintly and king like. Nobody would be able to harm him.

Malefic:

(1) Mercury in the 2nd house will create economic crisis.

(2) Native will be short tempered, impatient & will have ill health.

Remedial Measures:

(1) Never keep a white cloth in the house.

(2) Never live in the house facing south.

(3) Always eat something sweet and drink water before starting any new work.

(4) Throw copper coins in a burning pyre (Chita) whenever possible.

(5) Throw Gur (jaggery) in running water.

Sun in 9th House

Benefic :

(1) Native will be lucky, good natured will have good family life and will always help others.

(2) If Mercury is in the 5th house, the native will have fortune after 34 years.

Malefic:

(1) Native will be evil and troubled by his brothers.

(2) Disfavour from government and loss of reputation.

Remedial Measures:

(1) Never accept articles of silver as gifts or donation. Donate silver articles frequently.

(2) Ancestral pots and utensils of brass must be used and not sold.

(3) Avoid extreme anger and extreme softness.

Sun in 10th House

Benefic:

(1) Benefits and favours from government, good health and financially stronger.

(2) The native will get a government job and comforts of vehicles and servants.

(3) The native will always be suspicious about others.

Malefic:

(1) If the Sun is in the 4th house, the native's father will die in his childhood.

(2) If the Sun is in the 10th house and moon is in the 5th house the native will have a very short life.

(3) If the 4th house is without any planet, the native will be deprived of government favours and benefits.

Remedial Measures:

(1) Never wear blue or black clothes.

(2) Throwing a copper coin in a river or canal for 43 years will be highly beneficial.

(3) Abstain from liquor and meat.

Sun in 11th House

Benefic:

(1) If the native is vegetarian he will have three sons and will himself be head of the house and will get benefits from government.

Malefic:

(1) The Moon is in the 5th house and the Sun is not expected by good planets, the will have a short life span.

Remedial Measures:

(1) Abstain from meat and wine.

(2) Keep almonds or radishes near the head of the bed and offer it in the temple next day for long life and children.

Sun in 12th House

Benefic:

(1) If Ketu in the 2nd house the native will earn wealth after 24 years and will have good family life.

(2) If Venus and Mercury are together then one will benefit from business and the native will always have steady source of income.

Malefic:

Native will suffer from depression, financial loss from machineries and will be punished by the government.

If the other evil planet is in the 1st house, the native will not be able to sleep peacefully at night.

Remedial Measures:

(1) Native should always have a courtyard in his house.

(2) One should be religious and truthful.

(3) Keep a Chakki in the house.

(4) Always forgive your enemies

MICROSCOPY OF TRANSITING PLANETS SIMPLIFIED

VOLUME-5

CHAPTER SEVEN

Transit results of Moon from natal Moon

TRANSISTING MOON

Transit of Planet Moon from First House of Moon Sign

You could find yourself cast in an opposing position, and this might require compromise and understanding on your part. The flow of work at your work place will be smooth and satisfactory and you will achieve good progress in your undertakings. Your work will get recognition and appreciation. This period is also a good one financially. You will be able to recover the dues and attain your financial goals easily. Your married life will be good and there will be some improvement in your relationship with your spouse.

It is a great time to enjoy with friends and acquaintances, especially friendships with the opposite sex. Love and romance will be in the air. You will also get appreciation and respect from your friends and relatives. You will enjoy excellent and tasty food during this period. All types of physical comforts like good clothes, jewellery, perfumes etc. will keep you happy. You will be happy and contented. Peace and tranquillity will prevail during this time.

This is a time of good health for you and your family without out any physical ailments. It is a good time and travel will yield the desired results and will give you satisfaction and happiness.

Transit of Planet Moon from Second House of Moon Sign

You may not appreciate how others are handling your just now. Pushing it won't solve any problems. There will be obstacles at your work place. Bosses will be unhappy and co-workers will not be cooperative. Be careful in your dealing and avoid unnecessary fights and arguments. Avoid overwork as it is a period of physical and mental fatigue. From the financial point of view the expenses will be more and the income will be less and money will not come on time. Avoid all risky investments. Do not spend impulsively.

You would start new projects or push forward with those already in motion. You may enjoy a sense of creating your own opportunities. There will be disagreements and quarrels with spouse and friends. Social life will be poor. Control your frustrations as the time is against you. You will not be able to get the food of your choice and even if you do you will not be able to enjoy it. You will be frustrated and discontented during this time. Happiness will be at a premium. There will be a general sense of sluggishness. You will be prone to eye problems during this time. Avoid traveling. If you cannot avoid it, keep a tight check on expenses.

Transit of Planet Moon from Third House of Moon Sign
You may find yourself at odds with someone today, in particular at the gut or emotional level. Feelings could run strong, and this may require presence of mind and real patience in order to avoid a flare-up. You will get good success in your profession and will be able to achieve the

desired goals. Your work will get due appreciation, recognition and rewards from the bosses. This period is also a very rewarding one financially. You will be able to recover the past dues and will be lucky and gain well in all your financial ventures. Your personal life during this time will give you satisfaction and happiness.

Marital life will be happy. Relations with spouse, neighbours and relatives, especially your younger siblings will be good. Relations with the opposite sex will be good and rewarding. There will be gains of jewellery, gold and good clothes. You will enjoy the best food of your liking. You will be very happy and satisfied with life and will enjoy everything that comes your way. Health will be good and you will feel energetic and fit. A good time for short distance travels.

Transit of Planet Moon from Fourth House of Moon Sign
You may become aware of a conflict between the demands of your personal life and your professional life. You are expressing yourself more genuinely, and you are received well as a result. Progress of work will be slow and worrying. Expenses will soar and you must be very careful with your investment ventures as it is a period of losses. Control your spending. Relations will be sore and there will be a lack of understanding. There will be trouble from relatives, especially the ones from your mother's side.

This is likely due to the fact that you are not in touch with what it is you really want at this time. If you do know what you want, how to go about getting it doesn't come naturally to you right now. Some of your relatives may suffer loss of wealth and this may cause grief to you. You will be in general unhappy and will not be able to enjoy good food due to health problems. A sense of restlessness, grief, fear and doubt will prevail. Try your best to keep your cool and do not lose your mental balance. It is a bad time for health. Stomach and digestion problems and chest problems will plague you during this time. The health of family members will also be worrisome. Drive carefully as it is an accident prone period. The time is not suitable for travelling. If forced to travel take double care of your health and expenses.

Transit of Planet Moon from Fifth House of Moon Sign
You will find a way around almost any obstacle and are in control and able to guide yourself with ease. Your sense of inner direction is good and should lead to opportunities. Your intellect will be at a low and the quality of your work will suffer. As a result your respect and reputation at your workplace will suffer. It is a period of obstacles and progress will be very sluggish.

You feel more generous, optimistic, and sociable under this influence. From financial point of view this will be a trying time. You will not get any profitable deals and you may lose money due to bad investments. Lack of rapport and lack of love coupled with bad finances and health will make this a gloomy period for you. Even spouse and friends will not be able cheer you up. Keep your frustration under control or things will become sourer.

Decision-making can be challenging right now, as there is a basic conflict between your instincts and what you feel you should do. The general atmosphere of gloom and sorrow will not let you enjoy even good food. Dejection and self-pity will make you gloomy and irritable. Indigestion and mental depression are what you have to watch out for during this time. Travel is on the cards but you will face obstacles in your objective.

Transit of Planet Moon from Sixth House of Moon Sign
You feel successful and able to cope. Good advice from a guide or older person may be forthcoming. This transit represents hopefulness, good will, and increased influence. You will be in an energetic and enthusiastic mood and will work comfortably at a fast pace. You will get victory over your enemies and competitors and will be successful in finishing the stuck up undertakings. You will get good recognition and rewards from the bosses. Financially it is a very good period of gains and investments will yield good returns.

People in high places can be generous to your cause, and you could receive gifts or rewards. Relations with spouse and relatives will be cordial and enjoyable. Children will be affectionate. Social life will be good and you will make new friends – especially with the opposite sex. Overall it is a very happy period for enjoyments and fun. It is a good time for enjoying good food and clothes and other material comforts. You will be able to get good things at bargain prices. You will be happy and contented. Life will be full of love and affection. It is a good period for health without any worries.

Transit of Planet Moon from Seventh House of Moon Sign
You are emotionally charged now. You should be aware that your current state of mind can, in an indirect way, determine much about how you will be feeling in the month ahead. This period will give you success in all your undertakings. Any dealings with foreigners or foreign companies will yield favourable results. Your work will get recognition and you will be rewarded by your employers. You will have the upper hand over your enemies and competitors. The monetary gains will be good and from many sources. Love and romance will be in the air. You

will have a very happy conjugal life with your spouse. Your children will also give you happiness.

You are more sensitive and responsive than you are typically. You are more willing to take a risk or two, and you are motivated by a desire to impress others. You will enjoy a good social life and make new friends of the opposite sex. It is an excellent period for all types of enjoyments. You will enjoy very good comforts of bed, clothing, food and wine.

Overall good peace of mind and a feeling of contentment and joy will prevail during this time but romantic feelings will have the upper hand. Health will be fine. Do not indulge too much in drinking. Travel is on the cards and it will be a very fruitful and pleasurable one. Good time for foreign travel.

Transit of Planet Moon from Eight House of Moon Sign
A great time to reflect and understand your own situation, just how you feel about yourself. This could be a period in which you realize a long-term goal. There will be many obstacles in your path at your workplace. Avoid conflicts and disagreements with your seniors. Do not indulge in and secret dealings or scheming. Your enemies will increase and will give you troubles. Money will not come on time. Avoid all investments as it is a very bad period and possibility of losses is very strong. There will be quarrels and disagreements at home. Married life will suffer. Social life will be poor and love and romance will be at a premium. You will not enjoy good food and may go without food at times.

You may find opposition from others today to some plan of action or project of yours. You might find yourself struggling with someone older or even with yourself and goals. Comforts will be lacking. Unnecessary fear and anxiety, a sense of loss and gloom will prevail. Digestive troubles, diarrhoea and piles related diseases may trouble you during this period. Watch your step on the stairs, be careful while crossing the road and avoid all games, sports and activities involving physical risk. Avoid travelling as it is a very bad period for accidents and calamities.

Transit of Planet Moon from Ninth House of Moon Sign
Conflicting urges with regards to what you think you should do and what you want to do can be frustrating now. Progress of work will be slow and you may face intimidation from your seniors. Even hard work will not yield results and you may face some loss of reputation. Your enemies and competitors will have the upper hand. The flow of money will be bad and chances of some losses are strong and may cause some harm or losses. Life at home will not be very good either. Avoid disagreements or fights with your father and children.

The desire to experience something new, or the desire for more freedom to explore new possibilities, can amount to restlessness if you don't know what it is you want. Conjugal bliss will be lacking. However you may do some charity work or religious work which will be fruitful and may give you a good name. You will not enjoy good food during this time. Comforts will be lacking. Worry will be your constant companion during this time. Stomach disorders, tiredness and pains in the hips, thighs and legs will trouble you. You may indulge in some religious traveling but it will be quite tiresome.

Transit of Planet Moon from Tenth House of Moon Sign

You may well be reminded of your various responsibilities today. A good time to get down to the nitty-gritty and take care of some business you have postponed. This is a very good time professionally. Your work will yield the desirable results and you will get the appreciation of your bosses. Some kind of promotion or honour is also on the cards. Financially it is a rewarding period. It is also a very good time to start new projects. Money will come when needed and investments will get you good returns.

Serious matters may grab your attention now, or circumstances are such that you are required to show your more competent and responsible side. Self-restraint is characteristic of this influence. It is a very good time for a happy and contented family life. Conjugal bliss will be good and social life will be happy. You will gain a good reputation and respect in the society. You will enjoy excellent tasty food and material comforts during this period.

Transit of Planet Moon from Eleventh House of Moon Sign

It is easier for you to get in touch with your feelings and to recognize your inner resources now. Progress of work will be good and will get you the respect and appreciation of your bosses. You will also get some good rewards. It is an excellent period for financial gains. There will be a boost in your income and you will be able to recover old dues. All financial investments will be fruitful and will yield very good returns.

Making new commitments to old goals, shouldering responsibilities, and making careful use of your resources could feed your need for structure and order in your life. You will have a very social life with family reunions and getting together with friends. Eligible people may meet their future spouse. During this time you will have delicious food and enjoy many worldly comforts. Your mood will be upbeat with a sense of delight and happiness. This is a very good time for travel, especially long distance air travel. Travels will be fruitful and enjoyable.

Transit of Planet Moon from Twelfth House of Moon Sign

You will be able to tackle tasks that require real discipline or organization. You find yourself in a very practical mood and working with, instead of against, yourself. Your progress at the work place will be slow and sluggish. Your seniors will not be favourable. Avoid all underhand dealings and illegal activities. This is not a period to look for progress and prosperity but to do a damage control act and hang on to what you have. Expenses will increase and income will not be sufficient. Good food and comforts will be lacking. Jealousy and lethargy are what you have to watch out. Travel: Travels are there but will not be happy and watch your purse.

MICROSCOPY OF
TRANSITING PLANETS
SIMPLIFIED
VOLUME-5

CHAPTER EIGHT

MOON TRANSITS

URANUS NEPTUNE PLUTO

Moon conjunct Uranus
Opportunities could seemingly come from out of the blue.
Nobody can force you to do anything. Many may find you
especially witty and eccentric. You may have insights or
breakthroughs in regard to your living situation or life
circumstances. Your desire for change is stimulated now.
This is a period when you may act on a whim, or you could
encounter something surprising. You are only in the mood
to do things voluntarily. You are quick-witted, inventive,
and your moods may be contradictory. New friendships
sometimes form under this transit. Meetings with friends
and visitors or are possible now. A change of pace is likely.

Moon sextile Uranus
People and others will appreciate your unique or quirky
qualities. Everything conspires to out more unique and
unusual qualities. You may find that someone close to you
understands and is supportive of your aims and qualities.
You could come up with new solutions or inventions.
Breaking the routine is something that would please you
now. This transit indicates a pleasant surprise, a chance
meeting with an old acquaintance, an invitation, or some
other interesting event that enlivens your day.

Moon square Uranus

You may be going against tradition. You may find yourself at odds with others regarding matters of convention. You could get carried away under this kind of pressure and make mistakes you may regret. Some sudden, although likely minor, changes are in store. Family or friends may be erratic. Plans may change direction unexpectedly.

Moon trine Uranus

You are more inclined to take risks. You may find that someone close to you understands and is supportive of your ways. You could come up with new solutions or inventions. You may be the recipient of good news regarding family or domestic affairs. Than usual, although you are also unlikely to go over the top. With this transit you are open to progress and improvement. You are magnetically attractive to others, and they recognize and accept your unique traits.

Moon opposite Uranus

Task and work taken during this transit are likely to change in unexpected ways. Others may create obstacles and challenge your nonconforming attitude in some situation which results in opposition and blockage. Not perhaps a good time for you to try out new things or break away from the old routine. Keep your options open because your schedule is unlikely to materialize.

Moon conjunct Neptune

You may enjoy a reward for your past efforts. You may be able to bring a group together with words. Your feelings are boundless, you are easily touched, and however, you are more easily led astray and prone to disappointments. You are easily seduced, swayed, and even cheated. You attract attention in a quiet way now. Note that you may demonstrate impracticality when handling business and domestic affairs. It's better not to work against the transit.

Moon sextile Neptune
You are inclined to daydream and to make wishes. You might enjoy some kind of reward for your past efforts. Everything conspires to reveal you at your most elegant, particularly in social situations. You will have a grasp for abstract and spiritual ideas and the ability to present or communicate these to others. a strong influence for the arts, especially photography, music, drama, poetry, and any artistic field that appeals strongly to the emotions. You might take a trip down a pleasant, and perhaps wistful, one. If this transit occurs while you sleep, your dreams may be especially insightful or even prophetic.

Moon square Neptune
This transit's effects range from some feelings of wistfulness or confusion to emotional chaos. You may find yourself unrealistic, in a dreamy mood and at odds with your more pragmatic duties. Friends may not appreciate or go along with your dreamy side just now. You may not be able to lose yourself in your imaginings. Avoid money transactions or new business initiatives if you can, just for the time being, as you are unlikely seeing the whole picture. You may feel you have been deceived or misled, but self-deception is the more likely scenario. The desire to escape is strong now.

Moon trine Neptune
Although this influence is subtle, you are likely a little more charming, compassionate. Everything conspires to reveal you at your most elegant, particularly in social situations. You will have a grasp for abstract and spiritual ideas and the ability to present or communicate these to others. You are more vulnerable than usual, and open to outside influences. You could be taking a detour away from your routine. Your imagination is enhanced, and your

sympathy for others is strong. You can more confidently rely on your intuition under this influence.

Moon opposite Neptune
This is a less than ideal time to handle business. You could be lacking in willpower with this transit in effect. Your image and ideals could be challenged by another who sees you as impractical and not down-to-earth. You are more open to outside influences and energies right away. The desire to escape the daily routine is strong and domestic affairs, so if you can, put these off. Impracticality is what this transit is about, so it's best used for reflection, rest, and creative inspiration for imaginative thoughts.

Moon conjunct Pluto
It's a good time to quit a bad habit, as this transit energies you with more power than usual penetrating analysis, particularly with a group or in relation to your situation. This could be a time to make changes in your environment. Emotional entanglements are possible now, although many of these could only be happening inside of you. You could be driven now to alter your home environment, your relationships, or your business. If this transit occurs when other hard aspects also are in effect, you could become entangled in some form of power struggle.

Moon sextile Pluto
You are more able to influence others. You may be sought after for your advice and counsel regarding very personal issues. You will be able to be understanding and handle this very volatile situation. The ability to keep your emotions on the inside today may be a strategy that turns out to be most successful. This is a good influence for business, obtaining loans, taxes, and joint finances. Events occurring now might involve some kind of karmic repayment or benefit.

Moon square Pluto You may find yourself at odds with those around you or with your life situation regarding issues of great sensitivity very personal. Difficulties, blocks, and all manner of hot spots may be discovered and have to be worked through. If you can, avoid getting yourself entangled in messy, emotional struggles, as these are more likely to occur now than usual. You might get yourself into a disagreement about finances. Changes may occur now, but they are more likely to be internal changes. Intensity characterizes your relationships for the time being.

Moon trine Pluto
You may be very eloquent or forceful in speaking or communicating. You may find yourself having emotional differences with someone. You are more sensitive than usual to subtleties in your personal environment, and all the more vulnerable as a result. You have a new, intense, emotional outlook on life with the urge to get things done and to make a fresh start if necessary. Your attitude is that the old must now make way for the new. You will be able to be understanding and handle this very volatile material. Starting a new fitness routine, kicking a bad habit, or anything that requires willpower is more likely to enjoy success.

Moon opposite Pluto
This is a time when that which is hidden has a tendency to surface. Someone could challenge you on a very sensitive issue, resulting in an. An issue from the past may come up to haunt you now, or you could lose something. Intensity in your personal relationships and some sort of inner emotional turmoil is possible. You could have some difficulty in letting go of something, or could be dealing with people who are likewise struggling.

MICROSCOPY OF TRANSITING PLANETS SIMPLIFIED VOLUME-5

CHAPTER NINE

TRANSITING MOON

Overview

The Moon moves around the zodiac completing a cycle in approximately Twenty Eight days. They are brief in duration and not as meaningful and significant as outer planet transits. They are important while electing a date for any special event or function.

Moon Transits to Natal Planets & Points

Moon conjunct Sun

Your manner may not be warm or loving at the moment. Perhaps not the best time to present you to others or take a job interview. Projects begun today have a good chance in turning out well. This is a time when you can expect a little boost, some sort of extra support or recognition from those around you. You may feel that you are in touch and in harmony with others. The support you need is there. Your needs are aligned with your wants right now, and it's an opportune time to make a few resolutions. Things seem to play in your style, so you don't have to stress or strain. You may wish to do something special at this hour. Concentrate on what you want from your life, and where you want your life to head. The inner harmony you experience now is reflected in your outer experience and contributes to your personal success. You could experience some change or undergo inner changes that stimulate a new undertaking, relationship, or attitude change. You act with more confidence than usual. Without even trying, you are likely to draw attention to yourself or to receive support. This is an ideal time to establish inner peace and balance.

Moon sextile Sun
This transit offers you increased clarity derived from a feeling that what you want and what you need are in harmony. This is a good period for dealing with others in general, but particularly on professional levels or with those in charge. There is a chance to understand those around you and to have a special time with someone you love. General good feeling and a sense of support and harmony make this a happy time. Your intentions and actions harmonize, which improves your relationships with others and with your own body and spirit. You could experience an improvement in your family affairs or domestic circumstances, as well as your business pursuits.

Moon square Sun
Working with rather than against the flow should be easy to do. You may not find the support you flowing to you. Some sort of temporary obstacle may appear. You may feel frustrated. You may become aware of a conflict between what you want and what you need. Even if you are not aware of this inner imbalance, it could cause some tensions or feelings of being unsupported by others or by circumstances in your life.

You may find it very easy to overdo or work at cross purposes to yourself just now. You may feel slightly out of step or out of synch, which could make you edgy. There could be a noticeable discrepancy between the demands of your personal life and what is expected of you at work. Minor problems in relationships are more likely during this transit. Arriving at decisions is harder now because you feel torn between choices. There is a sense of testing the limits.

You might find you have to push a little harder during this transit than you normally would. If this transit occurs during the night, you could have a restless sleep. Examining bad dreams can help you understand what is bothering you. Use the dynamic energy of this transit to identify problems in order to find solutions to them, instead of harping on what is going wrong in your life or taking it out on others.

Moon trine Sun

You receive some sort of boost to your ego and confidence, perhaps through some form of recognition, however big or small. General good feeling and a sense of support and harmony make this a happy time. It's easy to put your best face forward and to cooperate with others because you are not conflicted on the inside. What you do and what you feel are in harmony, and you benefit from this clarity. The harmony that you feel between your body and spirit allows you to act more holistically and purposefully. As well, decision-making is improved. If this transit occurs during the night, you sleep better. You are expressing yourself more genuinely, and you are received well as a result.

Moon opposite Sun

This is a period when ego-gratifying circumstances are highlighted. You may find yourself somewhat at odds with those around you today. You may be unable to get the support you require or find that some of your supply lines have been diminished or cut off. Someone may challenge you. Decision-making can be challenging right now, as there is a basic conflict between your instincts and what you feel you should do. Inner imbalance between your body and your spirit can wreak a little havoc on your personal relationships.

Moon conjunct Moon

Your inner resources and emotions are accented. Expect a sense of support and good will from those around you. Perhaps you feel this is really you how you feel and are. This transit marks the start of your personal lunar month. You are emotionally charged now. You should be aware that your current state of mind can, in an indirect way, determine much about how you will be feeling in the month ahead. As such, make it as positive as you can.

You receive some sort of boost to your ego and confidence, perhaps through some form of recognition, however big or small. Honour your feelings, reach into your well, and pull out the feelings that support your larger goals. Familiarity, a sense of belonging, and emotional connections fuel your spirit now more than usual. You are more sensitive and responsive than you are typically. Relationships with significant women in your life may be especially prominent now.

Moon sextile Moon
This is a time when tensions with others can come from a lack of self-confidence or a sudden awareness of unfulfilled wishes and goals. A great time to reflect and understand your own situation, just how you feel about yourself. Emotions in particular, or the feelings of those around you, may be very clear. It is easier for you to get in touch with your feelings and to recognize your inner resources now.

Emotions are up, and you may even find yourself pondering a bit on the meaning of life. You feel at one with your situation. A feeling of contentment and satisfaction can lead to inertia, or it can create opportunities for you to express yourself to others the choice is yours. You are unlikely to break the routine for the time being, as a feeling of familiarity is a deep need. This is a good time for all things domestic--for bridging emotional gaps with family members, and for tending to domestic affairs with general success.

Moon square Moon You may feel blocked or frustrated emotionally by someone or by your own life situation in general. You might feel that some avenues of support have been cut off or blocked. Arguments of an emotional kind could be easy to find. Minor forced changes to your routine or habits may upset you now. Friends and associates may burden you, and indecision keeps you from making good financial or business decisions.

This can indicate a a brief period when you are not as popular as you normally are. Tempera mentality is your worst enemy for the time being. You may be feeling stressed or unsupported, which can negatively influence your health. Feeling emotionally at odds with others will pass soon enough. For now, avoid taking little upsets to heart. It's probably best to avoid new initiatives on the domestic front as well as business changes.

Moon trine Moon
You could feel real support and harmony at this time for circumstances and those around you. You are more receptive and are more able to rely on your instincts. New friends could be made. You are currently able to handle opportunities well by focusing your energy on constructive activities and goals. This can be a time of heightened yet manageable emotions. Family and financial affairs should run smoothly. Your personal popularity peaks. This is a good time for making business decisions, investing, and property deals, all things equal.

Moon opposite Moon
You may find yourself having emotional differences with someone. Those around you, or the situation you find

yourself in, may not feel right to you. You could be challenged. Decisions made now, if you can come to any conclusions at all, may not be sound. This is a time of conscious striving knowing what you want and working towards getting it. Feeling emotionally out of step with others may get the better of your spirits for the time being. Your reactions are presently strongly emotional, and it is easy for events or for people to trigger resentments or buried emotions.

Moon conjunct Mercury

Ideas and thoughts will have greater meaning and form just now. You may be very eloquent or forceful in speaking or communicating. People will understand just what you mean. Imagination is brought to your communications and your mental pursuits, and your ideas and thoughts flow smoothly. You are more inclined towards personal communications, social discourse, and sharing. As well, you may easily get caught up in reminisce.

You may have a sense of circumstances working against you or feel a lack of support and love from those around you. Your mind is more receptive and alert than usual, and you may find yourself especially busy and curious, but perhaps too scattered to concentrate for very long on any particular subject. Your memory is particularly sharp. Connections could be made or enhanced with younger people. You express your feelings in an honest way, and you are likely to be preoccupied with personal matters. Seeking advice could be a theme now, whether you are the one looking for it, or others are turning to you for answers.

Moon sextile Mercury

You could be most persuasive with others, and eloquent in speech and communication. The situation is a natural for self-expression and lends itself to your particular ideas and thoughts. A good conversation with those you love is possible. This influence brings imagination to your mental pursuits. In business terms, it's a strong influence for negotiation, trading, and communications. A positive connection to a younger person may be made now, whether it's a new connection or simply a boost to an existing relationship.

You are more excitable than usual, and less inclined to make rational, thought-out decisions. You are at your most persuasive. Circumstances and others tend to be less supportive than usual, and you might find you have to push yourself harder to achieve the same results. This is an especially favourable transit for public speaking and presenting your ideas with flair.

Moon square Mercury
Others may cut you off or make it difficult for you to express yourself today. You could find that you lack depth and feeling and the ability to move or communicate with others. Your ideas may not find the support you need. Don't sweat the small stuff. What feels right clashes with logic right now. What you say may be a misrepresentation of your true feelings and emotions. Car and other transportation troubles, as well as computer glitches, miscommunications, and dealing with red tape, are more likely now than usual.

Relationships with others may be strained for the time being. This is a good time to uncover issues of emotional unrest that have been bubbling under the surface. It takes extra effort for you to understand others, or they to understand you. You're less likely to be objective and prone to changing your mind frequently, so it would be better to postpone important decision-making. Although you are in the mood to talk about personal matters, you could be communicating with an air of defensiveness. Avoid getting stressed out over the little things.

Moon trine Mercury

You could be most persuasive with others, and eloquent in speech and communication. The situation is a natural for self-expression and lends itself to your particular ideas and thoughts. A good conversation with those you love is possible. Your head and your heart agree with one another now, so take advantage and open up the lines of communication with others. You are in a more sociable frame of mind. It's easier than usual to flaunt your talents without even trying, and articulating your feelings without upsetting anyone comes easily.

Moon opposite Mercury

Your current situation may demand some re-evaluation or otherwise challenge your ideas. It may be very hard for you to communicate what you mean to others. Minor disagreements, especially over domestic matters, are more likely than usual now. It can be hard to stick to the facts and to remain clear-headed under this influence, so do what you can to avoid scheduling negotiations, test-taking, or contract-signing now. Also, because you are not received as well, public relations initiatives should be postponed.

Moon conjunct Venus

You could feel real support and harmony at this time for circumstances and those around you. You may be moved to appreciate and discover the beauty in your life and in those around you. At the same time, everything could take on added value and importance. Be careful that you don't overspend or indulge too much just now. This is an affectionate and friendly influence not wild or exciting, but pleasing and perhaps a little self-indulgent. Your personal popularity moves up a notch.

Moon sextile Venus

You may be able to enjoy and value your own life situation today or feel especially kind towards a friend or loved one. Someone may compliment you on your tastes or belongings. Love and romantic matters are favourable for you now. You might enjoy a happy social event or other pleasurable activity. It's a good influence for beauty treatments, redecorating, and the arts; and favourable for scheduling dates. This transit increases intimacy and improves relationships with others, particularly with women.

Moon square Venus

A strong urge for the social life may find you out and about. However, you will walk a fine line today between good company and disapproval, so beware. You could find yourself working against the values of another, going against the flow. You are a little more vulnerable than usual, likely because you don't seem to know what you want for the time being. There could be clashes between your desire for familiarity and your need for pleasure right now. The possibility of some form of recognition or validation for what you do may come during this brief but effective period. Social upsets are possible, or you may find that you are unable to do something pleasurable even though you would really like to. This sometimes triggers an attraction to someone who is simply not right for you, or minor problems in existing love affairs. On other occasions, this can signal a new love affair or friendship, particularly with a female. Domestic matters could annoy you. Avoid money transactions if you can.

Moon trine Venus

You may be able to enjoy and value your own life situation today or feel especially kind towards a friend or loved one. Someone may compliment you on your tastes or belongings. This is a good influence for scheduling dates and for love in general. You are somewhat vulnerable, wearing your feelings on your sleeve. This can indicate happy social events, and is fortunate for beauty treatments, pleasurable outings, music, the arts, and holidays or gatherings. It's good for money as well, but you might spend it as quickly as you earn it! You are especially warm and friendly with people you meet, and others sense your sincerity.

Moon opposite Venus

Someone may challenge your values or good taste. Or, you could find it difficult to be appreciative of others at this time. Not the best time to shop, choose colours, and so on. You may not find much support for your particular tastes and values. Interference that prevents you from doing something pleasurable may be in store for you now. An unusual attraction to someone perhaps unsuitable is possible. There could be minor problems with money, and some hypersensitivity that undermines your good humour or that disrupts cooperation with others.

Moon conjunct Mars

Everything points to your taking the initiative today. You could feel great support from those around you, or circumstances could dictate your taking action. You feel healthy and natural. Your emotions intensify and you instinctively desire change and adventure. It would be wise to keep your cool and avoid confrontations. Excessive haste or rash behaviour can leave you vulnerable to accidents or injuries, but healthy risk-taking might simply serve to enliven you. This sometimes points to a passionate time, or a new relationship with a man.

It's a good time to mend relationship problems and to surround you with people. This is a good time to take a chance, say what you feel, or do something exciting outside of your normal routine. Taking the initiative is appropriate now. You are braver and more decisive. Your instinctive reactions are quick, your sexual appetite is voracious, and you naturally take the lead.

Moon sextile Mars

You could find that you are appreciated or valued for your feelings or your ability to act and get things done. Someone understands how you feel and is sympathetic today. This influence heightens your feelings, awakens your impulses, and stirs your passions, mostly in a positive way. This is sometimes an indication of connections made with men. You are more in tune with your natural impulses and less inclined to think things through before taking action. It's an excellent period for taking the initiative. Expressing your feelings comes naturally now, and you make no apologies for doing so! This transit gives you self-confidence and backbone without backlash from others.

Moon square Mars

This is a period when you are more inclined to be immature. This transit fires up your feelings and stirs up your need for action, activity, and challenges. You are more inclined to act on impulse now, and you could be quite temperamental. You could be feeling less vigorous than usual or more stressed. There could be problems with men. It could also be a rather passionate time, simply because, for the time being, you tend to be ruled by your passions. There could be an emotional overtone to all of this that may require understanding and flexibility on your part. Doing something rash is quite possible now, but it's not always a bad thing. The dynamic energy of this transit could give you just the right kick in the pants to push you out of a bad situation, for example. Still, it would be wise to use some caution, and don't push yourself too hard.

Moon trine Mars

You could find that you are appreciated or valued for your feelings or your ability to act and get things done. Someone understands how you feel and is sympathetic today. This transit boosts your self-confidence and ability to assert yourself without ruffling the feathers of people around you. Your desire nature and your emotions are cooperating beautifully just now, which increases your resourcefulness and independence. Others allow you to be yourself, and you feel "in sync" with your environment.

If circumstances call for an aggressive or forthright approach, you are more inclined to shy away or to fumble. You can more confidently rely on your instincts now, and you react well to competition. This influence heightens your feelings, awakens your impulses, and stirs your passions, mostly in a positive way.

This is sometimes an indication of connections made with men. As well, passionate liaisons sometimes begin under this transit. You're a natural leader under this influence, so it's an opportune time to take the initiative. Do something that breaks the routine or that you've always wanted to do but have been hesitating to do due to shyness or fear. You'll pull it off with finesse now.

Moon opposite Mars

Circumstances may seem to conspire to irritate you or cause you to become emotional. Someone could challenge you or find a way to anger you. It could be difficult to remain calm and within control. Acting on impulse is what this transit tends to spur you to do. On the negative side, you could be very temperamental and touchy. Used positively, you could possess just the right amount of verve to do something you've never done before.

You may feel like talking a bit more than usual, exploring new ideas or getting happily lost in a conversation. You might find that you attract challenging situations simply because you are overreacting emotionally. Be aware that you are ruled by your passions now. A new connection with a man, or problems with males, may feature. You could get caught up in a domestic squabble. Although overly hasty or rash actions taken now could rebound on you, some healthy risk-taking could simply help you to break the routine and get you out of a rut. This transit excites your passions, and you are less in control of them than usual.

Moon conjunct Jupiter
You may find yourself serving to guide someone younger than you in matters of importance. Or, you may perceive how to proceed with plans and decisions in regard to your life situation. This is a lucky expansive, happy, and prosperous period. Some sort of emotional relief is likely, particularly with regards to your personal life. Domestic changes and legal affairs are favoured, particularly dealings with property and renovations. It's a good time to write, teach, learn, publish, promote, and take tests.

You are especially sharp, communicative, and open at this time, as your wants are aligned with your thoughts. You may enjoy opportunities to do any of these things now. Your personal popularity increases, in direct proportion to your own elevated, positive mood, and some kind of recognition or honour may come your way. It's a better time of the month to buy a lottery ticket. Your desire for pleasure is strong. Occasionally, losses are required in order to see gains.

Moon sextile Jupiter

You may be sought after as just the person for a particular job. Your management and directional abilities are in high focus. This signals an emotionally upbeat period when you enjoy your family, friends, and social life. Legal and real estate matters proceed smoothly. Public relations and general good favour and approval are more likely now. You may stumble upon opportunities to expand your horizons through travel, higher education, or contact with those of a different background than your own.

It's a favourable time to work on improving your skills. You tend to say what you think now. This is a fortunate, albeit brief, period for achievement and recognition in business. This is a favourable influence for learning, teaching, taking exams, publishing, and promotion. Business opportunities may present themselves. Occasionally, a loss is necessary in order to achieve a gain. This sometimes indicates the beginning of a friendship, particularly with someone who expands your mind or your social circle.

Moon square Jupiter

New ways to communicate or an easy manner will make conversations and interactions go well today. You may find yourself more talkative and facile than otherwise. The bottom line is that you are not especially realistic due to moodiness. Minor annoyances, such as unexpected bills coming your way or arguments with others over personal philosophies, may be part of the picture. This is not an ideal time for publicity, promotion, or legal matters. You're not as inclined to consider the consequences of over-eating, over-drinking, or overdoing in general.

Moon trine Jupiter

You may be sought after as just the person for a particular job. Your management and directional abilities are in high focus. Your positive state of mind can attract others, as well as favourable circumstances, to you. It's a better time of the month to buy a lottery ticket or to engage in reasonable speculation. You are more tuned in to the big picture and less inclined to worry over details. Others might find you particularly wise right now, and you are more generous with your time, energy, and money.

Moon opposite Jupiter

You portray the more reasonable, refined, and likable side of your personality now, and others tend to respond warmly. Not perhaps the best time to make important decisions that affect your living situation or life circumstances. Others may challenge your authority or the direction you are taking. You're given to excesses just now, and it can be hard to think of the consequences of overdoing things when you're in such an elevated mood. If you can, hold off on publicity or promotion activities. Don't let differences of opinion get the best of you. Otherwise, this is a sociable and mostly pleasurable transit.

Moon conjunct Saturn

A good time to consolidate and organize your affairs or rearrange your living situation. You could be seen by others as just the person to be put in charge of some project requiring a conservative mind. A tendency towards isolation and starkness. Situations that require you to keep a cool head will work out well under this transit. You are not easily swept away by your feelings now, enabling you to effectively tend to business. Authority figures or people who are older than you could figure prominently now.

A heightened awareness of your responsibilities, or taking on new responsibilities, characterizes this influence. It's easier for you to buckle down and work, organize, and plan. What you output now will benefit you down the road, as it's likely to be solid and realistic. This is a good time to make plans and lists. Some of us feel lonely or unsupported under the influence of this transit. Others welcome the feeling of self-reliance that comes now. A domestic problem or a burden might drop into your lap now, but you are likely to handle it well.

Moon sextile Saturn
You may find yourself being put to good use by your friends, or it could be that circumstances force you to reorganize and be more conservative. All of this should go rather smoothly. Your more taciturn qualities are to the fore and found to be valuable. Although there isn't much in the way of instant gratification for the work you do now, you will see real benefits from your efforts down the road. Connections with older people or authority figures can be made and are generally positive now.

During this transit, you find it easier than usual to rationalize your own behaviour and that of others. Because you are not easily swept away by your feelings at this time, you can take advantage by making clear-headed and realistic decisions. You are more reliable than usual, and more willing to go it alone. Others might find you a little distant emotionally, but they also view you as responsible and competent.

Moon square Saturn

You may feel left out or passed over just now. Your own requirements may appear to limit and separate you from where the rest of the gang is headed. A sense of isolation and loneliness is not unusual. This is of short duration. You may need to work overtime, or you could feel a pinch with your finances. Some feelings of being blocked are possible now with Saturn, the great teacher, activated and urging you to slow down.

It's an excellent period for improving your skills and for opening up discussions on topics that you normally might sidestep. Domestic affairs may be a little messy. A feeling of being unsupported, alone, or too independent might grab hold of you for the time being. Expressing your feelings or your need for others is hard to do at the moment. Treat this period as a time when you are learning to rely on yourself.

Moon trine Saturn

You may find yourself being put to good use by your friends, or it could be that circumstances force you to reorganize and be more conservative. All of this should go rather smoothly. Your more taciturn qualities are to the fore and found to be valuable. New responsibilities may come your way now, or there can be a heightened awareness of existing ones. It's relatively easy to discipline yourself and work hard now.

You could find yourself struggling to communicate or being easily misunderstood. You may have a hard time concentrating on any one subject although it may not be immediately obvious. Others would be hard-pressed to sweep you off your feet or sway you from your path right now! Appeals to your emotions won't work as much as appeals to your common sense, logic, and sense of responsibility.

Moon opposite Saturn
You might like to ignore responsibilities and do some socializing, but realities may demand that you tend to business and forget your friends for the moment. The crowd may ignore you and leave you old sober-sides to take care of business. Feeling blocked from expressing yourself makes for a less than spontaneous period. Avoid clashes with authority figures or older people you simply aren't getting the recognition you deserve right now, but this influence will pass soon.

You are more willing than usual to bend and compromise. Remember that you get what you want by the forces of attraction during this period, rather than coming on strong. Your feelings are going against much of what you value, so make way for possible difficulty. Saturn often brings with it some blockage, hardship, or restriction.

Moon trine Ascendant
You can demonstrate great understanding and sensitivity to the needs of others just now and are in a good position to communicate concerning groups and society in general. This is a personally popular time when you are in good spirits, don an optimistic outlook, and enjoy supportive people and/or circumstances. This is a good time to start a new project or to start fresh in some manner. Business and domestic affairs tend to run smoothly.

MICROSCOPY OF
TRANSITING PLANETS
SIMPLIFIED
VOLUME-5

CHAPTER TEN

PLACEMENT OF PLANETS IN DIFFERENT HOUSES

MOON

In the Ascendant. – Fanciful and romantic, moderate eater, an attractive appearance, inclined to corpulence, windy temperament, much travelling, disease in private organs and ears, capricious, licentious, sociable, easy going, educated, warring, loved by the opposite sex, shy, modest, stubborn, proud, fickle-minded and eccentric.

Second house. – Wealthy, handsome, attractive, generous, highly intelligent, breaks in education, charming, poetical, great respect, sweet speech, persuasive, squint eyes and much admired.

Third house. – Sickly, dyspeptic and later on piles, mild, lean, disappointments, impious, many brothers, cruel, educated, consumption, famous, sisters, intelligent, unscrupulous, purposeless, miserly, fond of travelling and active-minded.

Fourth house. – Sickly mother, quarrels, unhappy home life, danger to father, domestic quarrels and conveyances, uncomfortable, coarse, brutal, tyrannical, vulgar

Fifth house. – Subtle, handsome wife, shrewd, showy, many daughters, intelligent, gains through quadrupeds, interrupted education, high political office.

Sixth house. – Submissive to the opposite sex, indolent, imperious, short-tempered, intelligent, lazy, slender body, weak sexual connection, widow-hunter, poor, drunkard, refined, tender, pilfering habits stomach troubles, many foes, worried by cousins.

Seventh house. – Passionate, fond of women, handsome wife, mother short-lived, narrow-minded, good family, pains in he loins, social, successful, jealous and energetic in several matters.

Eighth house. – Unhealthy, legacy, capricious, mother short-lived, few children, bilious, slender bad sight, Kinney disease, unsteady, easy acquisitions.

Ninth house. – Popular, educated, intelligent, well read, lover of fiction, builder of charitable institutions, wealthy, active, inclined to travel, godly, good children, immoveable property, religious, mystical, righteous, agricultural success, devotional, successful and good reputation.

Tenth house. – Persuasive, passionate, charitable, shrewd, adulterous, bold, tactful, ambitious, great position, active, trustee of religious institutions, obliging to good people, many friends, easy success, popular and able, wealthy, comfortable and long life.

Eleventh house. – Many children, powerful, philanthropic, polite, literary an artistic taste, helpful, influential, cultured, charitable, many friends, great position, reputation, good lands, easy success, liked and helped by the fair sex, giver of donations, man of principles.

Twelfth house. – Obstructed, deformed, narrow-minded, cruel, unhappy, obscure, powerless, deceived, solitary, and miserable.

MICROSCOPY OF TRANSITING PLANETS SIMPLIFIED VOLUME-5

CHAPTER ELEVEN

PLACEMENT OF PLANETS IN DIFFERENT SIGNS

Planets in Different Signs

MOON

In Aries. – Round eyes, impulsive, fond of travel, irritable, fond of women, vegetable diet, quick to decide and act, haughty, inflexible, sores in the head, dexterous, fickle-minded, war-like, enterprising, good position, self-respect, valiant, ambitious, liable to hydrophobia if the Moon is afflicted, large thighs, popular, restless, idiosyncratic, versatile.

Taurus. – Liberal, powerful, happy, ability to command, intelligent, handsome, influential, fond of fair sex, happy in middle life and old age, great strides in life, beautiful gait, large thighs and hips, phlegmatic afflictions, rich patience, respected, love-intrigues, inconsistent, wavering mind, sound judgment, voracious eater and reader, lucky, popular, influenced by women, passionate, indolent.

Gemini. – Well read, creative, fond of women, learned in scriptures, able, persuasive, curly hair, powerful speaker, clever, witty, dexterous, fond of music, elevated nose, thought reader, subtle, long life.

Cancer. – Wise, powerful, charming, influenced by women, wealthy, kind, good, a bit stout, sensitive;

impetuous, unprofitable voyages, meditative, much immovable property, scientist, middle stature, prudent, frugal, piercing, conventional.

Leo. – Bold, irritable, large cheeks, blonde, broad face, brown eyes, repugnant to women, likes meat, frequenting forests and hills, colic troubles, inclined to be unhappy, haughty, mental anxiety, liberal, generous, deformed body, steady, aristocratic, settled views, proud, ambitious.

Virgo. – Lovely complexion, almond eyes, modest, sunken shoulders and arms, charming, attractive, principled, affluent, comfortable, soft body, sweet speech, honest; truthful, modest, virtuous, intelligent, phlegmatic, fond of women, acute insight, conceited in self-estimation, pensive, conversationalist, many daughters, loquacious, astrologer and clairvoyant or attracted towards them, skilled in arts like music and dancing, few sons.

Libra. – Reverence and respect for learned and holy people, saints and gods; tall, raised nose, thin, deformed limbs, sickly constitution, rejected by kinsmen, intelligent, principled, wealthy, business-like, obliging, love for arts, far-seeing idealistic, clever, mutable, amicable, losses through women, loves women, just, not ambitious, aspiring.

Scorpio. – Broad eyes, wide chest, round shanks and thighs, isolation from parents or preceptors, brown complexion, straight-forward, frank, open-minded, cruel, simulator, malicious, sterility, agitated, unhappy, wealthy, impetuous, obstinate.

Sagittarius. – Face broad, teeth large, skilled in fine arts, indistinct shoulders, disfigured nails and arms, deep and inventive intellect, yielding to praise, good speech, upright, help from wife and women, happy marriage, many children, good inheritance, benefactor, patron of arts and literature, ceremonial-minded, showy, unexpected gifts, author, reflective mentality, inflexible to threats.

Capricorn. – Ever attached to wife and children, virtuous, good eyes, slender waist, quick in perception, clever, active, crafty, somewhat selfish, sagacious, strategic, liberal, merciless, unscrupulous, inconsistent, low morals, niggardly and mean.

Aquarius. – Fair-looking, well-formed body, tall, large teeth, belly low, youngish, sensual, sudden elevations and depressions, pure-minded, artistic, intuitional, diplomatic, lonely, peevish artistic taste, energetic, emotional, esoteric, mystical, grateful, healing power.

Pisces. – Fixed, dealer in pearls and fond of wife and children, perfect build, long nose, bright body, annihilating enemies, subservient to opposite sex, handsome, learned, steady, simple, good reputation, loose morals, adventurous, many children, spiritually inclined later in life.
MOON

MICROSCOPY OF TRANSITING PLANETS VOLUME-5

CHAPTER TWELVE

REMEDIES OF PLANETS PLANET MOON

Effects and Remedies

As explained in the preceding issue, the Sun is regarded as the generator of power that gives spirit and life to all planets, the Moon is considered to be the conductor of power lent by Sun and rules over the lives of the beings on this earth. Sun represents individuality, whereas Moon shows one's personality.

Moon governs over impregnation, conception, birth of a child and the animal instinct. She represents mother, mother's family, grandmother, old women, horse, navigation, agricultural land, Lord Shiva, love, kindness, mental peace, heart, services rendered for other's welfare and the 4th house.

The Moon's effect comes up in the 16th, 51st and 86th year of the native and similarly its 1st cycle falls in the 24th year, the 2nd in the 49th year and the 3rd cycle falls in the 94th year of the native. The Jupiter, Sun and Mars are Moon's friends, whereas Saturn, Rahu and Ketu are inimical to her. For her protection, the Moon sacrifices her friendly planets - Sun, Mars or Jupiter. Moon is the Lord of 4th house, stands exalted in the 2nd house of Taurus and becomes debilitated in the 8th house of Scorpio. The Moon provides very good results if placed in houses 1, 2, 3, 4, 5, 7 and 9 whereas the 6th, 8th, 10th, 11th and 12th houses are bad for the Moon. The death of a domestic milch animal or a horse, drying up of a person's well or pond, the loss of the senses of touching and feeling are the signs of moon turning malefic.

The placement of the Ketu in the 4th house causes i.e. mother's debt. In such a situation pieces of silver of equal weight and size be collected from every member of the family and the same should be thrown together into the running water of a river. Consequently all the ill effects would be warded off.

Moon in 1st House

In general, the 1st house belongs to Mars and Sun. When the moon is also placed therein, this house will come under the combined influences of the Mars, the Sun and the Moon i.e. all the 3 mutual friends will be treated as occupants of this house. The Sun and Mars will extend all friendly support to their natural friend Moon placed on the throne i.e. the ascendant house.

Such native will be soft-hearted and will inherit all the traits and qualities of his mother. He will be either the eldest brother or will certainly be treated so. As long as the native receives the blessings of his mother and keeps her happy, he will continue to rise and prosper in every way.

The things and the relatives as represented by Mercury, who is inimical to Moon, will prove harmful to the native, e.g., the sister-in-law and the green colour will affect adversely. Hence it is better to keep away from them.

Burning milk (for making Khoya) or selling milk for profit would reduce or minimize the power of the Moon placed in the 1st house, which means that the native's life and property would be destroyed if he engages himself in such activities. Such a native should serve others with water and milk freely for long life and all round prosperity. Such a native will get a life of about 90 years and will be bestowed with honours and fame by the Govt.

Remedies

1. Do not marry between the age of 24 and 27 years, i.e., marry either before 24 years of age or after 27 years of age.

2. Do not build a house out of your earnings between 24 and 27 years of age.

3. Keep away from the green color and sister-in-law. Do not keep a silver pot or kettle with a snout (Toti) in it in the house.

4. Offer water to the roots of a Banyan tree whenever you can afford.

5. Insert copper nails on the four corners of your bed.

6. Whenever crossing a river, always throw coins in it for the welfare of your children.

7. Always keep a silver Thali in your house.

8. Use Silver pots for drinking water or milk and avoid the use of glassware for the same.

Moon in 2nd House

The results of the 2nd house, when Moon is placed therein, will be influenced by Jupiter, Venus and the Moon, because this is the Puckka Ghar, the permanent house of Jupiter and Venus is the lord of the second Rashi Taurus. The Moon gives very good results in this house, as it becomes very strong here because of the friendly support of Jupiter against Venus.

Such a native may not have sisters, but will certainly be having brothers. In case he doesn't have, his wife will certainly have brothers. He will certainly receive his due share in parental properties. Whatever be the planetary position otherwise, but the Moon here will ensure male offspring to the native.

The native will receive good education, which will add to his fortune. The Business associated with the things of the Moon will prove highly advantageous. He may be a reputed teacher also.

The Ketu placed in the 12th house will cause eclipse of the Moon here, which will deprive the native either of good education or of male children.

Remedies

1. Temple within the native's house may deprive the native of male issue.

2. The things associated with the Moon, i.e., silver, rice, non-cemented floor of the house, the mother and old women and their blessings will prove very lucky for the native.

3. Offering green colour clothes to small girls continuously for 43 days.

4. Place the things associated with the Moon into the foundation of your house, e.g., a square piece of silver.

Moon in 3rd House

The results of the 3rd house, when the Moon is placed therein, will be influenced by the Mars, Mercury and Moon. Here the Moon proves highly beneficial to ensure a long life and great wealth or riches for the native.

If there are no planets in the 9th and 11th houses, then Mars and Venus will give good results to the native because of the Moon being in the 3rd house.

With the advancement of the native's education and learning, the economic condition of his father will deteriorate, but without affecting his education adversely. If Ketu's placing in the horoscope is auspicious and not harming the Moon in the 3rd, the education of the native will bear good fruits and prove advantageous in every manner.

If the Moon is malefic, it will cause great loss of wealth and money at the age of the malefic planet placed in the 9th house.

Remedies

1. Offer in donation the things associated with the Moon, e.g., silver or rice, after the birth of a daughter and the things associated with the Sun e.g., wheat and jaggery when a   son is born.

2. Do not make use of your daughter's money and wealth.
3. To avoid the evil effects of a malefic planet in the 8th house, serve the guests and others by offering them milk and water freely.

4. Worshipping Goddess Durga and obtaining the blessings of small girls by touching their feet after serving them food and sweets.

Moon in 4th House

The results of the 4th house are the general product of the total influences of Moon, the lord of the 4th Rashi Cancer and the permanent resident of the 4th house. Here the Moon becomes very strong and powerful in every manner.

The use of, and association with the things represented by the Moon will prove highly beneficial to the native. Offer milk in place of water to the guests. Obtain blessings of your mother or the elderly women by touching their feet. The 4th house is the river of income which will continue to increase expenditure. In other words, expenditure will augment income.

The native will be a reputed and honoured person with soft heart and all sorts of riches. He will inherit all the traits and qualities of his mother and will face the problems of life boldly like a lion. He will receive honour and favors from the government along with riches and will provide peace and shelter to others.

Good education will be ensured for the native. If Jupiter is placed in the 6th house and Moon in the 4th, parental profession will suit him. If a person has mortgaged certain valuables to the native, he will never come back to demand it.

If Moon be placed with 4 planets in the 4th house, the native will be economically very strong and wealthy. The male planets will help the native like sons and the female planets like daughters.

Remedies

1. Selling of milk for profit and burning of milk for making Khoya, etc., will have a very adverse effects on income, life span and mental peace.

2. Adultery and flirtation will be seriously detrimental to the native's reputation and prospects of wealth gains.

3. The more the expenses, the more the income.

4. Before beginning any auspicious or new work, place a pitcher or any container filled with milk in the house.

5. For warding off the evil generated by the Jupiter placed in the 10th house, the native should visit places of worship along with his grandfather and offer their oblations by placing their forehead at the feet of the deity.

Moon in 5th House

The results of the 5th house, when the Moon is placed therein, will be influenced by the Sun, the Ketu and the Moon. The native will adopt just and right means to earn wealth and will not yield to wrong doing. He may not do well in business but certainly receive favours and honours from the government. Anyone supported by him will win.

The Moon in the 5th house will give 5 sons if the Ketu is well placed and benefice even if the Moon is joined by malefic planets. By his education and learning the native will undertake several measures for others welfare, but the others will not do good to him.

Further, the native will be destroyed if he becomes greedy and selfish. If he fails to keep his plans a secret, his own men will damage him seriously.

Remedies

1. Keep control over your tongue. Never use abusive Language to ward off troubles.
2. Avoid becoming greedy and over selfish.
3. Deceit and dishonesty towards others will affect you adversely.
4. Acting upon the advice of another person before trying to harm anybody will ensure very good results and a life of about 100 years.
5. Public service will enhance income and reputation of the native.

Moon in 6th House

This house is affected by the Mercury and Ketu. The Moon in this house will be affected by the planets placed in the 2nd, 8th, 12th and 4th houses. The native will receive education with obstacles and will have to struggle a lot for reaping the benefits of his educational achievements.

If the Moon is placed in the 6th, 2nd, 4th, 8th and 12th houses it is auspicious. The native would enliven a dying person by putting a few drops of water in his mouth.

But if the Moon is malefic in the 6th house and Mercury is placed in the 2nd or 12th house, the native will have suicidal tendencies. Similarly, if the Moon is malefic and the Sun is placed in the 12th house, then the native or his wife or both will have severe eye defects and troubles.

Remedies

1. Serve milk to your father with your own hands.

2. Never take milk during night. But intake of milk during day time and use of even curd and cheese during night is permissible.

3. Do not offer milk as donation. It can be given only at religious places of worship.

4. Digging of wells for public will destroy the issues, but Digging of wells in a hospital or within the premises of cremation ground will not be harmful.

Moon in 7th house

The 7th house belongs to Venus and Mercury. When the Moon is placed here, the results of this house will be affected by the Venus, Mercury and Moon. Venus and Mercury combined together give the effects of the Sun. The 1st house aspects the 7th house. Consequently the rays of the Sun from the 1st house would be enlightening the Moon if placed in the 7th, which means that the things and the relatives represented by the Moon will provide highly beneficial and good results.

Educational achievements will prove fruitful for earning money or wealth. He may or may not have properties but will certainly have cash money in hand always. He will have good potential for being a poet or astrologer, or else he will be characterless and will have great love for mysticism and spiritualism.

The 7th Moon also denotes conflict between the native's wife and mother, adverse effects in milk trade.

Disobedience towards mother will cause overall tensions and troubles.

Remedies

1. Avoid marriage in the 24th year of your life.
2. Always your mother keeps happy.
3. Never sell milk or water for profit.
4. Do not burn milk for making Khoya.
5. Ensure that in marriage your wife brings silver and rice with her from her parents, equal to her weight.

Moon in 8th House

This house belongs to Mars and Saturn. The Moon here affects the education of the native adversely, but if education goes well the native's mother's life will be shortened and very often such a native loses both - education and the mother. However, the evil effects of the Moon in the 7th house will be mitigated if Jupiter and Saturn be placed in the 2nd house.

The 7th Moon often deprives the native of his parental properties. If there is a well or pond adjacent to the parental property of the native, he will receive adverse results of the Moon all through his life.

Remedies

1. Avoid gambling and flirting.
2. Perform Shraddha ceremony for to your ancestors.
3. Do not build any house after covering a well with roof.
4. Obtain blessings of the old men and children by touching their feet.
5. Bring water from the well or water tap situated within the boundaries of a cremation ground and place it within

your house. It will ward off all the evils generated by the Moon in the 7th house.

6. Offer gram and pulse in places of worship.

Moon in 9th House

The 9th house belongs to Jupiter, who is a great friend of the Moon. Hence the native will imbibe the traits and features of both these planets - good conduct, soft heartedness, religious bent of mind and love for virtuous acts and pilgrimage. He will live upto 75 years. A friendly planet in the 5th house will augment comforts and pleasures from the son and develops intense interest in religious deeds. A friendly planet in the 3rd house ensures great increase in money and wealth.

Remedies

1. Install the things associated with the Moon within the house, e.g., place a square piece of silver in the   almirah.
2. Serve the labourers with milk.
3. Offer milk to snakes and rice to fish.

Moon in 10th House

The 10th house is in every manner ruled by Saturn. This house is expected by the 4th house, which is similarly ruled by Moon. Hence the Moon in the 10th house ensures a long life of about 90 years for the native. Moon and Saturn are inimical, therefore, medicines in liquid form will always prove harmful to him. The milk will act as poison if taken during night. If he is a medical practitioner, dry medicines administered by him to the patient will have a magical effect for cure. If a surgeon, he will earn great wealth and fame for surgery. If the 2nd and 4th houses are empty money and wealth will rain on him.

If Saturn is placed in the 1st house, the native's life will be destroyed by the opposite sex, especially a widow. The things and business represented by Saturn will prove beneficial for the native.

Remedies

1. Visits to religious places of worship will enhance the Fortune of the native.
2. Store the natural water of rain or the river in a container and keep it within your house for 15 years. It will wash off the poisons and evil effects generated by the Moon in the 10th house.
3. Avoid taking milk during night.
4. Milch animals can neither live long in your house nor will they prove beneficial or auspicious.
5. Abstain from wine, meat and adultery.

Moon in 11th house

This house is strongly influenced by Jupiter and Saturn. Every planet placed in this house will destroy its inimical planets and the things associated with them. In this way the Moon here will destroy its enemy Ketu's things, i.e., the sons of the native. Here the Moon will have to face the combined power of its enemies Saturn and Ketu, which will weaken the Moon. Now if Ketu is placed in the 4th house, the life of the native's mother will be endangered. The business associated with Mercury will also prove harmful. Starting house construction or purchase of a house on Saturdays will strengthen the Saturn (the Moon's enemy) which will prove disastrous for the native. Kanyadan after the midnight and participating in any marriage ceremony on Fridays will damage the fortunes of the native.

Remedies

1. Offer milk in Bhairo Mandir and donate
   Milk to other liberally.
2. Ensure that the grandmother does not see her grandson.
3. Heat up a piece of gold in fire and put it in a glass of
   milk before drinking it.
4. Throw 125 pieces of sweet (Peda) in a river.

Moon in 12th house

This house belongs to Moon's friend Jupiter. Here the Moon will have good effects on Mars and the things associated with Mars, but it will harm its enemies Mercury and Ketu and the things associated with them. Hence the business and things associated with the house in which Mars is placed will provide highly beneficial effects. Similarly, the business and things associated with the houses where Mercury and Ketu are placed will be strongly damaged. The Moon in the 12th houses causes a general fear in the native's mind about numerous unforeseen troubles and dangers and thus destroys his sleep and peace of mind. Ketu in the 4th house will become weak and affect the native's son and mother very adversely.

Remedies

1. Wearing Gold in ears, drinking milk after inserting hot piece of gold in it and visiting religious places of worship will ward off the evils of the Moon in 12th house and also that of the Ketu in the 4th house.

2. Never offer milk and food to religious saints/sadhus.

3. Do not open a school, college or any other educational Institute and do not help children in obtaining free of cost

MICROSCOPY OF
TRANSITING PLANETS
SIMPLIFIED
VOLUME-5

CHAPTER THIRTEEN

Transit results of Mars from natal Moon

TRANSISTING MARS

Transit of Planet Mars from First House of Natal Moon Sign

1st house: Transit of Mars in the 1st house from Natal Moon

You could find that you lack depth and feeling and the ability to move or communicate with others. During this period, Mars will move through your first house from the Moon. This mostly connotes difficulties. This period may take you through a bumpy road in matters of your business or profession. You may find it difficult to finish your projects successfully on time. It is better not to start anything new during this particular period. If employed, try and avoid any kind of arguments and misunderstanding with your seniors, employers and government departments.

This is a good time to uncover issues of emotional unrest that have been bubbling under the surface. Some of you may also see a change of your position during this time. Keep an eye on your enemies as they may create more problems for you at this time. Your finances would also require proper attention, as you are likely to lose on undesired expenses. Cut down on your urge to spend money. This period also brings in ample opportunities or reasons to travel. Moreover, this period may also keep you away from your near and dear ones. Those who are married may have to stay away from your spouse and children, if any. Your health needs proper attention during this period. You are likely to feel lacklustre and be unenthusiastic about everything in life.

Although you are in the mood to talk about personal matters, you could be communicating with an air of defensiveness. Avoid getting stressed out over the little things. You are also susceptible to developing fever and some ailments related to blood and the stomach. Stay away from sharp weapons, fire, poisonous animals and from everything that might risk your life. You must keep up your spirits at this time, as you may suffer from bouts of depression, bewilderment and may develop unnecessary fear.

2nd house: Transit of Mars in the 2nd house from Natal Moon

You could be most persuasive with others, and eloquent in speech and communication. The situation is a natural for self-expression and lends itself to your particular ideas and thoughts. During this period, Mars will move through your second house from the Moon. This mostly suggests a period of loss. Take good care of your finances and focus on the safety of your valuables as you may suffer some losses due to theft during this period. You may also face a rutted phase at your work place due to several unpleasant happenings.

This transit could offer you the drive to do something new, but avoid making hasty, major decisions for the time being. Keep yourself away from arguments. Watch your words before uttering them to anybody. Your work or profession may see a very low phase during this time and some of you may even lose your position if not handled carefully.

Disrupted routines and plans figure now, which help to stimulate the adoption of new approaches. Beware of your old enemies and avoid creating new ones. You may develop the negative emotion of jealousy towards others during this time. Beware of any wrath of the government or the state authority. During this particular period, you are also likely to befriend some wicked people and get involved in quarrels with your family and dear ones.

3rd house: Transit of Mars in the 3rd house from Natal Moon

This is a dynamic and exciting period, one in which taking advantage of unusual or unconventional opportunities may reap rewards. During this period, Mars will move through your third house from the Moon. This brings in good times and could be regarded especially well for financial gains. During this time, you are likely to make money in your trade and profession. You are also likely to acquire valuable ornaments during this phase. Work should be on a smooth sail and you are likely to succeed in matters of importance. Your new endeavours would also see success. If employed, you are likely to be promoted to a position of greater authority and honour. Your unique approach to life is in order with this transit, and works to your benefit. Flexibility is the key to success at this time, and pleasant changes are in store. Your success would boost your self-confidence and strengthen your will power during this time.

Health would remain good and you would shine with health and vigour. Your enthusiasm is likely to be at its top and you would be relieved from all the past confusion or obstacles. This time also sees you indulging in exotic culinary delights. Your enemies would be defeated and you would be at peace with your mind. Avoid any trip abroad as it may not bring in the desired result during this time.

4th house: Transit of Mars in the 4th house from Natal Moon

During this period, Mars will move through your fourth house from the Moon. This brings in some hard times in a few of your life's segments. Most of you are likely to face a difficult time when it comes to managing your old enemies. You are also likely to encounter some new enemies who could also be from your own circle of family and friends. Some of you may also befriend some wicked people for whom you may suffer later. Keep an eye on your behaviour as it might become cruel during this phase. However, a few of you may also go in for some kind of settlement with your foes.

There will be an urge to communicate. Jupiter stimulates your drive, motivation, passions, and assertive powers. Your health would require more attention than usual as this period makes you susceptible to developing fever and discomfort in the chest. Some of you may also suffer from diseases mostly related to the blood and the stomach. Mentally you are likely to remain worried and under a spell of grief. Relationships would be demanding during this time. Make peace with your family and other relatives to avoid further sorrow during this phase. Hold on tightly to your honour and position in the society as well. Avoid any issues related to land and property especially during this time.

5th house: Transit of Mars in the 5th house from Natal Moon

You are especially sharp, communicative, and open at this time, as your wants are aligned with your thoughts. Your energy levels and your competitive spirit expand with this transit. During this period, Mars will move through your fifth house from the Moon. This signifies a ruffled time. It would be a wise move to curtail your expenses as much as possible as this period sees you losing control on your finances and expenses. Take care of your children as they may suffer from sickness. Avoid any kind of unpleasantness between you and your son, if any, as this may give you agony.

Be cautious of immoderation at this time, especially if your natal Mars is afflicted. Over-estimating your abilities is possible. Handle your enemies with care and be cautious enough to avoid creating some new ones. Your enemies are likely to give you some more harassment during this particular time. Your health would require more attention during this period. You are likely to feel lacklustre, weak and feverish. Some of you may catch some diseases that would require proper diagnosis. Take care of your food habits as well. Some of you may also go through a personal behavioural change during this time.

You could be feeling less vigorous than usual or more stressed. You might find that you attract challenging situations simply because you are overreacting emotionally. Some of you, though very unlikely of you, may become furious, apprehensive and very estranged from the near and dear ones. Some of you may even tend to lose their glory and fame during this phase. Development of some needless needs and urge to do some immoral deeds may land some of you in thick soup. Stay away from quarrel with family members during this time.

6th house: Transit of Mars in the 6th house from Natal Moon

Your personal popularity increases, in direct proportion to your own elevated, positive mood, and some kind of recognition or honour may come your way. During this period, Mars will move through your sixth house from the Moon. This denotes good times. This period would see you gaining wealth, acquiring gold, corals, copper and reaping unprecedented profit in your metal and other businesses. If employed, you may expect that much awaited promotion and honour at your work place. Most of you would see success in all your undertakings. The improvement in your overall financial condition would make you feel secure, comfortable and happy.

You may be sought after as just the person for a particular job. Your management and directional abilities are in high focus. You would also be able to live in with peace in mind and a sense of fearlessness would prevail in you. This is also the time to win over your enemies. You may also expect ceasefire of your previous quarrels. If you are caught up in any court case, you may expect a judgment that would favour you. Most of your enemies would withdraw and victory would be yours. You are also likely to command more respect and honour in the society. Some of you would also perform charitable deeds at this time. Health would be fine during this time. You would get rid of all your previous ailments.

7th house: Transit of Mars in the 7th house from Natal Moon

You may stumble upon opportunities to expand your horizons with those of a different background than your own. During this period, Mars will move through your seventh house from the Moon. This brings in a trying time mostly in matters of health and relationships. You may suffer from excess mental worry due to a health problem to yourself, your spouse and your near and dear ones. You are likely to feel fatigued and susceptible of developing eye discomfort, stomach ache and discomfort in your chest.

A tendency towards isolation and starkness. Situations that require you to keep a cool head will work out well under this transit. You may also have to take care of your spouse's health. You and your spouse are also likely to develop deep mental anxiety during this time. Most of you are likely to develop enmity with some noble person. Avoid any misunderstanding that may crop up due to hypothetical differences between you and your spouse. If not handled tactfully, this may lead to a big quarrel between the two of you.

A heightened awareness of your responsibilities, or taking on new responsibilities, characterizes this influence. Make peace with your friends and dear ones. You are also likely to be put to anguish by your kinships. Watch your behaviour, as you are susceptible of using bad words and being wrathful towards your siblings or children. Your finances would need a tight watch as well. Some of you may lose some of your riches due to your unnecessary indulgence in a competition.

8th house: Transit of Mars in the 8th house from Natal Moon

During this transit, you find it easier than usual to rationalize your own behaviour and that of others. Because you are not easily swept away by your feelings at this time, you can take advantage by making clear-headed and realistic decisions. During this period, Mars will move through your eighth house from the Moon. This mostly denotes physical danger to you. This period demands a strict watchfulness on any and all the developments related to your life, health and physique. Stay clear from diseases and all kind of addictions to maintain sound health.

You are more reliable than usual, and more willing to go it alone. Others might find you a little distant emotionally, but they also view you as responsible and competent. Avoid undertaking any task that might prove to be life risking for you. Finances would require proper vigilance during this particular period. Most of you are likely to face some steep decline in your finances If not handled carefully. However, avoid going for any loan and try and keep yourself debt free.

Your own requirements may appear to limit and separate you from where the rest of the gang is headed. A sense of isolation and loneliness is not unusual. At work, you may have to put in extra effort to see success in your endeavours. Keep up your hope and work on. Hold on to your position and honour at work, as this low phase shall also pass. Most of you are also likely to go on foreign trips and may even have to stay away from your family for a considerable time.

9th house: Transit of Mars in the 9th house from Natal Moon

This is a time when tensions with others can come from a lack of self-confidence or a sudden awareness of unfulfilled wishes and goals. During this period, Mars will move through your ninth house from the Moon. This signifies sufferings mostly due to ailments. This period makes you suffer from minor to major physical ailments and bodily pain. During this time, you are susceptible to dehydration and weakness or decayed physical power. You may also suffer from muscle pain and wounds caused by some weapon. Mentally you may feel worried and disappointment most of the time. Some of you may also have to go to a foreign land to experience a temporary painful living.

Finances would need better care and guarding, as you are likely to lose some during this particular time. Your professional life would require proper handling and more hard work. Some of you may also have to work in an uncomfortable work environment for a while. Work hard to maintain your position and respect at work or in your field of profession. Maintain peace and harmony at home and keep an eye for disguised foes within your near and dear ones. Some of you may also develop an urge to perform some activities that may not be acceptable in your religious confines.

10th house: Transit of Mars in the 10th house from Natal Moon

A great time to reflect and understand your own situation, just how you feel about yourself. Emotions in particular, or the feelings of those around you, may be very clear. During this period, Mars will move through your tenth house from the Moon. This signifies a ruffled path to success. You are likely to face a lot of trouble ranging from misbehaviour of your superiors, failure in efforts, sorrow, disappointments, and exhaustion and so on. However, you are also likely to meet with success in your field of work at the end. Some of you would be able to perform better than ever at work. You may also have to undertake some hopping about around places, as your work is likely to demand the same.

It is easier for you to get in touch with your feelings and to recognize your inner resources now. Emotions are up, and you may even find yourself pondering a bit on the meaning of life. You feel at one with your situation. This period is likely to bestow a rise in your prestige, position and authority at work. You are also likely to get scripted in the good books of your superiors and enlarge your circle of good friends. Your glory is also likely to bring in some new friends into your life. Health however, would require your attention. Keep note of what you are eating and keep up your mental health as well.

11th house: Transit of Mars in the 11th house from Natal Moon
During this period, Mars will move through your eleventh house from the Moon. This brings in happy times for you and your family. This period bestows you with landed property, and profit in your field of business or trade. Some of you are also likely to gain from your siblings during this time. This could also prove to be a good time for those who are employed. Some of you may expect a rise in your income or position at this time. Moreover, all your endeavours are likely to succeed bringing you more gains.

A feeling of contentment and satisfaction can lead to inertia, or it can create opportunities for you to express yourself to others the choice is yours. This could be regarded as a time when you would see improvement in not only your professional life but also in your personal day-to-day life. You may also expect an upward move in your social status, prestige and respect during this time. Your personality would glow reflecting your accomplishments.

Some of you may also expect the birth of a new member in your family bringing you more happiness and domestic peace. Your children and siblings would bring you more happiness. Health sector should be fine keeping you hale and hearty, free from diseases. You are also likely to feel more fearless than ever.

12th house: Transit of Mars in the 12th house from Natal Moon

You may feel blocked or frustrated emotionally by someone or by your own life situation in general. You might feel that some avenues of support have been cut off or blocked. During this period, Mars will move through your twelfth house from the Moon. This signifies body pain and general sufferings. This period may prove to be taxing for you if care is not taken in time. Pay attention to any health related issues, as you are likely to develop discomforts or ailments particularly related to eyes and stomach. Take care of your feet as well. This is the time when you must stay away from activities that might be risky to your life. Some of you may even suffer from nightmarish dreams or dream disorders.

You are currently able to handle opportunities well by focusing your energy on constructive activities and goals. This can be a time of heightened yet manageable emotions. Your work life could also be strenuous and you may also have to put in loads of hard work to see the face of success in your projects. If measures are not taken, some of you may even risk your position at work and be humiliated and dishonoured. Take care of finances and avoid any kind of unnecessary expenditure. Stay away from further conflicts with your enemies and be cautious enough not to create some new ones.

MICROSCOPY OF TRANSITING PLANETS SIMPLIFIED VOLUME-5

CHAPTER FOURTEEN

MARS TRANSITS URANUS NEPTUNE PLUTO

Mars conjunct Uranus

You feel like being different, trying something new and unusual. This is a good time for new ideas. You tend to act on impulses, or other sudden realizations. The desire to break free of a limiting situation is enlightened. You are more willing to experiment or take risks, and more conscious of a need to act independently. The best way to harness this exciting but erratic energy is to act rather than react.

Mars sextile Uranus

Decisions made now, if you can come to any conclusions at all, may not be sound. This is a time of conscious striving knowing what you want and working towards getting it. You may find yourself having emotional differences with someone. Those around you, or the situation you find yourself in, may not feel right to you. You want to do something that sets you apart from others or that makes you feel unique. You feel like being different, trying something new and unusual.

Mars trine Uranus

You are more willing to experiment or take risks in order to change your life's direction now. You feel like being different, trying something new and unusual. A good time for a breakthrough in terms of thinking positively. Your sense of independence is pleasantly stimulated now, and it can be a great time for doing something that requires courage or guts.

Mars opposition Uranus
Avoid taking foolish risks, but do try to remove yourself from the regular routine. Heated arguments could lead to going your own way when someone or something tries to confine you. Your own sense of independence and freedom is being challenged.

Mars square Uranus
Your desire for independence or to feel unique and original is strongly stimulated. Don't do too much dreaming just now. It would be very easy for you to get carried away with some fancy or another. You may find that you are impatient with anything that feels ordinary. You crave more glamor and drama in your life, and you might act on a whim now without considering the practical consequences. You are more sensitive to, and frustrated by, anything that makes you feel restricted, oppressed, or restrained. You may be especially impatient, impulsive, or prone to taking foolish risks.

Mars conjunct Neptune
You may find yourself becoming intensely personal and passionate in the way you appear or come on to others. This transit favours dancing, swimming, photography, arts, and entertainment. You feel as though you have been drifting along with the tide and following the crowd for too long, and your inner needs and motivations must assert themselves more strongly. You want something more imaginative and less mundane. You are especially sensitive to anything that reminds you that you are not in control now. You may feel that nothing is impossible now, or you could find yourself acting on a whim.

Mars sextile Neptune
You may be feeling pleasantly inspired. There can be letting go of anger, or a softening of the disposition now. You want something more imaginative and less irritating. A liking for some more form of love.

Mars trine Neptune

You could feel slighted as a result of others misunderstanding what you communicate or get offended over a difference of opinion. Your intuition, compassion, and idealistic impulses are pleasantly stimulated now. You want something less mundane. Practical concerns and routines are of little interest to you, so it's a good time to create something artistic, enjoy down time, and other such creative and entertaining endeavours.

Mars opposition Neptune

You may experience anxiety or worry over mundane affairs. It's best not to schedule tests or presentations now, as you can easily overlook important facts or find that you are easily distracted. You may enjoy a strong sense of purposefulness. Emotions, perhaps coming from another person oppose your life dreams and stifle any imagination you may have. This can result in an emotional confrontation. Your drive to succeed and excel, as well as to get your way, is stimulated now.

Mars conjunct Pluto

A drive to probe and penetrate may find you examining and working through some strong internal changes. Push too hard and you could be too dominating and even oppressive to yourself and others. You don't want to take no for an answer now. You are especially wilful and decisive. The desire to take control of something of your life in general is stimulated, and you can be especially determined and possibly impatient in the process. You might get involved with power struggles if someone seems to be in your way.

Mars sextile Pluto

You want to be the centre of attention right now so you may pay special attention to your charm. A change of mind down the road is likely. You can too easily misrepresent yourself with what you say or write now. The desire to act out a fantasy or to take action on a compassionate or idealistic level is very strong now. You need to push too hard and you could be too dominating, even oppressive, to yourself and others.

Mars trine Pluto

You might throw yourself wholeheartedly into something now, and when your determination is strong. A drive to probe and penetrate may find you examining and working through some strong internal changes. Your drive to succeed, excel, and control is stimulated now with positive results.

Mars opposite Pluto

Pleasurable activities are emphasized, and relationships with others tend to be gratifying and agreeable. It's an excellent period for negotiations and smoothing over of differences. A tendency to bully and confront may dominate. Efforts to make changes could be thwarted, or power struggles emerge. A real power struggle could be in the wind. An emotional person or event challenges your sense of privacy and inner growth. Someone may get very personal with you.

Mars square Pluto

It would be wise to observe whatever powerful feelings that confrontations or conflicts arouse under this influence Intense emotional drama is available if that is what you need. Your emotions are not in tune with the more sensitive and private areas of your life.. Your desires are intense and difficult to satisfy under this influence. The desire to get the upper hand is strong, but it's unlikely to happen under this influence.

MICROSCOPY OF TRANSITING PLANETS SIMPLIFIED VOLUME-5

CHAPTER FIFTEEN

TRANSITING MARS

Overview:

A time of much energy and drive, perfect for starting something out some new. The transits of Mars to planets and points in the natal chart are brief influences, lasting approximately 2-3 days. Mars acts to energizer and activate the conditions surrounding the planets and the points it touches.

Mars Transits

Mars conjunct Sun
You may be especially dynamic and assertive just now. There is a lot of energy and drive available, and you may have an urge to push forward. Taking action is the theme now. You may jump into something impulsively, do something you normally don't have the courage to do, or something you have always wanted to do but haven't had the chance to act out. Competitive activities are favoured. Males or traditionally masculine activities figure prominently.

Mars trine Sun
You may be especially dynamic and assertive just now. There is a lot of energy and drive available. You may be especially dynamic and assertive just now. There is a lot of energy and drive available. Taking action on an instinctive

level is the theme now. This is a good time to do something that requires additional bravery or courage, as this influence tends to release some of your inhibitions. You are living spiritedly now. It's an excellent influence for competitive activities, such as sports or business.

Mars opposite Sun

You are at a peak of physical energy now. Your enthusiasm runs high, and so does your courage. You may have an emotional confrontation with someone older than you or with an authority figure. Your feelings and emotions may be running against your best interests.

Mars square Sun

Emotions may flare up or arguments occur that work against your own best interests. Be prepared, and walk softly. You are taking things quite personally now, and something that someone says or does now can easily rile you up. Challenges with those in authority or with males could figure. Impatience and impulsiveness tend to rule. You are in no mood to compromise just now. A tendency to be more accident-prone could be due to stress or physical exhaustion.

Mars conjunct Moon

You take things more personally now, and issues that have been stewing beneath the surface reveal themselves now. You have a lot of energy for improving your surroundings or life situations. You are very motivated to improve. There could be some hard feelings, especially from younger persons, if you become too aggressive. Acting upon your emotions in some manner, or taking action in your home, could figure now with the fiery planet stimulating your emotional, domestic Moon.

You have all the drive and energy you could want, and it should be easy to channel it. You are looking to expand something right now the bigger the better. You are confident, straightforward, direct, and ambitious. .You are likely to feel especially energized and enthusiastic about what you believe in or regarding business ventures.

Mars sextile Moon
You have all the drive and energy you could want, and it should be easy to channel it. You possess willpower, verve, and energy that you can direct toward achieving your more lofty goals. You are very motivated to improve. There could be some hard feelings, especially from younger persons, if you become too aggressive.

Mars trine Moon
You are very motivated to improve. There could be some hard feelings, especially from younger persons, if you become too aggressive. A pleasing emotional or sexual experience can be part of the picture now. Your emotional drive and sense of things may be at odds with your best interests, the way to proceed. The desire to take action for the good or to better your life is strong now. Your emotions are spirited, your lust for life is strong, and you are willing to act on a hunch. There's nothing neutral about your feelings now, yet you still manage to come across as level-headed. This is a good time for projects around the home, sexual activity, and anything that involves putting your heart into what you do.

Mars opposite Moon
Positively, however, you might feel much enthusiasm for getting your life into order in some significant manner. Your feelings, or the feelings of someone who supports you, may be hurt.

Mars square Moon

Emotional flare-ups, especially with younger people or those you spend time with are, possible right now. You could push too hard and damage your living situation or means of support. You are acting on your feelings right now, but it might get you into hot water if you are not truly in touch with what you want. You are capable of some childish or impulsive reactions during this transit. Tempers may flare, domestic squabbles are possible, and you could be feeling under the weather. If you are feeling particularly disgruntled, this could be a good time to get in touch with what has been brewing inside.

Mars conjunct Mercury

You may be very forceful in what you say and think. With all of this emotional energy, you could speak or communicate very well. You have mental drive. You are very busy and potentially very productive during this transit. Your ambition to complete projects, for example, is stimulated. You could be itching to express yourself, but not very receptive to others' points of view. As such, it can be hard to carry a satisfying and healthy conversation. Others might find you too aggressive when it comes to expressing your point of view. You are also inclined towards impulsive decision-making and off the cuff remarks.

Mars sextile Mercury

You are especially aware of the process right now, and this gives you a sense of responsibility and purposefulness. There is a lot of energy available for disciplined work, but push too hard and you may break something. You may be very forceful in what you say and think. With all of this emotional energy, you could speak or communicate very well. You have mental drive.

Mars trine Mercury
You may be very forceful in what you say and think. With all of this emotional energy, you could speak or communicate very well. You have mental drive. It's easier than usual for you to make quick decisions, communicate with others directly and effectively, and to make serious progress in any projects or mental work now. You could be enthusiastic about a particular idea or concept. Lively conversations can figure. Your desire to solve problems is strong and your mental energy levels high. You are proactive, and willing to put your ideas into action.

Mars square Mercury
On the negative side, your relationships with others could be strained. You could be feeling less vigorous than usual or more stressed. It's a good time to temper your energy or apply yourself, using traditional methods. Excessive emotional energy could produce flare-ups, harsh words, and arguments. Your mind is very during this time and can cause as much harm as good.

Mars opposite Mercury
You might find that you attract challenging situations simply because you are overreacting emotionally. Managed well, this can be a time in which you arrive at increased self-understanding of your innermost needs and wants. You may have words and possible hurt feelings with someone during this time. You won't accept opposition to your ideas right now, although you are likely to encounter it. You could be coming on too strong with your opinions or point of view. Resist turning an intellectual debate into an argument.

Mars conjunct Venus
You may feel like talking a bit more than usual, exploring new ideas or getting happily lost in a conversation. Your

desires are strong and you will want to enjoy yourself. Spending is very possible. There is a basic drive to appreciate and taste life. Sexual and creative energy is high now. You are hungry for experience--you want to put into action many of your wants and desires. Although you might be a little too eager, and perhaps come across as insensitive, this could also be a time when you take the lead and make your move.

You could meet with some opposition. Someone's emotional state may block your own interests. be impulsive with your affections and your pocketbook during this transit. You have an opportunity now to take the initiative in order to achieve harmony and sexual fulfilment. Social relations are impassioned, and perhaps demanding or extreme. Your romantic impulses may be more forceful and pressing. Some level of competition is present in your interactions with others.

Mars sextile Venus
You have just emerged from a period in which you were less forthright or in which you were considering new plans but not quite ready to take action. This is a time in which you are especially sensitive to the limitations or blocks in your path, which can point to frustration or stress. Your own drive and emotions are hard set against the way things are, your particular set of realities.

Mars trine Venus
Your desires are strong, and you will want to enjoy yourself. Romance is very possible. There is a basic drive to appreciate and taste life. You may find it easy to go after your heart's desire right now, whether that's a person, circumstance, or object! Sexual and romantic activities may be initiated or simply feel. Your sense of timing is strong. The desire to enjoy life, for comfort and pleasure as well is

stimulated. Creative endeavours are favoured at this time. Sensuality is also strong now.

Mars opposite Venus

You are especially sharp, communicative, and open at this time, as your wants are aligned with your thoughts. You may be a little too forward-looking, forgetting or ignoring important details. Now, you are ready to go forward, push personal plans, or go after what you want. You can really communicate and convey yourself to others right now. Others may oppose or confront your value system. Their push or drive may tend to conflict with the way you feel and do things. Your own desires may be ignored.

Mars square Venus

You could find yourself driven by a restless desire to do something. You could be especially defensive and emotional, or possessive and protective of loved ones. With all of this emotional energy, you could speak or communicate very well. Powerful desires and amorous feelings are stimulated now perhaps through an enticing interaction or personal encounter. Strive for a balance between taking the initiative and being sensitive and aware of others' needs and wants. You might feel the need to take charge or lead a project.

Mars conjunct Mars

A time of much energy and drive, perfect for starting something out or taking care of business. Exercise or romance is in order. You are at a peak of physical energy now. Your enthusiasm runs high, and so does your courage. It's a time of decisiveness, taking the initiative, handling problems directly and straightforwardly.

Mars sextile Mars

You may find yourself at odds with someone today, in particular at the gut or emotional level. You are drawn to physical activity, and if you are involved in a competitive event, you are more likely than usual to come out a winner. It's a good time to take the initiative and to act on things that you've only been thinking about doing. A time of much energy and drive, perfect for starting something out or taking care of business.

Mars trine Mars

A time of much energy and drive, perfect for starting something out or taking care of business. Exercise or romance is in order. You have excellent rhythm and timing right now. You are confident, straightforward, direct, and ambitious. You might enjoy competition at this time in your life. Enthusiasm runs high, and you easily find motivation to do something physical or brave.

Mars opposite Mars

During this transit, you find it easier than usual to rationalize your own behaviour and that of others. You tend to say what you think now. Keep in mind that what you say or write now has impact, for better or for worse. Feelings could run strong, and this may require presence of mind and real patience in order to avoid a flare-up.

Mars square Mars

Harsh energy could leave you feeling emotionally blocked and frustrated. Don't try to push too hard. You are only fighting yourself. Wait this one out. A sense of frustration is likely now, possibly because you are feeling out of step with your natural rhythm. Buried angers can surface now as tension or impatience. You are touchy and over-sensitive now, and it is very easy to take offence.

Mars conjunct Jupiter

A perfect time to be assertive and to move forward in your career decisions. You have all the drive and energy you could want, and it should be easy to channel it. The path is open and clear. You are likely to feel especially energized and enthusiastic about what you believe in or regarding business ventures. The desire to do something about your beliefs or ideals is strong now, or you are in a position to stand up for your beliefs.

This is likely due to the fact that you are not in touch with what it is you really want at this time. If you do know what you want, how to go about getting it doesn't come naturally to you right now. Your sense of timing is excellent, all things considered. You more readily take chances, and you feel especially strong, positive, adventurous, confident, and energetic. You are looking to expand something right now--the bigger the better. You are competitive in a friendly manner, and you readily rise to a challenge now.

Mars sextile Jupiter

It's an excellent period for improving your skills and for opening up discussions on topics that you normally might sidestep. You will find a way around almost any obstacle and are in control and able to guide yourself with ease. A perfect time to be assertive and to move forward in your career decisions. You have all the drive and energy you could want, and it should be easy to channel it. The path is open and clear.

Mars trine Jupiter

You have all the drive and energy you could want, and it should be easy to channel it. The path is open and clear. All systems go! This is a strong aspect for beginning a new enterprise or endeavour. Decisive action comes naturally now. You possess willpower, verve, and energy that you can direct toward achieving your more lofty goals. You have the urge to expand, branch out, or take on more challenges. The desire to take action for the good or to better your life is strong now.

Mars opposite Jupiter
You feel more generous, optimistic, and sociable under this influence. Emotional considerations may block or oppose how you proceed with a project or plan. Someone may get pushy or obscure the real choices and the right path.

Mars square Jupiter
Your emotional drive and sense of things may be at odds with your best interests, the way to proceed. You could make some bad decisions, be too generous, or squander your resource. You may be boastful or arrogant in manner right now, and you tend to overestimate your capabilities. The tremendous energy you have at your disposal now should be used constructively or you might find you are just spinning your wheels. You may be a little too forward-looking, forgetting or ignoring important details. Your ideas or plans may be too big.

Mars conjunct Saturn
Irresistible force meets immovable object. Proceed with caution! There is a lot of energy available for disciplined work, but push too hard and you may break something. You may be particularly aware of, and frustrated by, slowness, blocks to your plans, limitations, and other realities right now. Positively, however, you might feel much enthusiasm for getting your life into order in some significant manner. Eliminating waste or excess may be the focus now, for which you can channel tremendous energy.

Mars sextile/trine Saturn

This transit suggests you now have a stronger sense of who you are and the principles you represent. Irresistible force meets immovable object. Proceed with caution! There is a lot of energy available for disciplined work, but push too hard and you may break something.

Mars trine Saturn
New ways to communicate or an easy manner will make conversations and interactions go well today. You may find yourself more talkative and facile than otherwise. There is a lot of energy available for disciplined work, but push too hard and you may break something. This is a good time to appreciate determined effort and actions. You are especially aware of the process right now, and this gives you a sense of responsibility and purposefulness. It's a good time to temper your energy or apply yourself, using traditional methods.

Mars opposition Saturn
You can translate your thoughts into actions readily now decisiveness helps you to say what you think and think what you say. The trick is to realize that pushing matters right now simply won't do you any good. Try to think about the long term instead of pushing for immediate results. You will find a way around almost any obstacle and are in control and able to guide yourself with ease. Your sense of inner direction is good and should lead to opportunities.

Mars square Saturn
Making plans, presenting your work or ideas, and communications of all kinds are favoured. Others tend to value your opinions and ideas under the influence of this transit. Your own drive and emotions are hard set against the way things are, your particular set of realities. Push on now and you risk breaking something. Be patient, and let this one blow over. This is a time in which you are

especially sensitive to the limitations or blocks in your path, which can point to frustration or stress. You may be especially impatient with protocol, red tape, traditional methods, superiors, and rules that seem oppressive.

Mars conjunct Ascendant

You can really communicate and convey yourself to others right now. You have a lot of energy and come across as assertive and dominant. You have just emerged from a period in which you were less forthright or in which you were considering new plans but not quite ready to take action. Now, you are ready to go forward, push personal plans, or go after what you want. You are more direct, courageous, and initiating.

MICRCOSCOPY OF
TRANSITING PLANETS
SIMPLIFIED
VOLUME-5

CHAPTER SIXTEEN

PLACEMENT OF PLANETS IN DIFFERENT HOUSES

MARS

In the First house. – Hot constitution, scars in the body, pilfering habits, big navel, early danger to father, reddish complexion, active, adventurous, powerful and low-minded.

Second house. – Quarrelsome, extravagant, harsh speech, adulterous, short-tempered, wasteful, sharp-tongued, broken education, satirical, large patrimony, bad-tempered, aggressive, unpopular and awkward.

Third house. – Pioneering, few brothers, sex-morals weak, courageous, intelligent, reckless, adventurous, short-tempered, unprincipled, easy morals, unpopular.

Fourth house. – Sickly mother, quarrels, unhappy home life, danger to father, domestic quarrels and conveyances, uncomfortable, coarse, brutal, tyrannical, vulgar.

Fifth house. – Unpopular, no issues, ambitious, intelligent persevering, unhappy, bold, unprincipled, decisive.

Sixth house. – Successful, good lands, rich success over enemies, intelligent, political success, powerful, worry from near relations.

Seventh house. – Two wives or friction with wife, dropsy, rash speculations, unsuccessful, intelligent, tactless, stubborn idiosyncratic, peevish, passionate, tension in married life.

Eighth house. – Short life, few children, danger to maternal uncles, widower later, and hater of relations, bad sight, and extra marital relations.

Ninth house. – Unkind worldly, successful trader, loss from agriculture, sickly father, naval merchant, dependent life, self-seeking, acute, stubborn, impetuous, logical.

Tenth house. – Founder of institutions and towns, energetic, adventurous, wealthy, active, healthy, famous, self made man, good agriculturist, good profits, clever, successful loved by relations, decisive.

Eleventh house. – Learned, educated, wealthy, influential property, crafty, happy, commanding.

Twelfth house. – Unsuccessful, poor, rotten body, unpopular, incendiary diseases, suffering, stumbling, active, fruitless, liable to fraud and deception, dishonest, unseen, impediments, deformed eyes.

MICROSCOPY OF
TRANSITING PLANETS
SIMPLIFIED
VOLUME-5

CHAPTER SEVENTEEN

PLACEMENT OF PLANETS IN DIFFERENT SIGNS

MARS

In Aries. – Organizing capacity, commanding, rich, social, scars in the body, sensual, dark, mathematician, rich social, scars in the body, sensual, dark, mathematician, active, powerful, inspiring, pioneering able, statesman, frank, generous, careful not economical in domestic dealings, vague imaginations, combative tendencies, hard-hearted.

Taurus. – Influenced by women, timid, rough body, stubborn, sensual, liking for magic and sports, somewhat unprincipled, selfish, tyrannical, not soft-hearted, and rash, emotional, animal instinct strong sensitive.

Gemini. – Loving family and children, taste in refinement, scientific, middle stature, well built, earned, ambitious, quick, rash, ingenious, skilled in music fearless, tactless, peevish, unhappy, subservient, diplomat, humiliating, detective.

Cancer. – Intelligent, wealthy, rich travels and voyages, wicked perverted, love of agriculture, medical and surgical proficiency, fickle-minded, defective sight, bold, dashing, headlong, speculative unkind, egoistic.

Leo. – Tendency to occultism, astrology astronomy and mathematics, love for parents, regard and respect for elders and preceptors, independent thinking, peevish, liberal, victorious, stomach troubles, worried by mental complaints, generous, noble, author early in life, successful, combative, restless.

Virgo. – Imitable, explosive, trouble in digestive organs, no marital harmony, general love for the fair sex, revengeful, self-confident, conceited, affable, boastful, materialistic, ceremonial-minded, positive, indiscriminative, pretentious, deceptive, scientific enterprises.

Libra. – Tall, body symmetrically built, complexion fair and swarthy, ambitious, self-confident, perceptive faculties, materialistic, live for family, self-earned wealth, affable, warlike, foresight, business-like, deceived by women, sanguine temperament, king, gentle, fond of adulation, easily ruffled, boastful.

Scorpio. – Middle stature, clever, diplomatic, positive tendency, indulgent, tenacious memory, and malicious, aggressive, proud, haughty, great strides in life.

Sagittarius. – Gentlemanly, many foes, famous minister, statesman, open, frank, pleasure loving, few children, liable to extremes, conservative, indifferent, exacting, impatient, severe, quarrelsome, litigation troubles, good citizen.

Capricorn. – Rich, high political position, many sons, brave, generous, love for children, middle stature, industrious, indefatigable, successful, penetrating, bold, tactful, respected, generous, gallant, influential.

Aquarius. – Unhappy, miserable, poor, not truthful, independent, unwise, wandering, impulsive, controversial, combative, well-versed in dialects, free, quick in forgiving and forgetting, conventional, danger on water, morose, meditative.

Pisces. – Fair complexion, troubles in love affairs, few children, passionate, restless, antagonistic, exacting, and uncertainty of feeling, faithful, unclean, colic, indolent, and wilful.
PLANET

MICROSCOPY OF TRANSITING PLANETS SIMPLIFIED VOLUME-5

CHAPTER EIGHTEEN

REMEDIES OF PLANET MARS

Effects and Remedies

Mars is a dry, red and fiery planet. Masculine by nature it signifies energy, both constructive and destructive depending upon his position as Mars positive and Mars negative. If Sun and Mercury are placed together in one house, Mars would be positive but if Saturn and Sun are placed in one house Mars becomes negative.

Mars acts on the extremes - either soft like a wax or hard like a stone. The Sun, Moon and Jupiter are his friends, whereas Mercury and Ketu are his enemies. Rahu and Saturn are neutral to Mars. The first cycle of Mars runs between the ages 28 and 33, the 2nd between 63 and 68 years and the 3rd between 98 and 103 years. The 1st and 8th houses are the own houses of Mars and he gets exalted in the 10th house of his debilitation. Mars acts as a malefic in the 4th and 8th houses, but he is benefic if placed in the 1, 2, 3, 5, 6, 7, 9, 10, 11 and 12th houses.

Mars is the signification of sex, brothers, land and property and rules over the animal instincts in man. A benefic Mars offers self-confidence, sharp wit, faculty of argumentation and adventurous spirit, strong determination and qualities of leadership in all human pursuits. On the contrary, a weak and afflicted Mars makes the native lose temper quickly, fool hardy, quarrelsome and brutal. Such a Mars makes the native a sexual pervert.

The general effects and remedial measures of Mars according to Lal Kitab can be delineated as follows :

Mars in 1st House

Mars in the 1st house makes the native good natured, truthful and richer from the 28th year of age. He wins favours from the government and victory against the enemies without much effort. He earns large profits from the business associated with Saturn i.e., iron, wood, machinery etc. and the relatives represented by Saturn i.e., nephews, grandsons, uncles etc.

Spontaneous curses from the mouth of such a native will never go waste. Association of Saturn with Mars provides physical trouble to the native.

Remedies

1. Avoid the acceptance of things free of cost or in charity.
2. Avoid evil deeds and telling lies.
3. Association with saints and Faqirs will prove very harmful.
4. Things of ivory will give very adverse effects. Avoid them.

Mars in 2nd House

The native with Mars in the 2nd house is generally the eldest issue of his parents, or else he or she would always like to be treated so. But living and behaving like a younger brother would prove highly beneficial and ward off several evils automatically. Mars in this house provides great wealth and properties from the in-laws' family. Mars negative here makes the native a snake in disguise for others and causes his death in war or quarrels.

Mars with Mercury in the 2nd house weakens the will power and undermines the importance of the native.

Remedies

1. The business associated with Moon, e.g., trade in cloth, will provide great prosperity, hence strengthen Moon.
2. Ensure that your in-laws make arrangements for providing drinking water facilities to the common people.
3. Keep deer skin in the house.

Mars in 3rd House

The 3rd house is affected by Mars and Mercury, who provide brothers and sisters to the native i.e., he will not be the only issue of his parents. Others will be highly benefited from the native, but he will not be able to receive benefit from others. Humbleness will bring rewards. In-laws will become richer and richer after the native's marriage. The native believes in the principle eat, drink and be merry" and suffers from blood disorders.

Remedies

1. Be soft hearted and avoid arrogance. Be good to brothers for prosperity.
2. Keep articles of ivory with you .
3. Put on silver ring in the left hand.

Mars in 4th House

The 4th house is overall the property of Moon. The fire and heat of Mars in this house burns the cold water of Moon i.e., the properties of the Moon are adversely affected. The native loses peace of mind and suffers from jealousy to others. He always misbehaves with his younger brothers. The native's evil mission gets strong destructive powers. Such a native affects the life of his mother, wife, mother-in-law etc very adversely. His anger becomes the cause of his overall destruction in various aspects of life.

Remedies

1. Offer sweet milk to the roots of a banyan tree and put that wet soil on your navel.
2. To avoid havoc from fire, place empty bags of sugar on the roof of your house, shop or factory.
3. Always keep a square piece of silver with you.
4. Keep away from black, one-eyed or disabled person.

Mars in 5th House

The 5th house belongs to the Sun, who is a natural friend of Mars. Hence Mars ensures very good results in this house. The sons of the native become instruments of wealth and fame for him. His prosperity increases manifold after the birth of sons. The things and relatives represented by Venus and Moon will prove beneficial in every manner. Someone of his forefathers must have been a doctor or Vaidya.

The prosperity of the native will continue to grow more and more with the growth in age. But romance and emotional affairs with the opposite sex will prove highly disastrous for the native, which will destroy his mental peace and night sleep too.

Remedies

1. Maintain a good moral character.
2. Keep water in a pot below the head side of your bed at night and drop it in a flower pot in the morning.
3. Offer Shraddha to your ancestors and plant a Neem tree in the house.

Mars in 6th House

This house belongs to Mercury and Ketu. Both are mutual enemies and inimical to Mars also. Hence Mars in this house will keep himself away from both. The native will be courageous, adventurous, lover of justice and powerful enough to set fire into water. He will be highly benefited by the trade and business associated with Mercury. His pen will wield more power than the sword. If Sun, Saturn and Mars are placed together in one house, the brothers, mother, sisters and wife will be affected very adversely.

Remedies

1. Distribute salt in place of sweets on the birth of a male child.
2. His brothers should keep the native happy by offering him something or the other for their protection and prosperity. But if he does not accept such things, the same should be thrown in water.
3. The male children of the native should not wear gold.
4. Adopt remedies of Saturn for family comfort. Worship Ganesh for parents' health and destruction of enemies.

Mars in 7th House

This house belongs to the influences of Venus and Mercury, who combined together provide the effect of Sun.

If Mars is placed therein, the 7th house will be affected by Sun and Mars both, which ensures that the native's ambition will be fulfilled. Wealth, property and family will increase.

But if Mercury is also placed here along with Mars, very adverse results will follow regarding the things and relations represented by Mercury e.g., sister, sister-in-law, nurses, maid servant, parrot, goats etc. Hence it would be better to keep away from them.

Remedies

1. Place solid piece of silver in the house for prosperity.
2. Always offer sweets to daughter, sister, sister-in-law and Widows.

3. Repeatedly build a small wall and destroy it.

Mars in 8th House

The 8th house belongs to Mars and Saturn, who jointly influence the properties of this house. No planet is considered good in this house. Mars here affects very adversely the younger brothers of the native. The native sticks to commitments made by him without caring for profit or loss.

Remedies

1. Obtain blessings of widows and wear a silver chain.
2. Offer sweet loaves of bread prepared on Tandoor to dogs.
3. Take your meals in the kitchen.
4. Build a small dark room at the end of your house and do not allow sun light to enter it.

5. Offer rice, jaggery and gram pulse at religious places of worship.
6. Fill an earthen pot with 'Deshi Khand' and bury it near a cremation ground.

Mars in 9th House

This house belongs to Jupiter, a friend of Mars. Mars placed in this house will prove good in every manner to the native by virtue of the help and blessings of the elders. His brother's wife proves very fortunate for him. Generally he will have as many brothers as his father had. Living with brothers in a joint family will enhance all round happiness. The native will gain a highly prestigious administrative post upto the 28th year of his age. He may earn large profits in the trade of goods associated with warfare.

Remedies

1. Obedience to elder brother.
2. Render services to your Bhabhi i.e., brother's wife.
3. Do not become an atheist and follow your traditional Customs and rituals.
4. Offer rice, milk and jaggery at religious places of worship.

Mars in 10th House

This is the best position of Mars in a horoscope, the place of his exaltation. If the native is born in a poor family, his family will become rich and affluent after his birth. If he is born in a rich family, his family will grow richer and richer after his birth. If the native is the eldest brother he will gain a more distinct recognition and reputation in society. He will be bold, courageous, healthy and competent enough to set traditions, norms and rules in society. However, if malefic planets Rahu, Ketu and Saturn or Venus and Moon are placed in the 2nd house, the aforesaid beneficial effects are reduced. Further if a friendly planet is placed in the 3rd house, it will also affect the results of Mars in the 10th house adversely. If Saturn is placed in the 3rd house, the native will gain huge wealth and large properties in the later part of his life along with a kingly position. Mars in the 10th house but no planet in the 5th house provides all round prosperity and happiness.

Remedies

1. Do not sell ancestral property and gold of the house.
2. Keep a pet deer in your house.
3. While boiling milk, please ensure that it should not overflow and fall on the fire.
4. Offer help to one-eyed and childless persons.

Mars in 11th House

Mars gives good results in this house, because this house is influenced by Jupiter and Saturn. If Jupiter is in exalted position, Mars gives very good results. Native is courageous and just and usually a trader.

Remedies

1. One should never sell one's ancestral property.
2. Keeping Sindoor or honey in an earthen pot will give well Results.

Mars in 12th House

This house is inhabited by Jupiter, so now both Mars and Jupiter will give good results. This is also considered as the

"Pukka Ghar" of Rahu, so now Rahu will not trouble the native notwithstanding its position in native's horoscope.

Remedies

1. Take honey the first thing in the morning.
2. Eating sweets and offering sweets to another person will increase the wealth of the native.

MICROSCOPY OF
TRANSITING PLANETS
SIMPLIFIED
VOLUME-5

CHAPTER NINTEEN

Transit results of Jupiter from natal Moon

TRANSISTING JUPITER

Transit of Planet Jupiter from 1st house of Natal Moon Sign

You may find yourself having emotional differences with someone. Those around you, or the situation you find yourself in, may not feel right to you. The unemployed will have difficulty in getting a job and the employed will have a tough time at work. The bosses and seniors will be against you and you will face disgrace and loss of position at work.

Keep your irritability under check and avoid quarrels of arguments at work or you face humiliation and mental anguish at work. You will have to work doubly hard to achieve the targets. Monetarily too the period is a troublesome one and you have to keep a tight check on your purse and do a tight rope dance.

This is a time of conscious striving knowing what you want and working towards getting it. Feeling emotionally out of step with others may get the better of your spirits for the time being. Your spirits will be at a low and your love and domestic life will be at low ebb. Avoid clashes with the family members and try to keep your cool. Friends and relatives will not be favourable. However it is a good time for studies and religious and charity work. It is a good time to plan a child too. Your health will give you repeated nagging problems. Avoid adventures and risky games which may cause life threatening risks. There will be constant ental agony and depression. Avoid travel as it will only cause trouble without giving any results.

Transit of Planet Jupiter in the 2nd house from Natal Moon

It's a good time to take the initiative and to act on things that you've only been thinking about doing. This transit is a very favourable one. Your bosses and seniors will appreciate your work and you will have a say in the important matters. You would have the upper hand over your enemies and competitors during this period. Financially also this will be a rewarding time for you and you are will be able to gain well from investments in shares and agriculture. It is a very good time to invest in real estate. All your pending dues will be recovered and you will clear all your debts.

This is the day to start new projects or push forward with those already in motion. You may enjoy a sense of creating your own opportunities. A happy period from love and relations point of view and you will enjoy a good conjugal life. Peace and harmony will prevail in your family. There could be a birth in the family. On the social front also you will enjoy a good time with friends and relatives. You will lend your support to charitable causes and will enjoy more respect and admiration of people.

Transit of Planet Jupiter in the 3rd house from Natal Moon.

You may not find the support you flowing to you. Some sort of temporary obstacle may appear. You may feel like exercising or getting out and about. At your work place things will not be smooth and you will face the opposition of your employer and your colleagues. Your enemies will try to dethrone you from your position. You will have to face many obstacles in executing your work. Financially also it is a bad phase and you must avoid speculation or you will lose money. Do not give or take loans. While relations with spouse will be all right, the health of spouse will be a cause for worry.

There could be a noticeable discrepancy between the demands of your personal life and what is expected of you at work. You may feel frustrated. There will be disputes and argument with your siblings and friends. Avoid clashes as much as possible. You may lose a relative or a friend during this transit. While worries and anxiety will be there, it is a good period for marriage and there will be some auspicious events at home. Your health needs extra care as you will be susceptible to headaches, diseases and mental anxiety. Avoid journeys as they will not yield the desired results and you may incur losses.

Transit of Planet Jupiter in the 4th house from Natal Moon

It's time to take the initiative, to apply your confidence and energy to something constructive. This is a period in which you are living spiritedly, indulging your desires without going overboard, and acting spontaneously. This transit is a worrisome one for you at work. You have to concentrate and do a lot of hard work. In spite of that you cannot expect and recognition or rewards. Your bosses will be over demanding and will not be favourable. Enemies will increase and will give you mental worries and anguish.

Money will not come when needed. Avoid wasteful expenditure. There will be disturbed relations with spouse and happiness will be lacking at home.

You could find yourself driven by a restless desire to do something; but without a well-defined goal, you tend towards impulsive actions and get yourself into needless arguments. You must make extra efforts to maintain cordial relationships with your friends and relatives. Avoid disputes and litigations as you may face humiliation. The health of your mother will not be good. Make sure you avoid arguments or you will antagonize people and make enemies. There will be lack of vigour and vitality and you will suffer from a feeling of weakness and unhappiness.

Transit of Planet Jupiter in the 5th house from Natal Moon

It's easy to put your best face forward and to cooperate with others because you are not conflicted on the inside .Circumstances spur you into action. This is a very happy and successful transit for you. You will be able to work with enthusiasm and dedication and work will yield the desired results. Your superiors will appreciate your work and will reward you for your good efforts. Those in trade and business can expect good profits. Money will come on time and investments will get you good returns. It is a very good period for studies also. On the domestic front you will enjoy good conjugal relations and life at home will be a happy one.

You could be a little too eager to impress others with an aggressive or inappropriate stance. You will enjoy a good time socializing and will meet important people through whom you will gain. You will enjoy success, a good reputation and status in whatever you do. Physically and mentally you will be at your peak and will enjoy peace, happiness and contentment. Travels will be fruitful and enjoyable. This is a very good time for pilgrimages.

Transit of Planet Jupiter in the 6th house from Natal Moon

The natural confidence that you exude during this transit doesn't come across as offensive. This is a very troublesome transit for you. You have to be extremely careful at work as your superiors and co- workers will not be favourable. Theft, fire and loss of property at your work place is likely. Postpone all new ventures as it is a wrong time to start anything new. It is not the time to look for any advancement but to hang on to what you have.

Careless or impulsive behaviour can be a problem under this transit. You could find yourself feeling thwarted, frustrated, or restless. On the domestic front also there will be troubles. Relations with your spouse will be strained and conjugal bliss will be lacking. Avoid heated arguments and showdowns with your spouse. Your enemies will have the upper hand so avoid any disputes and quarrels and especially avoid litigations.
Health needs extra attention during this one year transit. Tension and restlessness will plague you. Do not neglect any health issue and go for immediate treatment. Avoid travel as much as possible. Take extra care of your belongings, cash and your health if forced to travel.

Transit of Planet Jupiter in the 7th house from Natal Moon

You will find a way around almost any obstacle and are in control and able to guide yourself with ease. Your sense of inner direction is good and should lead to opportunities. This is a very good transit for you. Your superiors will be favourable and the flow of work will be smooth and enjoyable. Businessmen can look for new partnerships and alliances. Financially it is a happy rewarding period and money will come on time and investments will yield good returns. You may go abroad in connection with your work and it will be a successful trip. You will meet men in power and authority and will gain through their acquaintance. Love and romance point of view it is a great time for conjugal bliss with your partner. Relations with spouse and children and relatives will be good and enjoyable.

Vitality increases now as your confidence in your effectiveness builds. You feel more generous, optimistic, and sociable under this influence. It is a very good transit for singles to get engaged or married. Married people may consider an addition in the family. You will enjoy all bodily and material comforts and enjoy good food. You will have a great social life and will be admired and respected. You will be active and intelligent and people will notice and admire you. Health will be good and your body will acquire a new vigour, vitality and lustre. You will feel active, confident and happy. Travels will be fruitful and pleasurable. A foreign trip is quite likely during this one year transit.

Transit of Planet Jupiter in the 8th house from Natal Moon

Decision-making can be challenging right now, as there is a basic conflict between your instincts and what you feel you should do. The realization of a long-term goal may come now. This is a period of disappointments for you. There will be unnecessary arguments and disputes at the workplace. If you get distracted and don't concentrate on your work, there may be loss of reputation, position and honour. A lot of extra efforts are required for completion of work. Avoid all illegal activities and be careful of your commitments and written documents as you may get into trouble with the authorities and may face legal action or imprisonment. Your finances need closes watch and avoid unnecessary expenses. Be extra careful with money and valuables as loss due to theft is likely.

Not a great day to make plans or decisions. It could be hard to figure out the right move. You may feel frustrated as to where you are headed in life just now. Watch your behaviour as you will be irritable, rude and rash during this transit. Try to maintain your calm at this time. Relations with spouse and family of spouse will be strained. Avoid arguments with your family members and friends. If you do not watch your behaviour you will lose friends and make more enemies. Health would need close watch too as you will have constant health problems during this time. You will be tired and exhausted with a lazy lacklustre feeling. Avoid travel as much as possible as it will not give the desired results and will be tiresome and a waste of time and money.

Transit of Planet Jupiter in the 9th house from Natal Moon

A very lucky period for making plans or decisions and finding your way through just about any problem you may discover. You feel successful and able to cope. This is an excellent period for professional and financial growth. Your bosses will be favourable and appreciative and you can expect a good promotion and increment. Your investments will be profitable. Income will be good, plentiful and continuous. It is a very good time to buy property. Those in business can expect a good jump in profit. This is a very good time for people in the teaching, writing and publishing line. There will be peace and tranquillity at the home front and your relations with spouse, children and the elder will be cordial and enjoyable. You will have a good social life and will enjoy a good reputation, status and honour in the social circles.

Good advice from a guide or older person may be forthcoming. This transit represents hopefulness, good will, and increased influence. You may be especially sociable, tolerant, and generous. You will take a lot of interest in religious activities, yoga, meditation etc. and will get the blessings of gurus and saints. It is a very good time for singles to consider engagement or marriage and a very good time to plan a baby too. You will enjoy good health and good food during this time and will feel happy and energetic. A very good time for travels, especially for religious and foreign travels.

Transit of Planet Jupiter in the 10th house from Natal Moon

Not a great day to make plans or decisions. It could be hard to figure out the right move. You may feel frustrated as to where you are headed in life just now. This is a bad transit for you. Avoid disputes and arguments with your superiors at your work place as they will not be receptive to your views. Your enemies will have the upper hand and you may lose your position and honour. They may get you transferred to a far off place. Your finances need a close watch. Avoid all risky investments. It is a bad period from love and romance point of view. You will be disturbed and will have will develop negative thoughts.

Someone older or in authority may disapprove of your actions or decisions. You may feel vague restlessness and discontent with life as it is. This will disturb your family life and your relations with your spouse and children will be strained. Avoid irritability and watch your behaviour with your elders. Relations with your in-laws will be strained. Your health will not be good and the health of your children also needs watching. You will be prone to eye infections and cough and throat troubles. Avoid travelling as travels will be tiresome and will not yield the desired results.

Transit of Planet Jupiter in the 11th house from Natal Moon

You are emotionally charged now. You should be aware that your current state of mind can, in an indirect way, determine much about how you will be feeling in the month ahead. This is a very good transit for you. Work will yield the desired results and appreciation. Your superiors will be favourable and you may expect a promotion or increment at the workplace. The businessmen will gain in trade. Investments will fetch you good returns. You will have the upper hand over your enemies and competitors. It is a very good time for buying property, jewellery, new vehicles and other material comforts.

Your mood may be elevated, but somewhat unstable as the source of your enthusiasm may not be based on reality. If eligible it is a very good time for love and marriage. Those who are married may expect a new member in their family. Relations with family members and friends will be good and you will have a good social life. You will enjoy a good status in the society. is likely to be heightened. There will be gains from your friends and relatives too. You will take good interest in religious activities, yoga, meditation and mantras etc. During this transit you will enjoy very good health and peace of mind. Travels will bring you both pleasure and yield the desired results. Long distance travels are likely.

Transit of Planet Jupiter in the 12th house from Natal Moon

You may find opposition from others today to some plan of action or project of yours. You might find yourself struggling with someone older or even with yourself and goals. Those in employment will have a difficult time at work. Your employers and bosses will not be in your favour. You must hang on to what you have and try to maintain status quo by doing a damage control act. Do not expect any promotion, increment or even appreciation. You may be forced to go to a foreign land. It is the same with the people in the trade and business also. Avoid all risky investments. Expenditure will be more than income. It is a very bad time for people in the cattle business.

Your behaviour and conduct may go astray during this period. Avoid negative thoughts and approach and be careful in your attitude with your near and dear ones or you will have to face humiliation and loss of face at home and in the society too. Avoid showdowns and unpleasant situations. Relations with children will be strained. Your mental and physical health needs watching. It is a period of grief and fear so try to keep your cool and control your emotions as you may become a victim of worry and mental affliction. Avoid all activities or games that may put your life at risk. You may undertake long distance travels. You may also be forced to stay away from your place and your children. Visits to temples and holy places is quite likely too.

\

MICROSCOPY OF
TRANSITING PLANETS
SIMPLIFIED
VOLUME-5

CHAPTER TWENTY

JUIPTER TRANSITS URANUS NEPTUNE PLUTO

Transit Jupiter Conjunct Uranus

This is a positive time when you express your deepest feelings openly and intensely. You seek new or exotic places to visit and will delight in meeting people who are very different from you. During this period your difficulty during this time is to manage these changes without completely disregarding your responsibilities. Time will bring many chances to expand your life in ways that you weren't expecting. You may have the go to travel but won't be satisfied by the same old experiences. You may also be more interested in social reform, politics or humanitarian causes.

Transit Jupiter Opposition Uranus

You seek intensity in your life and in your relationships, and you become more aware of hidden sides of your personality. Your energy level is very high but you're more impulsive and impatient than usual, and need to be more cautious when handling electronic equipment. You may also have more problems in your business relationships, as you have a need to balance your responsibilities to others with your own need for freedom. You may have the opportunity to travel but will find more surprises than you bargained for. You may also be more interested in social reform or business ventures that help other people find the freedom to express themselves.

Transit Jupiter Sextile Uranus

You may be more involved to share your opinions through writing. This can be a very creative time and your mind is stimulated by the possibility of achieving more personal freedom and independence. Your conversations with other people will be fresh, exciting and very progressive, and you truly enjoy sharing your idealistic vision. You may teach or inspire with original ideas, or encourage others to complete the task assigned to them.

Transit Jupiter Square Uranus

Your interactions with other people are more stimulating and you'll enjoy any opportunity to meet new people who are very different from you. You'll feel extremely restless and bored in any situation that doesn't allow you total freedom or independence, and complete change may seem to be your only solution. Your challenge during this time is to manage these changes without completely disregarding your responsibilities or rebelling against necessary and normal restrictions of everyday business.

Transit Jupiter Trine Uranus

There can be a tendency to go overboard and to indulge in extravagances. The desire to experience something new, or the desire for more freedom to explore new possibilities, can amount to restlessness if you don't know what it is you want. New ways to communicate or an easy manner will make conversations and interactions go well today. This is a great time to travel to foreign places, and the people you meet will give you a broader view of the world. You may also be tempted to mislead others with the best of intentions, but should avoid it as much as possible. You enjoy sharing your idealistic vision and may have the opportunity to teach or inspire others with original and progressive ideas.

Transit Jupiter Conjunct Neptune

You should avoid intentionally deceiving them to accomplish your goals, even if you think you're doing so in their best interest, as exaggerations and innocent white lies can still backfire. You may be tempted to trust the idealistic or glamorized version of a project without testing the merits or questioning other people's motives. You may strive to enlighten or teach the people around you about the true meaning and purpose of life, or you may be the one in need of a spiritual rebirth.

Transit Jupiter Opposition Neptune

You're a great salesperson now and may be tempted to mislead others with the best of intentions, but should avoid it as much as possible. You may idealize your own behaviour and are more gullible to flattery. If your heart's in the right place you can achieve a greater level of faith in life now – just remember to keep one foot firmly planted on solid earth. As you're subject to more susceptible to being deceived by a glamorized version of a project without testing the merits or questioning other people's motives.

Transit Jupiter Sextile Neptune

You're concerned with higher ideals and finding the truth, but may become confused by what is truth and what is illusion. Your compassion and sense of idealism are greatly enhanced during this time, and you may become involved with projects that serve to help others less fortunate. Your conversations are likely to be idealistic and concerned with finding the truth, and you may explore belief systems that are more spiritual or metaphysical than traditional religion. You're more capable of discerning the real truth from the illusion in your business dealings, but still need to watch trusting a glamorized version of a project without testing the merits or questioning other people's motives.

Transit Jupiter Square Neptune

You may be drawn to teaching other people about the true meaning and purpose of life, or you may be the one in need of a spiritual rebirth and may meet someone who helps restore your faith .You may be drawn to the true meaning and purpose of life, or you may be the one in need of a spiritual rebirth and meet someone who helps restore your faith. Your compassion and sense of idealism are greatly enhanced during this time, and you may become involved with projects that serve to help others less fortunate. This is not the best time to rush into adopting belief systems that you haven't had a chance to test in your reality, or to believe simply on faith.

Transit Jupiter Trine Neptune

You may strive to enlighten or teach the people around you about the true meaning and purpose of life, or you may be the one in need of a spiritual rebirth and meet someone who helps restore your faith. You may also be the one to initiate change, out of boredom and a need for more exciting and stimulating challenge. You may be tempted to trust the idealistic or glamorized version of a project without testing the merits or questioning other people's motives, leaving you open to be taken advantage of.

Transit Jupiter Conjunct Pluto

Your difficulty during this time is to manage these changes without completely disregarding your responsibilities or overthrowing any existing structure in your situation. But where we find truth we often find illusion as the other side of the coin, and evaluating new information can be very tricky during this time, especially in business. You seek new or exotic places to visit and will delight in meeting people who are very different from you. You may also be more interested in social reform, politics or humanitarian causes, or business ventures that help other people find the freedom to express themselves.

You may have the opportunity to travel but won't be satisfied by the same old experiences. You may also be tempted to mislead others with the best of intentions, but should avoid it as much as possible. This period of time will bring many opportunities to expand your life in ways that you weren't expecting. You may not have felt restricted up to this point, but the unexpected events that occur now will awaken your need for personal freedom and independence.

Transit Jupiter Opposition Pluto

You may achieve a position of power or influence but need to stay very aware of your motives and work toward the good of the whole, rather than for your own personal interests. You should approach all contracts and agreements with caution and avoid useless power struggles. Your ambition and drive for success are extremely powerful during this time, and the level of sheer physical energy, determination and optimism you feel needs to be handled carefully.

Transit Jupiter Sextile Pluto

It's very tempting and easy to use this energy solely to promote your own agenda, but the more you do for others now, the more you'll gain in return. Your drive for success is very powerful during this time and you seem to have unlimited energy, determination and optimism. You can easily effect change in your environment to give you more room to expand and grow, and are guided by a strong sense of personal honour and integrity. - the more you do for others, the more success you'll find for yourself. You have great powers of persuasion and can inspire other people to support your efforts.

Transit Jupiter Square Pluto

If you can remain humble and use your significant personal power for the betterment of your life and the lives of others, you'll enjoy great satisfaction and fulfilment from your efforts, as well as attracting the support of influential people and the possibility of financial success. It's important that you keep your eye on what's best for the larger situation and avoid acting solely for your own best interest, which is very tempting now. You'll find more positive results if you use your personal power in a conscientious way, and have respect for the power of other people as well. You feel justifies any action you take, but run the risk of using your significant powers of persuasion to dominate others in order to elicit their support.

Transit Jupiter Trine Pluto

Your energy level is very high but you're also extremely impatient, and need to proceed with caution and watch impulsive action. Your ambition and drive for success are very strong during this time, and you enjoy unlimited energy, determination and optimism. You find that other people feel lucky in your efforts. While you certainly have more potential for achieving success this is a time of reaping what you've sown and if you've acted in the best interest of other people in the past. You can effect positive changes or reform in your business surroundings, or may have a desire to teach, empower or enlighten other people.

MICROSCOPY OF TRANSITING PLANETS SIMPLIFIED VOLUME-5

CHAPTER TWENTY ONE

TRANSITING JUPITER

We must always remember that Jupiter transits to benefit us to the utmost, we need to get hold of the opportunities that are being offered to us. We cannot wait for things to happen to us. At the same time, we must know of the potential for overdoing, for glossing over details to feed our optimism and greed.

Jupiter-Sun Transits

Jupiter transits conjunct Sun

This is a highly auspicious aspect, but much will depend on the condition of the Sun at birth. If the Sun is challenged naturally, Jupiter transiting conjunct the Sun may bring about some opportunities, but they may not be easy to grab unless you have built your self-confidence before the transit occurs. Sometimes, unexpected windfalls come during this transit, but don't count on it. It's an excellent time to start new long-term projects. You might find that you feel more vital, confident, and optimistic about the future at this time. It's a good time to resolve conflicts. Events may give your ego a boost, and you could be feeling quite vital and alive.

Jupiter transits sextile Sun

Your work will bear very good results. You will overcome obstacles easily and will get victory over your enemies and competitors. This can be an excellent time for financial transactions, making plans for the future, making investments, resolving conflicts with others, and boosting your self-confidence. You may be feeling particularly vital and confident, and this inner can bring its rewards.

Jupiter transits square Sun

Financially a very good month and you will gain through investments and speculation however there may be a tendency to wastefulness during this transit, as well as faulty decision-making due to over-optimism or arrogance. Avoid making any large purchases during this transit, as you might find that once Jupiter passes, you didn't really need the item. Jupiter is infusing you with a boost to your ego at this time, and it is up to you how to handle it.

Jupiter transits trine Sun

This transit represents considerable opportunity. You are likely to feel very good at this time, and reasonably confident. This is a time to find ways to improve your life and your satisfaction from life. Resolving conflicts with others is favoured, and you do come across in a more favourable light than usual. It's generally a good time to invest. Jupiter is giving your ego a boost, and it's likely a much-needed boost.

Jupiter transits opposite Sun

You could be feeling less vigorous than usual or more stressed. You might find that you attract challenging situations simply because you are overreacting emotionally. This is a very good period or networking and improving your social contacts. You are likely to be feeling quite powerful and optimistic. The problem with the transit is that you might over-reach as a result of these inflated feelings of importance. This need not be the case at all. In fact, you might find that you receive a much-needed boost to your ego at this time

Jupiter transits to the Moon

There will be opposition and clashes with your superiors at the workplace and this may result in disgrace and humiliation. During these transits, you are especially aware of what you need to feel secure. You may tend towards self-indulgence, and you may encounter issues surrounding your need to commit versus your need to be free. Problems from your past may re-surface. You are likely to want to improve your domestic affairs and relationships.

Jupiter transits conjunct Moon At your work place you may be forced to take up undertakings beneath your current level and dignity. You may be looking to improve your home life and domestic affairs when Jupiter transits your Moon. At the root of this is a desire for more security and a stronger home base or foundation. This is a friendly transit period when you may find yourself more amiable and personally popular. Take advantage of this time by resolving conflicts with others in your personal circle.

Jupiter transits sextile Moon

Avoid getting involved in any kind of arguments or quarrels with your enemies as you will be the loser. Your sense of humour is improved, your ability to derive pleasure from life is augmented, and you come across as considerably more friendly and popular during this transit. Follow your heart, expand your personal circle, spice up your home, and improve your close relationships.

Jupiter transits square Moon

Relations with friends and relatives will also be not cordial and social life will be dull. You might be feeling somewhat dissatisfied with your domestic environment or your personal circle at this time, or you might be dealing with personal issues that tug you in two different directions. Avoid the tendency to splurge or to pamper yourself for no other reason except to tame your moodiness. What you are really looking to do is to expand your emotional life with joy and pleasure, and the best way to find satisfaction is to weed out what is making you unhappy on a spiritual level.

Jupiter transits trine Moon

This can indicate a a brief period when you are not as popular as you normally are. Friends and associates may burden you, and indecision keeps you from making good financial or business decisions. You might be feeling quite personally popular and well-received by others at this time. If it's not immediately apparent to you, dig deeper and appreciate your relations with your family and close friends. Good will and optimism characterize this period of time.

Jupiter transits opposite Moon

It's probably best to avoid new initiatives on the domestic front as well as business changes. Some of us experience swings from optimism to self-pity. Problems rooted in the past and with family and early childhood are apt to surface during this period, and productivity may be adversely affected as you nurse your wounds. Your emotions are stable with this influence. Feelings of contentment and a generally good mood help you to deal with changes effortlessly.

Managed well, this can be a time in which you arrive at increased self-understanding of your innermost needs and wants. There can be a tendency to put on weight or to be financially extravagant. If this is the case, recognize that it's a sign that you are looking for emotional satisfaction in the wrong places. You may be questioning the amount of support you are receiving from others, but be aware that your judgment on this matter is likely skewed. You might be setting others up on some level to prove to yourself how unsupported you are. We all need to feel emotionally supported, and this transit makes us more aware of that need.

Jupiter Trine Natal Mercury

As with other Jupiter Trines you are more receptive and are more able to rely on your instincts. That is why it is important to stay focused and to take the initiative and keep active. Grand and lavish ideas that are profitable. Good for signing and formulating contracts. Good for communicating about opportunities and business matters that involve dealing with authority. Good for traveling and possible to make money through traveling, foreign countries or foreigners.

Jupiter transits to Mercury

Occasionally, this influence brings you before the public in some manner. This can be a time of heightened yet manageable emotions. Stimulate and expand your curiosity, and offer the opportunity for growth through learning, self-promotion, and increased chances to get your ideas across. You are more alert than usual to possibilities, and your curious spirit is aroused. You begin to think in big ways. You feel more confident of your capacity to communicate and of your intellectual capabilities.

Jupiter transits conjunct Mercury

You may find yourself having emotional differences with someone. This is a good time for making business decisions, investing, and property deals, all things equal. This transit brings a generally positive state of mind. Good for all mental business, negotiating skills, learning something new, languages and art. Dealings with the law are favourable. This is a time when your usual way of thinking and seeing the world is infused with a grander, bigger perspective.

Feeling emotionally out of step with others may get the better of your spirits for the time being. Emotional desire is strong, but could very well conflict with the demands of your personal life. This is a time when your usual way of thinking and seeing the world is infused with a grander, bigger perspective.

You see the big picture now, but be careful that it is not at the expense of critical details. Details may be glossed over, and you may tend towards over-optimism at this time. This transit presents an excellent opportunity to grow mentally and intellectually. Your positive attitude lies at the heart of this opportune time.

Jupiter transits sextile Mercury

This is a time when you have an opportunity to learn things that will expand your vision, improve your business or business dealings, and boost your confidence. Hold off on making business decisions or embarking on new projects on the domestic front. Ideas and thoughts will have greater meaning and form just now.

Your life may feel a little easier as you now entertain more pleasant and inspiring thoughts, and your communications are well-received. You may find that you are inspired to do more and to be more. Take advantage of this opportunity to put your best foot forward and to learn something that will benefit your working life and your personal relationships.

You are more inclined towards personal communications, social discourse, and sharing. This is a time when you have an opportunity to learn things that will expand your vision, improve your business or business dealings, and boost your confidence. It's generally a good time to buy and sell, sign contracts, and promote yourself and your ideas. Your life may feel a little easier as you now entertain more pleasant and inspiring thoughts, and your communications are well-received. You may find that you are inspired to do more and to be more. Take advantage of this opportunity to put your best foot forward and to learn something that will benefit your working life and your personal relationships.

Jupiter Square Natal Mercury

New information enters your mind causing you to revaluate certain ideas and plans. May also indicate an absentminded and mentally lazy time. If you are now encountering some problems in your communications with others, it may be because you are not listening very well. Likewise, if your business dealings are frustrating at this time, it could be because you are not seeing the trees for the forest. With everything that is going on around you, it can be hard to keep track of everything.

Jupiter transits trine Mercury

You may feel like talking a bit more than usual, exploring new ideas or getting happily lost in a conversation. This is a time when you handle opportunities that come your way very well. Take this opportunity to learn something new. The possibility of some form of recognition or validation for what you do may come during this brief but effective period. Your attitude is generally positive. Your interests are increased, and you are mentally busy during this period.

Jupiter transits opposite Mercury

It's a good time to mend relationship problems and to surround you with people. Positive new connections may be made now. The possibility of some form of recognition or validation for what you do may come during this brief but effective period. This could also be a time when you are prone to making miscalculations based on an avoidance of critical details.

Jupiter-Venus Transits

Favourable trends in your domestic or professional affairs may be noticeable. A positive frame of mind does wonders now. Jupiter transits to Venus stimulate your desires to share pleasures with significant others and with friends. They urge you to find enjoyment in your life through leisure activities and romance. You may want to acquire new material goods as well.

Jupiter transits conjunct Venus

There could be an emotional overtone to all of this that may require understanding and flexibility on your part. You have a strong urge to socialize and to improve your enjoyment of life through leisurely activities and romantic connections during this transit. You might find yourself feeling lazy with regards to work and business matters, preferring to enjoy and indulge yourself. On the other hand, you might pour a lot of energy into creative activities and hobbies, and if you happen to love your work or do creative work, then you might find this a particularly busy and satisfying time. Otherwise, you might want to schedule a vacation at this time. You might end up spending too much money on frivolous items.

Jupiter transits sextile Venus

This transit may pass you by largely unnoticed, save for feeling rather friendly and sociable and a bit lazy. However, if you plan for it, you might want to grab the opportunities of the positive energies generated. Expand your social circle or simply make sure you get out there. Why? You are more friendly than usual, and you come across in a better "light" on a social and romantic level. You have the opportunity to make a good impression, so schedule an interview, ask for that raise, or make time for social activities. It may be subtle, but your demeanour is more friendly and sincere than usual. You are that much more charming and you are feeling generous as well. It is also possible that you will attract money at this time.

Jupiter transits square Venus

This is a period when you are more inclined to be immature or childish if you have not been managing or acknowledging your emotions in a healthy manner. Overindulgence is the theme of this transit. Your desire for pleasure increases dramatically, and you are likely to overestimate your ability to indulge and get away with it. You may overspend or over eat both symptoms of your inner restlessness. It can be hard to focus on your responsibilities at this time due to a desire to spoil yourself with pleasurable activities. You need to exercise some moderation at this time.

Jupiter transits trine Venus

You are feeling generous and romantic during this transit. This positive attitude can help you attract positive experiences and situations. You are very creative, and your social life is activated or enhanced. Jupiter is acting to expand your desire for pleasure, romance, and material goods as well. This is a favourable time to start a new endeavour, especially one that is intended for profit (unless, of course, there are other serious afflictions). This is also a favourable time to start a new relationship. The only potential problem associated with this transit is the tendency to be a little too carefree and to pass opportunities away with an overly optimistic attitude. Keep your eyes open to potential opportunities.

Jupiter transits opposition natal Venus

You could be feeling less vigorous than usual or more stressed. You might find that you attract challenging situations simply because you are overreacting emotionally. This is not a good influence, although being an aspect between two beneficial planets, its power for ill is slight. It will, however, tend to cause some loss, whether financial, through travel or through dealing with religious people. This is not a good aspect for domestic affairs, or for any relationships that may be formed at this time. It is not, on the whole, a good influence for pleasure; in fact there is usually a mixture of pleasure and sorrow combined under this aspect. However, with care it will not affect you seriously.

Jupiter-Mars Transits

You may feel like talking a bit more than usual, exploring new ideas or getting happily lost in a conversation. There will be an urge to communicate. Jupiter stimulates your drive, motivation, passions, and assertive powers.

Jupiter transits conjunct natal Mars

You are especially sharp, communicative, and open at this time, as your wants are aligned with your thoughts. Your energy levels and your competitive spirit expand with this transit. Be cautious of immoderation at this time, especially if your natal Mars is afflicted. Overestimating your abilities is possible. However, if some level of moderation is employed at this time, this is an excellent time to gather the courage to start something new or enterprising. At this time, you are drawn to traditionally male qualities and strength.

Jupiter transits sextile natal Mars

Your spirits are high during this transit. You are especially sharp, communicative, and open at this time, as your wants are aligned with your thoughts. You are hungry for a bit of adventure. There may be an opportunity presented to you through a male acquaintance. Your powers of assertion are strong at this time, but they go over well with others. You are dynamic at this time, and it's a good idea to recognize opportunities and seize them.

Jupiter transits square natal Mars

New ways to communicate or an easy manner will make conversations and interactions go well today. You may find yourself more talkative and facile than otherwise. You may be overconfident at this time. Success and progress can be had during this transit, but only if you apply moderation to your efforts. You are restless in physical terms and with regards to your desire nature. You are looking for more from life, but you may have a hard time satisfying your urges.

Jupiter transits trine natal Mars

During this transit, you find it easier than usual to rationalize your own behaviour and that of others. It's an excellent period for improving your skills and for opening up discussions on topics that you normally might sidestep. You feel more confident than usual, and you have a dynamic energy that should be harnessed and directed into something productive. Be aware of opportunities that may present themselves at this time, possibly from a male acquaintance or with regards to travel, business, or physical activities. Your competitive spirit is high, but it's a non-grating kind that goes over well with others.

Jupiter transits opposition natal Mars

An inner restlessness can dominate this period in your life. What you do with this extra energy is very much up to you. Don't be surprised if you are not in top mental gear today. You could find yourself struggling to communicate or being easily misunderstood. Hard words are possible with an authority figure or an older person. However, be aware that you will have a tendency to overestimate your abilities. Be cautious with regard to putting yourself at physical risk, as accidents are more likely at this time. Avoid the tendency to boast or to come on too strong, as you may end up rubbing important people in your life the wrong way.

Jupiter-Saturn Transits

You may have a hard time concentrating on any one subject. Either you are easily distracted or a whole slew of information and demands are thrown upon you at once.

Jupiter transits to Saturn test the balance between your desire to grow and to expand, and your awareness of your personal limitations. You become more aware of opportunities, and your desire is to grow, but at the same time you are reminded that there are limitations to what you can do.

Jupiter transits opposite Saturn

It may be challenging to get in touch with what you truly want to do as you tend to live in your brain rather than your heart for the time being. You have a desire to grow and expand, but your attitude is tempered with some caution and feelings of restriction. Perhaps what you want to do is not exactly feasible at this time. It is a good time to breathe new life into old plans rather than to strike out with a new plan altogether. Some caution is in order regarding your finances, although you might find that you are able to get some help from older or more stable individuals at this time. Something is telling you to push forward and to expand and grow, but with a close eye on your limitations. Take steps to grow, but don't overextend yourself at this time or you are bound to face frustrations.

MICROSCOPY OF TRANSITING PLANETS SIMPLIFIED VOLUME-5

CHAPTER TWENTY TWO

PLACEMENT OF PLANETS IN DIFFERENT HOUSES

JUPITER

In the first house. – Magnetic personality, good grammarian, majestic appearance, highly educated, many children, learned, dexterous, long-lived, respected by rulers, philologist political success, sagacious, stout body, able, influential leader.

Second house. – Wealthy, intelligent, dignified, attractive, happy, fluent speaker, aristocratic, tasteful, winning manners, accumulated fortune, witty, good wife and family, eloquent, humorous, and dexterous.

Third house. – Famous, many brothers, ancestors, devoted to the family, miserly, obliging, polite, unscrupulous, good agriculturist, thrifty, good success, energetic, bold, taste for fine arts and literature, lived by relatives.

Fourth house. – Good conveyances, educated, happy, intelligent, wealthy, founder of charitable institutions, comfortable, good inheritance, good mother, well read, contented life.

Fifth house. – Broad eyes, handsome, states manly ability good insight, high position, intelligent, skilful in trade, obedient children, pure-hearted, a leader.

Sixth house. – Obscure, unlucky, troubled, many cousins and grandsons, dyspeptic, much jocularity, witty, unsuccessful, intelligent.

Seventh house. – Educated, proud, good wife and gains through her, diplomatic ability, speculative mind, very sensitive, success in agriculture, virtuous wife, pilgrimage to distant places.

Eighth house. – Unhappy, earnings by undignified means, obscure, long life, mean, degraded, thrown with widows, colic pains, pretending to be charitable, dirty habits.

Ninth house. – Charitable, many children, devoted, religious, merciful, pure, ceremonial-minded, humanitarian principles, principled, conservative, generous, long-lived father, benevolent, God-fearing, highly cultured, famous, high position.

Tenth house. – Virtuous, learned, clever in acquisition of wealth, conveyances, children, determined, highly principled, accumulated wealth, founder of institutions, good agriculturist, non-violent, ambitious, scrupulous.

Eleventh house. – Lover of music, very wealthy, states manly ability, good deeds, accumulated funds, God-fearing, charitable, somewhat dependent, influential, many friends, philanthropic.

Twelfth house. – Sadistic, poor, few children, unsteady character, unlucky, life lascivious later life inclined to asceticism, artistic taste, pious in after-life.

MICROSCOPY OF TRANSITING PLANETS SIMPLIFIED VOLUME-5

CHAPTER TWENTY THREE

PLACEMENT OF PLANETS IN DIFFERENT SIGNS

JUPITER

In Aries. – Love of grandeur, powerful, wealthy, prudent, many children, courteous, generous, firm, sympathetic, happy marriage, patient nature, harmonious, refined, high position.

Taurus. – Stately, elegant, self-importance, liberal, dutiful sons, just, sympathetic, well read, creative ability, despotic, healthy, happy marriage, liked by all, inclination to self gratification.

Gemini. – Oratorical ability, tall, well-built, benevolent, pure-hearted, scholarly, sagacious, diplomatic, linguist or poet, elegant, incentive.

Cancer. – Well read, dignified, wealthy, comfortable intelligent, swarthy complexion, inclined to social gossip mathematician faithful.

Leo. – Commanding appearance, tall, great, easily offended ambitious, active, happy intelligent, wise, prudent, generous broad-minded, literary, harmonious surroundings, likes hills and dales.

Virgo. – Middle stature, ambitious, selfish, stoical, resignation, affectionate, fortunate, stingy, lovable, a beautiful wife, great endurance, learned.

Libra. – Handsome, free, open-minded, hasty, attractive, just, courteous, strong, able, exhaustion from over-activity, religious, competent, unassuming, pleasing.

Scorpio. – Tall, somewhat stooping, elegant manners, serious, exacting, well built, superior air, selfish, imprudent, weak constitution, passionate, conventional, proud, zealous, ceremonious, unhappy life.

Sagittarius. – Pretty, wealthy, influential, handsome, noble, trustworthy, charitable, good executive ability, weak constitution, artistic qualities, poetic, open-minded, good conversationalist.

Aquarius. – Learned, not rich, controversial figure, philosophical, popular, compassionate, sympathetic, amiable, prudent, humanitarian, melancholic, meditative, dreamy, dental troubles.

Pisces. – Good inheritance, stout, medium height, two marriages if with malefic, enterprising, political diplomacy, high position.

MICROSCOPY OF TRANSITING PLANETS SIMPLIFIED VOLUME -5

CHAPTER TWENTY FOUR

REMEDIES OF PLANETS

REMEDY OF PLANET JUPITER

Effects and Remedies

Jupiter is a fiery, noble, benevolent, masculine, expansive, optimistic, positive and dignified planet. Higher attributes of the mind and soul, generosity, joy, jubilation and joviality along with high reasoning ability and the power of right judgments are all governed by Jupiter.

Jupiter rules educational interests, law, religion, philosophy, banking, economics and indicates the extent of one's love and longing for religion, scriptures, elders and preceptors. He is also a signification of wealth, progress, philosophic nature, good conduct, health and children.

Jupiter represents `Thursday' and the yellow color. He is regarded as 'Karaka' for 2nd, 5th and 9th houses. The sun, mars and moon are his friends, whereas Mercury and Venus are enemies to him. Rahu, Ketu and Saturn adopt neutrality to him. He stands exalted in the 4th house and the 10th house is the house of his debilitation.

Jupiter provides good results if placed in houses 1, 5, 8, 9 and 12, but 6th, 7th and the 10th are the bad houses for him. Jupiter gives bad results when Venus or Mercury get placed in the 10th house of a horoscope. However, Jupiter never gives bad results if placed alone in any house. A malefic Jupiter affects the Ketu (son) very adversely. Jupiter offers malefic results if he is placed with Saturn, Rahu or Ketu in a horoscope.

Jupiter in 1st House

Jupiter in the Ist house makes the native necessarily rich, even if he is deprived of learning and education. He will be healthy and never afraid of enemies. He will rise every 8th year of his life through his own efforts and with the help of friends in the government. If the 7th house is not occupied by any planet success and prosperity will come after the marriage of the native. Marriage or construction of a house with one's own earnings in the 24th or 27th year would prove inauspicious for the longevity of the father's life. Jupiter in Ist house along with the Saturn in the 9th house causes health problems for the native. Jupiter in the Ist house and Rahu in the 8th causes the death of the native's father because of heart attack or asthma.

Remedies

1. Offer the things of mercury, Venus and Saturn to the religious places.
2. Scrving cows and helping untouchables.
3. If Saturn is placed in the 5th house, don't build a house.
4. If Saturn is placed in the 9th house, don't buy machinery associated with Saturn.
5. If Saturn is in 11th or 12th house, avoid use wine, meat and eggs strictly.
6. Ward-off the evil effects of mercury by putting on silver in the nose.

Jupiter in 2nd House

The results of this house are affected by Jupiter and Venus as if they are together in this house, though Venus may be placed anywhere in the chart. Venus and Jupiter are inimical to each other. Hence both will affect each other adversely. Consequently, if the native engages himself in the trade of gold or jewellery, then the things of Venus like wife, wealth and property will get destroyed.

As long as the wife of the native is with him, the native will continue gaining honour and wealth despite the fact that his wife and her family may be suffering because of ill health and other problems. The native is admired by females and inherits the property of his father. He may be benefited by lottery or property of a person having no issues, if the 2nd, 6th and 8th houses are auspicious and Saturn is not placed in the 10th.

Remedies

1. Charity and donations will ensure prosperity.
2. Offer milk to snakes for warding off the evils of Saturn placed in the 10th.
3. Fill up the pits if any on the road side, in front of your house.

Jupiter in 3rd House

The Jupiter in the 3rd house makes the native learned and rich, who receives continuous income from the government all through his life. Saturn in the 9th makes the native live long, whereas if Saturn is placed in the 2nd the native becomes extremely clever and crafty. However Saturn is the 4th indicates that the native will be robbed of money and wealth by his friends. If Jupiter is accompanied by inimical planets in the 3rd the native is destroyed and becomes a liability on his closer ones.

Remedies

1. Worship of Goddess Durga and offering sweets and fruits to small girls and obtaining their blessing by touching their feet. Avoid sycophants.

Jupiter in 4th House

The 4th house belongs to Moon, a friend of Jupiter, who stands exalted in this house. Hence Jupiter here gives very good results and provides the native the powers of deciding the fate and fortune of others. He will possess money, wealth and large properties along with honour and favours from the government. In times of crisis the native will receive divine help. As he grows old his prosperity and money will increase. How so ever if he has built a temple at home Jupiter will not give the above mentioned results and the native will have to face poverty and disturbed married life.

Remedies

1. The native should not keep a temple in his house.
2. He should serve his elders.
3. He should offer milk to snake.
4. He should never bare his body before anyone.

Jupiter in 5th House

This house belongs to Jupiter and sun. Native's prosperity will increase after the birth of his son. In fact, more sons a native has, the more prosperous he will become. 5th house is the own house of Surya and in this house Surya, Ketu and Brihaspati will give mixed results. However if

Mercury, Venus and Rahu is in 2nd, 9th, 11th or 12th houses then Jupiter sun and Ketu will give bad results. If the native is honest and laborious then Jupiter will give good results.

Remedies

1. Do not accept any donations or gifts.
2. Offers your services to priests and sadhus.

Jupiter in 6th House

6th house belongs to Mercury and Ketu also has its effect on this house. so this house will give combined effects of Mercury, Jupiter and ketu. If Jupiter is benefic the native will be of pious nature. He will get everything in life without asking. Donations and offerings in the name of elders will prove beneficial. If Jupiter is in 6th and Ketu is benefic then native will become selfish. However, if Ketu is malefic in 6th house and mercury is also malefic the native will be unlucky up to 34 years of age. Here Jupiter causes asthma to the native's father

Remedies

1. Offer things connected with Jupiter in a temple.
2. Feed the cocks.
3. Offer clothes to the priest.

Jupiter in 7th House

7th house belongs to Venus, so it will give mixed results. The native will have rise in luck after marriage and native will be involved in religious works. The good result of the house will depend upon position of moon. The native will never be a debtor and will have good children. And if the sun is also in 1st house the native will be a good astrologer and lover of comforts.

However if Jupiter is malefic in 7th house and Saturn is in the 9th the native will become a thief. If mercury is in the 9th then his married life will be full of problems. If Jupiter is malefic native will never get support from brothers and will be deprived of favours from the government. Jupiter in 7th house causes differences with the father. If so one should never donate clothes to anyone, otherwise one will certainly get reduced to extreme poverty.

Remedies

1. Offer worship to lord Shiva.
2. One should not keep idols of god in ones house.
3. Keep gold tied in a yellow cloth always with you.
4. One should stay away from yellow clad sadhus and faqirs.

Jupiter in 8th House

Jupiter does not give good results in this house, but one will get all the worldly comforts. In the time of distress, one will get help from god. Being religious will increase native's luck. As long as the native is wearing gold he will not be unhappy or ill. If there is Mercury, Venus or Rahu in 2nd, 5th, 9th, 11th and 12th house, native's father will be ill and native himself will face loss of prestige.

Remedies

1. Offer things connected with Rahu, like wheat, barley, coconut into running water.
2. Plant a pipal tree in a cremation ground.
3. Offer ghee and potatoes and camphor in temple.

Jupiter in 9th House

9th house is especially influenced by Jupiter. so the native will be famous, rich and will be born in a rich family. The native will be true to his words and will have long life and have good children. In case Jupiter is malefic the native will have none of these qualities and will be atheistic. If the native has any planet inimical to Jupiter in the 1st, 5th and 4th house then Jupiter will give bad results.

Remedies

1. One should go to temple everyday
2. Abstain from drinking alcohol.
3. Offer rice to running water.

Jupiter in 10th House

This house belongs to Saturn. So the native will have to imbibe the qualities of Saturn only then he will be happy. the native should be cunning and sly. only then the can enjoy the good results of Jupiter. If sun is in the 4th house Jupiter will give very good results. Venus and Mars in the 4th house ensure multi-marriages for the native. if friendly planets are placed in the 2nd, 4th and 6th houses, Jupiter provides highly beneficial results in matters of money and wealth. A malefic Jupiter in the 10th makes the native sad and impoverished. He is deprived of ancestral properties, wife and children.

Remedies

1. Clean your nose before beginning any work.
2. Throw copper coins in the running water of a river for 43 days.
3. Offer almonds to religious places.

4. A temple with idols must not be established in home.
5. Put tilak of saffron on the forehead.

Jupiter in 11th House

Jupiter in this house affects the things and relatives of his enemies Mercury, Venus and Rahu very adversely. Consequently, the wife of the native will remain miserable. Similarly, sisters, daughters and father's sisters will also remain unhappy. The native will be a debtor even if mercury is well placed. The native will be comfortable only as long as his father lives with him in a joint family along with brothers, sisters and mother.

Remedies

1. Always keep gold on your body.
2. Put on a copper bangle.
3. Watering a pipal tree would prove beneficial.

Jupiter in 12th House

The 12th house would provide the combined influences of Jupiter and Rahu, who are inimical to each other. If the native observes good conduct, wishes good for all and observes religious practices he will become happy and enjoy a comfortable sleep at night. He would become wealthy and powerful. Abstaining from evil acts of Saturn will make the business of machinery, motor, trucks and cars highly beneficial to him.

Remedies

1. Avoid furnishing false evidence in any matter.
2. Render services to sadhus, pipal gurus and pipal tree.
3. Place water and Saunf on the head side of your bed during nights.

MICROSCOPY OF TRANSITING PLANETS SIMPLIFIED VOLUME -5

CHAPTER TWENTY FIVE

Transit results of Saturn from natal Moon

TRANSISTING SATURN

Transit of Planet Saturn from 1st house of Natal Moon Sign

Transit of Saturn from natal Moon

This is a good period for dealing with others in general, but particularly on professional levels or with those in charge. We all know that Saturn is a slow moving and large planet in the Solar system, its transit has a strong impact on our lives. The following are the effects of Saturn's placement as per your moon sign as per the Indian Astrology. However they can vary quite a bit based on your individual horoscope.

Transit of Planet Saturn in the 1st house from Natal Moon.

Your seven and half cycle of Saturn is at its peak and this peak of Saturn's transit is bad in every way. Professionally the going will be tough time and targets will be difficult to achieve. Your enemies and competitors may deceive you and you may have to face transfer to a far off place on a punishment posting. The bosses will not be favourable. This is not the time to look for progress and prosperity but to do a careful damage control act and hang on to what you have. Finances will be in a bad shape and money will not come when it is needed. The expenditure will be heavy. Avoid taking unnecessary loans.

You are especially aware of the process right now, and this gives you a sense of responsibility and purposefulness. There would be some problems at home too. Love and understanding at home will be at a premium. Your relations with spouse and children will not be good and there will be frequent misunderstandings. There will be quarrels with your friends and relatives and your reputation will take a beating. Mental agony, physical pains and a sense of despondency will constantly haunt you. The health of your spouse will also be troublesome. Travels are there but they will be tiresome and will not bear the desired results.

Transit of Planet Saturn in the 2nd house from Natal Moon

The peak of Saturn's cycle is over and you'll get some relief but this last phase of this transit will still give you a few pin pricks. The progress of work will be slow and will not produce the desired results. Avoid any underhand dealings and do not harm or antagonize others. Control your expenses and avoid impulsive spending. Relations with spouse and children will not be cordial Avoid harsh words. Stay away from family disputes. Your social life needs watching as you are likely to get involved in unnecessary quarrels and may end up making more enemies. Your health needs watching. A general sense of weakness and getting tired easily is the main problem. Travel is quite possible during this period, including foreign travel, but the journeys will be a tiresome and will not be fruitful.

Transit of Planet Saturn in the 3rd house from Natal Moon

You will be able to discharge your duties with renewed vigour and enthusiasm. Your courage, confidence and communication skills will be at their best and you will have success in the existing assignments and also in new ones. A promotion to a position of authority or a good increment is on the cards. It is an auspicious time to look for better opportunities too. Financially it's a very good time and you will have income from many sources. A very good time to invest in property and agriculture. poultry farming or agriculture. Your domestic life during this time will also be very happy. You will enjoy good conjugal bliss and relations with spouse and children will be very good. You will enjoy a good social life and will have the upper hand over your enemies. An excellent time for health and you enjoy comforts and happiness. Travel is on the cards and it will be fruitful and enjoyable.

Transit of Planet Saturn in the 4th house from Natal Moon

Disenchantment with regard to work will be your main enemy. Unless you shake it off you may face the displeasure of your superiors. Avoid Transfer to another place is possible during this time. Your finances will need careful watching during this period. Control your expenses or you my land up in some hot soup. Domestic life will not be smooth. Do not get involved in any illegal affairs. Avoid clashes with relatives and friends.

Your social life will not be happy and if you don't watch your behaviour you may face public disgrace. Stay away from your enemies as they will have the upper hand. Extra care should be taken about your health and also the health of spouse and children. Lethargy, stomach disorders, anguish, mental agony, fear and a general sense of disorientation will prevail during this period. Death of a relative is possible. Avoid travelling as the results will not be favourable. If travel is unavoidable, take extra care about your food and health.

Transit of Planet Saturn in the 5th house from Natal Moon

Your profession needs some very careful handling. Exercise financial caution during this time. Avoid risks and new assignments during this period as you may not get the desired results and the chance of losing your job or reputation is possible. Avoid arguments and watch your behaviour and language at your workplace. Financially you have to do a careful budgeting and be ready for a tight rope dance. Avoid all risky investments in stocks and shares during this period. A sense of despondency and grief will be prevalent at home. Your relations with the opposite sex will not be good. Trust and understanding will be lacking.

Working with rather than against the flow should be easy to do. Increased vitality and self-confidence come from a sense of peace on both body and spirit levels. Avoid getting involved in any imprudent activities and avoid quarrels and arguments with your friends and relatives. Avoid getting involved in any type of litigation with your relatives. Your health, the health of your spouse and family members will be troublesome. Watch out for heart, eye and urinary track disorders. Mental peace will also be at a premium during this time. Travel is likely but will not be fruitful. If forced to travel watch your purse.

Transit of Planet Saturn in the 6th house from Natal Moon

You will complete the unfinished projects and will initiate new projects and will gain the appreciation. A general sense of energetic well- being will prevail during this time. Both professionally and financially it is a very good time for you. The bosses and seniors will be supportive and helpful. During this period you will be settling all your outstanding debts, bills and other dues. The inflow of money will be smooth and you will be financially quite comfortable. It is a very favourable time to buy land or a house or building a house. You will have the upper hand over your enemies and competitors.

This is a period when ego-gratifying circumstances are highlighted. You receive some sort of boost to your ego and confidence, perhaps through some form of recognition, however big or small. This period is a very good one for love and romance related matters. You will enjoy cordial and enjoyable happy relations with your partner. Love and marriage related proposals will get a favourable response and will fructify into concrete ties. You will have a great time socializing and will make new friends. You will enjoy good health and mental peace during this time. Travels will yield the desired results and enjoyable. Good time for going abroad.

Transit of Planet Saturn in the 7th house from Natal Moon

Saturn in the seventh house of your Moon sign denotes a low point in your life. Your enemies and competitors will not be able to have the upper hand and will create obstacles in your path. Almost all the aspects of your life will require extra focus. Your income may suffer and you may even lose some of your money due to treachery or deception. Avoid taking any kind of loan during this time, as it will take longer to pay off than you expect. Work will be hard. You will need to go that extra mile to experience success in your endeavours. This can result in a frustrating and stressful day. There is a sense of testing the limits. You might find you have to push a little harder during this transit than you normally would. Beware of being deceived if you are in any kind of partnership or joint business enterprise.

Those employed should avoid doing anything that might cause them to lose their jobs. It would be wise to avoid any kind of litigation. This may not be a good time to fight a court case or stand in an election. Students may find it difficult to concentrate on their studies. At home, you need to consciously maintain peace and harmony.

Most of you are likely to develop feelings of severe anxiety and restlessness. Challenges you face now are actually quite revealing if you look at them as learning experiences. Some are likely to suffer from diseases related to the kidneys, sex organ and the urinary tract. Do not neglect any health complaints of your spouse or your children, as they may become life threatening later on. Some of you may go to a foreign land during this time. However, if possible, avoid going on trips, as they could be troublesome. You might lose your home and be forced to live elsewhere. All areas of personal and family health need attention.

Transit of Planet Saturn in the 8th house from Natal Moon

This transit of Saturn will be a highly disturbing one for you. Unnecessary fears and anguish will have their effect on you. An important relationship, perhaps an older person or someone in authority, may come into focus You will have a tough time at work and your efforts will not get you the desired results. Your bosses will not be favourable at all and if you are not careful you may face disgrace at your workplace or even lose your job. Stay away from the vices and bad company or you may land up in jail. Money will not come on time and what comes will not be enough. Love and romance will be at a premium during this time.

This is a time when tensions with others can come from a lack of self-confidence or a sudden awareness of unfulfilled wishes and goals. Avoid disagreements and clashes or there may be a break with your spouse. Social life will be a disaster and there will be clashes and enmity with your family members. Avoid all illicit activities or you may face the law and disgrace in the society. A gloomy, suspicious and resigned attitude will prevail. Be extremely careful as you may develop some serious long lasting health troubles. Your spouse may lose a family member. Travel is there but that too will be troublesome. Be very careful and drive carefully as it is an accident prone period.

Transit of Planet Saturn in the 9th house from Natal Moon

You may wish to do something special at this hour. Concentrate on what you want from your life, and where you want your life to head. This transit will cause hard work with frustration and distress at your work place. A transfer to a far off place is likely. Your competitors and enemies are likely to have the upper hand and you need to watch your back. Your bossed will not be favourable and appreciation and rewards will be hard to come by. Control your purse carefully as you are likely to indulge in wasteful expenditure during this transit. Income will not be sufficient and attempts to earn extra money will encounter a lot of obstacles. Avoid all kinds of underhand dealings and litigations or you may have to face legal actions.

You could experience some change or undergo inner changes that stimulate a new undertaking, relationship, or attitude change. There will be disturbances at home and relations with spouse and children will not be cordial. Conjugal life will suffer. Relations with elders will be spoiled. Social life will take a back seat and you may face some disgrace in the society. Your friends will not give you support. There may be a death of a relative of your father's side. You need to watch out for throat troubles and pain in the thighs and hips. Health of spouse and father will not be good either. Travel is there but will not be fruitful or happy. Watch your health and purse during travels.

Transit of Planet Saturn in the 10th house from Natal Moon

This transit offers you increased clarity derived from a feeling that what you want and what you need are in harmony. This transit will give you professional suffering and distress. The execution of work will not be smooth and there will be repeated obstacles. The bosses will not be favourable and you will have serious differences with them. You may be forced to change your job but even the new job will be troublesome. Your enemies and competitors will have the upper hand. Your income will not be adequate to meet your expenses. Control your expenses and avoid taking loans or you will fall in to a debt trap.

There is a chance to understand those around you and to have a special time with someone you love. Your marriage and love life will be full of disagreements and disputes. Make sure that you do not cross the limits due to frustration. Do not look for any new romance as it will frustrate you even more. Your relations with relatives, especially your mother's side, will be spoiled. Your social life will be frustrating and your dignity in the society may suffer. Take extra care of your health, especially chest and knee joint problems. Take proper care of your knees and chest at this time. Your mother's health needs watching too. Profession related travel is on the cards but will not be rewarding.

Transit of Planet Saturn in the 11th house from Natal Moon

This transit of Saturn is a jolly good one for you. You could experience an improvement in your family affairs or domestic circumstances, as well as your business pursuits. Professionally work flow will be smooth and will yield the desired results. Your work will get recognition and the bosses will be appreciative and you are likely to be promoted to a higher position with more authority and can expect significant jump in salary. Your office may also send you for higher training or higher studies. Financially this period will give you income from many sources. Investments will yield very good returns and you will recover all your pending dues. You will also acquire some property during this period.

There is a chance to understand those around you and to have a special time with someone you love. General good feeling and a sense of support and harmony make this a happy time. Love and romance will be in the air and you will have a very enjoyable time with spouse and the opposite sex. Your children will do well and a source of happiness. Socially it is a great time for partying and you will make good new friends. You will enjoy good respect and honour in your social circles. Your friends and elders will be cordial and helpful. There will be sense of well-being in your life. You will enjoy good health and be cheerful and energetic. Travels will be there and will be fruitful and pleasurable too.

Transit of Planet Saturn in the 12thhouse from Natal Moon

Your seven and half cycle of Saturn has started. Working with rather than against the flow should be easy to do. You may not find the support you flowing to you. Some sort of temporary obstacle may appear. The bosses will not be favourable and your competitors will be at your throat. If not careful you may have lose your position and may be forced to change your job. There will be unnecessary expenses and waste of money. Income will not be sufficient and money will not come when required. Especially it is a bad time for agriculture related dealings. Peace at home will be at a premium and there will be constant disputes and arguments with your family members.

You may become aware of a conflict between what you want and what you need. Your love life will take a beating. Your social life will not be smooth either and you may lose your reputation. Think carefully and weigh all the pros and cons before taking any serious decision as your mind will be a bit fuzzy during this period. This is a bad time for your health and also the health of your spouse and your children. Have a full health check-up as do not neglect any health problem. You r may suffer from eye troubles and injuries to your feet. The journeys will be tiresome, unproductive and will cause a hole in your pocket.

MICROSCOPY OF
TRANSITING PLANETS
SIMPLIFIED
VOLUME-5

TRANSITING PLANETS

CHAPTER TWENTY SIX

SATURN TRANSITS URANUS NEPTUNE PLUTO

Transit Saturn Conjunct Uranus

If the situation has indeed become too restrictive and can't be fixed a complete change may be warranted, but you should work as patiently as possible when making necessary changes. Even if you haven't felt restricted in the recent past, you'll now feel extreme pressure to break out of situations that limit you in any way. You may feel the need to leave an oppressive job or relocate, but tend to be more impulsive and erratic when making changes and need to be prepared for the consequences of your actions. Very often, a complete break will be warranted and you may feel that you have no choice but to follow your feelings.

Transit Saturn Opposition Uranus

During this period of time, your desire for personal freedom and new experiences will be intense and urgent, and you're likely to spend most of this year extremely restless. In fact, the main source of difficulty during this time is the surfacing of inner tensions that you've ignored in the recent past, and you may feel like you'll burst if you don't change your situation to relieve some of the pressure. If partnerships are truly not functional, it may be best that they end. Extreme restlessness, nervous tension and lack of sleep can be problems and you should find a healthy outlet for your frustration rather than repressing it inside your body.

Transit Saturn Sextile Uranus

Unfortunately, you're much more reckless and impatient now, and may act prematurely; if your temper's a problem, get it more under control. This affords you a more patient and disciplined approach to making necessary changes and you won't feel the need to completely disrupt your everyday life. You may work more with other people and will be cooperative when working toward a common goal. You may be interested in technology or science as a way to explore.

Transit Saturn Square Uranus

There will be an urge to communicate. Also, perhaps a short trip or a special phone call is in order.

You are especially sharp, communicative, and open at this time, as your wants are aligned with your thoughts. During this period of time, your desire for personal freedom and new experiences will be intense and urgent, and you'll rebel against any limitations imposed on you, even the normal responsibilities you live with every day. In fact, the main source of difficulty during this time is the surfacing of inner tensions that you've ignored in the recent past, and you may feel like you'll burst if you don't change your situation to relieve some of the pressure.

Transit Saturn Trine Uranus

You may indeed need to change your circumstances and as hard as it is to slow down and act responsibly, that's the best way to move forward. You need to work as patiently as possible to make necessary changes and deal with your frustration. You crave new experiences but also see the need to act responsibly in order to preserve the stability that's necessary and healthy in your life.

Saturn Conjunct Neptune

This period of time will bring disillusionment and perhaps disappointment, as the cold facts of reality come crashing into your illusions about certain aspects of your career. Circumstances tend to show you how to put into form what before you only could imagine. To the extent that you are off track or uncertain, however, this cycle can force you to take a look at what you ordinarily overlook or avoid. It typically is a reality check that can be uncomfortable if you are in the habit of hiding things from yourself and others. In the areas of life affected by this cycle, you prefer to see the most idealistic picture you can and will tend to neglect the more concrete aspects of reality. You may feel that you have a mission that involves self-sacrifice or playing the martyr, believing that you're doing a good thing for everyone. While that can occur now, you can strengthen your position by taking your share of responsibility for any shortcomings that may appear in front of you at this time.

Underlying motives come to the surface and relationships become deeper and more meaningful. Indeed, this can be a time where you can put particular aspects of your life in order that have been in disarray by taking steps to arrive at the truth of any matter. Making distinctions between what is important and what is ephemeral can help you to clear away all that is unnecessary so that you can make a new start with a clear perspective of what matters to you.

Transit Saturn Opposition Neptune

You may realize that you've been used or taken advantage of and will strive to blend this new insight and view of reality into your present situation. While this process is often painful, it's very necessary to bring your life into more of a balance. Sometimes this period highlights vulnerabilities and weaknesses that seem to stand in the way of what you wish to attain. Often it is easy to blame others for whatever is lacking. You may place your faith in other people and trust in their goodness, and believe what you want to believe.

You express great intensity and passion in the way you appear and express yourself to others. You almost transfix those who meet you with your fixedness and sense of power. But during this time, challenges and obstacle will surface that directly test your belief system - and your faith. New information may reveal deception in your partnerships or you may discover that you've been working toward a goal that was unrealistic or impractical. The potential exists to make dreams a reality during this cycle especially if you have a clear vision of what you seek.

Emotions are up, and you may even find yourself pondering a bit on the meaning of life. You feel at one with your situation. This period of time will bring disillusionment and perhaps disappointment, as the cold facts of reality come crashing into your illusions about certain aspects of your career. You should also be more cautious of your health, as your energy level is low and you may be more susceptible to chronic fatigue, allergies and infections. You should also be more cautious of your health, as your energy level is low and you may be more susceptible to chronic fatigue, allergies and infections.

Transit Saturn Opposition Neptune

While this process is often painful, it's very necessary to bring your life into more of a balance. Be especially careful when dealing with contracts and negotiations, as it's more difficult to assess the real value of agreements and you may not have all the facts. This can be a time to focus on what is vague and to get a handle on certain areas of your life that are elusive. You want closeness but you do not want to be dominated or restricted by the other person.

You can benefit now from a more confident manner and increased certainty about your goals in life. You may realize that you've been used or taken advantage of and will strive to blend this new insight and view of reality into your present situation. In the areas of life affected by this cycle, you prefer to see the most idealistic picture you can and will tend to neglect the more concrete aspects of reality. You may feel that you have a mission that involves self-sacrifice or playing the martyr, believing that you're doing a good thing for everyone.

Transit Saturn Sextile Neptune

You may feel that you have a mission that involves self-sacrifice or playing the martyr, believing that you're doing a good thing for everyone. You'll find more balance between the practical and spiritual concerns of your life. You want to be fulfilled in your work, but it's not enough to just make money or succeed in business. You want to know that there's some higher purpose to what you're doing and can now make any adjustments you feel are necessary to allow more harmony within yourself.

Transit Saturn Square Neptune

This period will bring calmness, clarity and stability to your mind, and you gain more confidence and security through facing mental challenges. Business projects are more demanding now, but you have great confidence in your abilities and can communicate your ideas clearly. You may place your faith in other people and trust in their goodness, and believe what you want to believe, whether or not your assessment is valid.

Transit Saturn Trine Neptune

Sometimes this is a significant period since it can force you to focus on only what is necessary to the exclusion of all else. If you like to surround yourself with many things, you may find that they lose their appeal or that some are removed altogether. New information may reveal deception in your partnerships or you may discover that you've been working toward a goal that was unrealistic or impractical.

You could feel real support and harmony at this time for circumstances and those around you. You're logical, critical and exacting when dealing with details and will be more accurate and precise when performing any sort of analysis or calculation. You're willing to apply mental discipline and a patient attitude to your work, and your ideas will start developing better form now.

Transit Saturn Conjunct Pluto

Whatever leaves usually is not needed, however, even if it appears otherwise. In time, you tend to recognize clearly that what you released during this period was in your best interest no matter what your attachment. You may also embark on a journey of self-empowerment or gain more experience in your line of work.

A keen awareness of what you have and what you lack may emerge now. However, there's considerable limitation in place right now that will make these changes more difficult to achieve. You may have more difficulty with money and the normal resources that you count on may not be available; you should avoid amassing debt during this time.

Saturn Opposition Pluto

You may want to eliminate old structures in your life to clear the way for new cycles of growth, or your present situation may need a complete overhaul. Generally, this is a time of endings so that a chapter of your life may close now, especially if it is overdue. Yet you can accomplish a great deal at this time because you can bring matters to completion, although it often is difficult due to your resistance to change.

You may have the tendency to hold all your feelings inside when obstacles become frustrating, but this will tend to build up and if you don't have a healthy outlet, you may erupt with anger or resentment, which can be quite intense. Usually life is easier when you realize that after something finishes, space is available for something new to take its place. It is possible that this cycle, in its effort to limit you to what is essential, may demand more than you are willing to give.

Transit Saturn Sextile Pluto

Even when you think you're containing it, other people will sense this power in you and may put up their defences or attempt to hold you back out of a fear of being run over. Try to develop more patience during this time, and work diligently but cautiously when effecting important changes in your situation. You may have auspicious interactions with authority figures and are more comfortable being in the presence of powerful people.

Transit Saturn Square Pluto

This is a positive time when you express your deepest feelings openly and intensely. You have a strong desire to make changes in your life that will gain you more success, power or wealth, but rather than acting impulsively, you'll take your time to initiate a well-calculated plan of action. Your powers of strategy are very sharp and you can bite your time and wait for the perfect opportunity to put your plans into action.

Very important people come into your life now. You meet someone who becomes a strong influence on you you're careful to change only what needs to be changed and will find resources and support that other people would miss. Make good use of this time to secure the foundations of your career path, and gaining more experience will empower you and increase your earning potential in the business world.

A time of real inner growth through other people, the social life. You have a strong desire to make changes in your life that will gain you more success, power or wealth, but this process is slower than you'd like and you may become very impatient with waiting. You feel great ambition and drive, and will experience tremendous frustration with anything that stands in your way.

Everything seems to take longer than it should and you may feel that you have no outlet for your tremendous energy. You tend to react to these frustrations with anger and resentment, but will try to hold it all inside rather than erupt in an explosive way. You may have auspicious interactions with authority figures and are more comfortable being in the presence of powerful people.

Transit Saturn Trine Pluto

This period of time may bring difficult conflicts with those in power, as one or both of you try to dominate the other. You have a strong desire to make changes in your life that will gain you more success, power or wealth, but rather than acting impulsively, you'll take your time to initiate a well-calculated plan of action. Your powers of strategy are very sharp now, and you can abide your time and wait for the perfect opportunity to put your plans into action.

MICROSCOPY OF TRANSITING PLANETS SIMPLIFIED VOLUME-5

CHAPTER TWENTY SEVEN

TRANSITING SATURN

Saturn Transits to Planets

When transiting Saturn trines or sextile our natal Moon,

Most of you would see success in all your undertakings. The improvement in your overall financial condition would make you feel secure, comfortable and happy. We feel more in control of our emotions, our domestic affairs, and our personal habits. We feel considerably more mature and capable of handling our personal lives. Family matters assume more importance in our lives now, and we meet our responsibilities with maturity and competence.

When Saturn transits trine or sextile Mercury,

We are more apt to organize our lives and to improve our skills. Progress made during this transit period is likely to bring us rewards in our careers and/or our social lives if not now, in the future. Our thinking is clear, and we can study and absorb information, perhaps not more readily, but certainly more deeply. What we learn now, we retain. Our thinking is more realistic and practical. We are less inclined to jump to conclusions or to make poor judgments, simply because we take into consideration the consequences, the probable outcome, and the bottom line. This is not a time when we take risks unless they are very educated risks. We tend to rely on time-honoured, traditional approaches to new ventures. We are able to formulate plans, lists, and budgets and we think things through.

When Saturn transits trine or sextile Venus,

Most of you would see success in all your undertakings. The improvement in your overall financial condition would make you feel secure, comfortable and happy This is also the time to win over your enemies. Your romantic lives and our financial lives become more grounded. This is a good time to formulate a plan to curb spending and to cut away some accumulated debt, as our outlook is more reasonable and practical in these matters. We might begin a more serious romance, or our current relationship may take on a more responsible, mature, or serious tone. Relationships begun during this transit have a good chance of being long-term.

You would also be able to live in with peace in mind and a sense of fearlessness would prevail in you. We may be more inclined to socialize with older or more mature people, or we may cut back on socializing of our own doing, perhaps to reserve more energy and time for serious creative endeavours or romantic relationships. We might find that circumstances are such that we mix business and pleasure in pleasing ways, or we make social contacts that lead to business propositions, or we turn an artistic hobby into a business. Our overall manner in social situations is more mature, and we can easily make a good impression with our peers and with those older than us.

When Saturn transits trine or sextile to Mars,

Most of your enemies would withdraw and victory would be yours. You are also likely to command more respect and honour in the society. We experience a period of time when disciplining ourselves is easier. We are more in touch with our bodies in the sense that we see them for what they are, and many begin exercise programs during this transit.

When Saturn trine Ascendant

Make peace with your friends and dear ones. You are also likely to be put to anguish by your kinships. Self-discipline and self-motivation, a necessary cooling of the passions, increased focus in work and activities, and a sense of purpose are themes now. We feel in control of our passions and our impulses, and we face life with more purpose and maturity. We are more practical than usual, and our progress in most projects is perhaps slow but steady. This can be a very productive time in our lives. While the changes come quite naturally and flowingly with the trine, the sextile represents opportunities that need to be grabbed.

Saturn Transits to Personal Planets:

Conjunctions Saturn's influence is direct and personal when it transits conjunct a personal planet

When Saturn transits conjunct the Sun,

You would also be able to live in with peace in mind and a sense of fearlessness would prevail in you. Our level of maturity, realism, and responsibility come up for inspection. The goals we have set for ourselves, as well as our very character, are now re-evaluated for strength and purpose, and tested against reality. Saturn has a way of slowing down our life, as if it is forcing us to take a really good look at it. Because the Sun rules our vitality, we may feel that our energy is somewhat depleted.

Most of your enemies would withdraw and victory would be yours. You are also likely to command more respect and honour in the society. We may be assessing our achievements to date, and we are extremely sensitive to whether or not we have been recognized on a professional level as well as on a personal level. Whether our talents and abilities, and our unique individuality and character, are recognized by others becomes especially important to us.

Some of you may even tend to lose their glory and fame during this phase. This may be a time when we cut out projects or possibly relationships that are no longer working for us, or that have been built on weak foundations. We are essentially conserving our energy for those things that do work for us, and we work on building and strengthening them

When Saturn transits conjunct the Moon:

Take care to keep your respect and position in the workplace intact. Make sure you don't have to regret any of your actions done at this time. An increased awareness of the flaws or weaknesses in our support system is likely now. This can lead to some feelings of isolation or a feeling of being un-parented and alone in this world. This is a strong period for introspection. We might discover that we have not left enough doors open to our inner worlds, or that we have not been supportive of others in tangible ways.

Watch out for probable hurdles before venturing into something new. Demands from family and loved ones might be, or seem, greater now than usual. Or, you might be pulling yourself back from others, perhaps in self-pity or due to fear that your needs will not be met. If you are going through a self-pitying phase, allow it to happen for as long as it serves its purpose. Sometimes we can draw great strength from these phases. In fact, this transit eventually leads us to discover our own inner courage and strength. Take some time to be alone, to reflect, and to understand what it is you want back from life on an emotional level.

During this period you are susceptible to become irritable and may try to find out faults in all matters. Deeply ingrained personal habits are also something to re-assess. Some might need to be left behind in order for you to move forward in a healthier manner. You might feel a little hardened or toughened up, but as long as this puts you in a more realistic state rather than a resentful one, this may not be such a bad thing. In fact, it may very well be exactly what you need right now.

When Saturn transits conjunct Mercury

This period may also demand more labour from you in order to accomplish any task undertaken Seriousness of thought is likely now, as you crave simple answers and truths. You may doubt many of the ideas you've had to date, or the projects you've been putting your energy into. The purpose of this transit is to pare down your thinking process, improve your communication skills, and simplify your tasks.

This denotes contentment and good times for you. You would be happy and successful in all your endeavours others might notice that you are a little withdrawn socially, perhaps sarcastic or negative in your speech, and less available in general. You might be pouring more of your energy into a particular project, study, or course and have little time for others as a result. This is not the best time for presenting your ideas, as you might be finding that others are not supportive of them.

You would be able to finish off the work given to you successfully on time. However, it's an excellent period for reviewing, reassessing, perfecting, and improving ideas, projects, skills, and communication so that in the future, you will be more confident about all of these things. Some projects or ideas might need to be left behind so that you can conserve your energy for those that truly work for you, and that you can feel honestly confident about. You are becoming more mature in your thinking, and while you may be swinging to a more negative or critical outlook in the initial stages of this transit, this process may be necessary in order to reach a balanced, mature, and realistic state.

When Saturn transits conjunct Venus

Possibility of gain from this person is also indicated during this particular time. What has carried you to date in the world of your social and romantic relationships may no longer feel satisfying or worthwhile for you during this transit. It's time to assess your relationship needs, attitudes, and capabilities. Some of you may also expect to spend some passionate time with someone new of the opposite sex. You may be withdrawing yourself emotionally as you become more serious, critical, and concerned about a significant relationship in your life.

This period may also bring in a rise in your status in the society. You are likely to be honoured and may command more respect in the society. Letting go of things that truly do not work for you anymore may be necessary, but there is also a strong probability that an existing partnership can be redefined and strengthened. This can also be a time when you begin to question your ability to attract others or what you want from life. Questions of beauty, attractiveness, social charm and grace, and financial power can be themes now.

You may expect to receive higher monetary gains from different sources. Your personal endeavours, businesses and investments are likely to bring in higher financial gains and more profits. This can all take place in your inner world, but for many, there is an external trigger in the form of an event or circumstance that changes your perception of things. Eventually, you will come to a point where you are more confident of how you go about attracting love, money, favours, and pleasure into your life, and this comes from arriving at truths and realities. It's a strong period for reassessing your spending habits. Financial stresses may be part of the picture now, leading to a more conservative, mature, and realistic approach to handling your finances.

When Saturn transits conjunct Mars

You are likely to prosper in your field of activity especially during this time. You may become more soft-spoken and very cordial in your behaviour. You may also expect to get some favourable news. The purpose of this transit is to cool your passions in some manner, to conserve your energy for what truly matters, and to discipline your approach to getting what you want from life. Circumstances may be such that you are required to exercise restraint in your life now. You may be encountering resistance or blockages if you push yourself too hard, assert yourself too strongly, or express anger in an excessive manner.

You are likely to be surrounded by material comfort. Socially this is a good phase as well. You would be able to command more respect in the society. As the transit progresses, you will be learning to direct your energies into endeavours that are truly helpful and useful to you. You might also be learning to curb some of the excesses in your life, as well as to go about getting what you want in a more mature, temperate, and moderate manner. You will be examining the ways you express your anger, how that has hindered you in the past, and how you might better do so in the future

When Saturn transits square or opposition the Sun,

You may also have to work extra hard to accomplish any of the task undertaken by you. Beware of your enemies and stay out of their way in order to avoid any humiliation. We may experience some form of disillusionment with regards to an important person in our life, with authority figures, with personal plans and achievements, or with aspects of our own personality. We may feel blocked from advancing in our chosen life path, and lacking in energy and confidence.

You are susceptible to worries and restlessness during this particular time. You are also likely to be distressed and feel discontented during this phase. It is also associated with mechanical breakdowns in your life. However, these generally happen because you haven't been managing your life effectively, and Saturn calls upon you to identify the weaker areas of your life, and to fix or strengthen them. Take the time to sort out your life, improve your work, and to become more efficient. If things or people leave your life, it is likely because the connection between you was weak, or they somehow no longer serve a healthy purpose in your life.

When Saturn transits square or opposition the Moon,

Some may be displaying bouts of jealousy or holding something over your head. Intensity characterizes your relationships for the time being. feeling overlooked, left out, on our own, and even uncared for. Domestic problems may be part of the picture, often connected to women and sometimes the mother. It can be hard for us to take risks at this time, and we are likely to focus on the negatives in our lives. Fears and insecurities of all kinds are magnified during this period--fear of rejection, fear of what the future might bring, fear that we won't be able to handle our lives masterfully, and so forth.

You will be able to be understanding and handle this very volatile material. You are able to cut through the red tape and get at what is beneath and behind. You may be given to sulking, feeling sorry for ourselves, dredging up the past, and focusing on what we haven't done or can't do. We may be feeling awkward and self-conscious, and consequently less sociable as spontaneity is lacking for us now. It is important to remember that this is very much our perception at this time, and it can be managed if we are aware of the general meaning of Saturn's influences. It is a time when we are called upon to take a realistic look at our personal and emotional lives. This is a great period for getting organized, downsizing, or otherwise improving your anything that requires willpower is more likely to enjoy success. This is a period when progress on the domestic front is slow, delayed, or denied. Our personal popularity is weakened temporarily, and business may also be affected. The best way of handling this energy is to recognize that it's a time to slow down and re-evaluate our personal lives, and that pushing ourselves to do too much will be frustrating and possibly costly. We need more rest than usual, and we need to learn to rely on ourselves for the time being. This is a time when we are called upon to examine our priorities and make necessary changes to our daily routines in order to improve our lives.

When Saturn transits square or opposition Mercury,

You have a new, intense, emotional outlook on life with the urge to get things done and to make a fresh start if necessary. This is a time when we are called upon to examine our thinking patterns to find rigid or negative attitudes that have been holding us back from advancing. We are ridding ourselves of projects that no longer serve their purpose, and learning to cut out the fluff in our lives so that we can focus on projects that truly matter. It's not the best time to present your ideas, but rather to reassess them, and work on perfecting them for presentation at a later date. You are seeking truths now, and in the process, you might experience many doubts.

When Saturn transits square or opposition Venus

This is a time to engage in some sort of transformation in which you weed out the bad in order to more effectively use the good. This might be a time of relationship tests, struggles, or trials. You may not be attracting things and people that you want in your life as easily as you were before this transit and this can be eye-opening. It's a signal to work on improving your manner as well as the things that you offer to others in partnership.

Someone could challenge you on a very sensitive issue, resulting in an argument or, at the least, a very intense discussion. You are working towards ridding yourself of self-delusions when it comes to close partnerships, socializing, finances, and attractiveness. In the process, you might feel disdain for superficial interactions and resent "going through the motions" on a social and/or emotional level. Your goal is to find deeper connections to others. Relationships built on weak foundations may not survive, but other relationships can be improved and strengthened.

Financial matters might be stressful for the time being, which forces you into a position of conservation and moderation.

When Saturn transits square or opposition Mars

This is a time when that which is hidden has a tendency to surface. Someone close to you might be dredging up the past. Excessive or wasteful endeavours and personality traits may need to be tempered now. You are becoming more cautious now, and you might experience a temporary loss of enthusiasm or setbacks that make you doubt your ability to win in life. You are learning to live life in moderation, but it may be frustrating at first as you face tests, rejections, or trials that remind you that pushing too hard or too fast doesn't always yield the results you crave.

Saturn Transits to Other Natal Points

Transiting Saturn conjunct, square, or opposition Jupiter

You have a new, intense, emotional outlook on life with the urge to get things done and to make a fresh start if necessary. Transits of Saturn to Jupiter deal with your life priorities, and how they can better be organized or structured, as well as your expectations and general outlook on life, and how you can come to a more realistic, mature, and balanced state of mind. You may be required to re-align your plans and goals, particularly in business, towards more realistic avenues.

Transiting Saturn sextile or trine Jupiter

It's easier for you to employ strategy, and you tend to read between the lines rather than accept life at face value. Your expectations and outlook on life are considerably more realistic now as you naturally seek balance between too negative and overeager attitudes. It's a strong time for realigning your projects and getting your life priorities straightened out. You are concerning yourself with the long term now, and practically preparing yourself for a better future.

Saturn Trine Natal Saturn

You are more able to influence others, and you are personally popular in an understated, quiet way. A time when clear indications and realizations of what is working and what is not working in your life is shown. Things can get back on tract with this aspect. Emotionally eases your life and brings general contentment. Opportunities a good time to move forward with long range plans that will bring future success. Possibilities of being in the best place for achievements now. A transit that makes up for lost time or opportunities gone by. Also success may come because of seeds planted earlier.

Saturn Square Natal Saturn

A time when you are no longer sure of the directions and choices you've taken to fulfil ambitions. This is a shake-up of your structure. Feeling apprehensive and insecure is normal now allowing you to question and search for your true desires. Insist of yourself to let go of your worries and have faith that the best of your life will remain after this transit is done. Socially limiting with job and career difficulties. Problems with authority, government, legal affairs, bills and/or property. Money is scarce. Worry and anxiety especially about the future. A time to reassess however doesn't throw the baby out with the bath water.

Saturn conjunct Sun

Difficulties, blocks, and all manner of hot spots may be discovered and have to be worked through. A crucial time during which, depending upon what age this takes place; you may reach new highs of determination and accomplishment. This will bring great discipline and a concentration or focus that could make or break you the ability to work hard.

MICROSCOPY OF TRANSITING PLANETS SIMPLIFIED VOLUME-5

CHAPTER TWENTY EIGHT

PLACEMENT OF PLANETS IN DIFFERENT HOUSES

SATURN

In the first house. – Foreign customs and habits, perverted mind, bad thoughts, evil-natured, tyrannical, unscrupulous, well-built thighs, strong-minded, cunning, thrifty, unclean, passionate, aspiring, curious, deformed, sickly, exploring, flatulence, licentious, addicted to low-class women.

Second house. – More than one marriage, diseased face, unpopular, broken education, weak sight, unsocial, harsh speech, stammering, addicted to wine.

Third house. – Intelligent, wealthy, wicked, loss of brothers, polite, adventurous, bold, eccentric, cruel, courageous, obliging, agriculturist.

Fourth house. – Danger to mother if with the Moon, unhappy, sudden lodes, colic pains, narrow-minded, crafty, estates encumbered, good thinker, success in foreign countries, political disfavour, licentious, interrupted education.

Fifth house. – Narrow-minded, mediocre life no children, perverted views, taleteller, government displeasure, troubled life, clear-minded.

Sixth house. – Obstinate, sickly, deaf, few children, quarrelsome, sex diseases, clever, active, indebted.

Seventh house. – More than one wife, enterprising, sickly, colic pains, deafness, diplomatic, stable marriage, ambitious, political success, travelling, dissimulator, foreign honours, deputation.

Eighth house. – Seeking disappointments, big belly, few issues, corpulent, inclined to drinking, friendship with women of other castes, colic pains, defect in sight, seductive, clever, well-informed, impious, danger by poisons, asthma, consumption, dishonest, ungrateful children, cruel, long life.

Ninth house. – Legal success, founder of charitable institutions, very miserly, thrifty in domestic life, scientific, irreligious, logical, ceremonial-mined.

Tenth house. – Visits to sacred rivers and shrines, great worker, bilious, good farmer, sudden elevations and depressions, residence in foreign countries uncertain, later on in life an ascetic.

Eleventh house. – Learned, feared and respected, very wealthy, much landed property, broken education, conveyances, political success, influential, political respect.

Twelfth house. – Deformed, squint eyes, losses in trade, learned in occult science, poor, spendthrift, many enemies, dexterous, unpopular, attracted towards yoga in later life.

MICROSCOPY OF TRANSITING PLANETS SIMPLIFIED VOLUME-5

CHAPTER TWENTY NINE

PLACEMENT OF PLANETS IN DIFFERENT SIGNS

SATURN

In Aries. – Idiotic, wanderer, insincere, peevish, resentful, cruel, fraudulent, immoral, boastful, quarrelsome, gloomy, mischievous, perverse, misunderstanding nature.

Taurus. – Dark complexion, deceitful, successful, powerful, unorthodox, clever, likes solitude, voracious eater, persuasive cool, contagious diseases, many wives, self-restraint, worried nature.

Gemini. – Wandering nature, miserable, untidy, original, thin, subtle, ingenious, strategic, few children, taste for chemical and mechanical sciences, narrow-minded, speculative, logical, desperado.

Cancer. – Poor, weak teeth, pleasure-seeking, few sons, cheeks full, slow, dull, cunning, rich, selfish, deceitful, malicious, stubborn, devoid of motherly care.

Leo. – Middle stature, severe, obstinate, few sons, stubborn, unfortunate, conflicting, hard worker, and good writer evil-minded.

Virgo. – Dark complexion, malicious, poor, quarrelsome, erratic, narrow-minded, rude, conservative, taste for public life, weak health.

Libra. – Famous, founder of institutions and the like, rich, tall, fair, self-conceited, handsome, tactful, powerful, respected, sound judgment, antagonistic, independent, proud, prominent, charitable.

Scorpio. – Rash, indifferent, hard-hearted, adventurous, petty, self-conceited, reserved, unscrupulous, violent, unhappy, danger from poisons, fire and weapons, wasteful, unhealthy.

Sagittarius. – Pushing, artful, cunning, famous, peaceful, faithful, pretentious, apparently generous, troubles with wife, courteous, dutiful children, generally happy.

Capricorn. – Intelligent, harmony and felicity in domestic life, selfish, covetous, peevish, intellectual, learned, suspicious, reflective, revengeful, prudent, melancholy, inheritance from wife's parties.

Aquarius. – Practical, able, diplomatic, ingenious, a bit conceited, prudent, happy, reflective, intellectual, philosophical, vanquished by enemies.

Pisces. – Clever, gifted, polite, happy, good, wife trustworthy, scheming, wealthy, helpful.

MICROSCOPY OF TRANSITING PLANETS SIMPLIFIED VOLUME-5

CHAPTER THIRTY

REMEDIES OF PLANETS

REMEDY OF PLANET SATURN

Effects and Remedies

As the slowest moving planet and the chief signification for longevity, Saturn is a barren, binding, cold, dry, hard, defensive and secretive planet. Its effects and influences are felt with greater intensity and for longer periods than any other planet. Saturn is considered to be very favourable for people born in the signs owned by Venus, whereas Saturn is evil to those born in the signs owned by Mercury.

The astrological thesis of Lal Kitab describes Saturn as a serpent, whose head or mouth is Rahu and Ketu is its tail. If Dragon's Tail is posited in earlier houses than Saturn, the latter becomes a great benefit for the native. However, if the position is otherwise, the Saturn throws highest poisonous results on the native. Further, Saturn never gives malefic effects if posited in houses of Jupiter i.e. 2, 5, 9 or 12, whereas Jupiter provides bad results if posited in the house of Saturn.

Saturn is considered good in houses 2nd , 3rd and 7th to 12th, whereas 1st, 4th, 5th and 6th houses are bad for Saturn. Sun, Moon and Mars are its enemies, Venus, Mercury and Rahu are friends and Jupiter and Ketu are neutral to it. Saturn gets exalted in 7th house and the 1st house is the house of its debilitation. Venus and Jupiter placed together act like Saturn in that house. Similarly Mars and Mercury placed in a single house act like Saturn in that house. In the former case Saturn behaves like Ketu, while in the latter case it behaves like Rahu.

Venus gets destroyed if Saturn is being expected by the Sun in any horoscope. The aspect of Venus on Saturn causes loss of money and wealth, but the aspect of Saturn on Venus proves highly beneficial. Collision of Saturn and Moon causes operation of the eyes of the native. Saturn gives good results if posited in house earlier than sun.

Saturn can never give malefic results if posited with Sun or Jupiter in a single house, but highly adverse results would follow if posited with Moon or Mars in any house. Saturn releases its poisonous results on the sign and Mars, if it is posited in 1st house, on Mars only if posited in 3rd house, on moon if posited in 4th house, on sun if posited in 5th house, and on Mars in posited in 3rd house. Saturn in 3rd house deprives the native of the accumulation of cash money and kills the children of the native when posited in 5th house and 10th house is empty. It becomes highly benefic in 12th house if friendly planets are posited in 2nd house. Saturn provides very good results if placed in houses 1 to 7 on the condition that 10th house is empty. Saturn in 1st house and sun in 7th, 10th or 11th houses causes all sorts of troubles for native's wife. Combination of Mars and Saturn gives adverse results al through.

Saturn in 1st House

1st house is influenced by Sun and Mars. Saturn in 1st house will give good results only when 3rd, 7th or 10th houses are not inhabited by any planet which is inimical to Saturn. If Mercury or Venus, Rahu or Ketu is in 7th house,

Saturn will always give good results . In case Saturn is malefic and the native has a hairy body, the native will remain poor. If native celebrates his birthday it will give very bad results However the native will have a long life.

Remedies

1. Abstinence from alcohol and non-vegetarian meals.
2. Burying Surma in the ground will be beneficial for Promotion in service and business.
3. Serving monkey will lead to prosperity.
4. Offering sweet milk to the roots of a banyan tree will give good results as regards education and health.

Saturn in 2nd House

The native will be wise, kind and just. He will enjoy wealth and will be of religious temperament. However, whether Saturn is benefic or malefic in this house, it will be decided by the planets placed in 8th house. The state of finance of the native will be decided by 7th house, the number of male members in the family by 6th house and age by 8th house. When Saturn is malefic in this house, after the native's marriage his in laws will face problems.

Remedies

1. Going barefoot to temple for forty three days.
2. Putting a tilak of curd or milk on the forehead.
3. Offering milk to snake.

Saturn in 3rd House

In this house Saturn gives good results. This house is the pukka Ghar of Mars. When Ketu aspects this house or is placed here Saturn will give very good results. The native will be healthy, wise and very intuitive. If the native is wealthy he will have few male members in the family and vice versa. As long as the native abstains from wine and non-vegetarianism, he will enjoy a long and healthy life.

Remedies

1. Serve three dogs.
2. Distributing medicines for eyes free.
3. Keeping a dark room in the house will prove highly beneficial.

Saturn in 4th House

This house belongs to Moon. So it will give mixed results in this house. The native will be devoted to his parents and will be of loving nature. Whenever the native is suffering from bad health, the use of things associated with Saturn will give good results. In native's family someone will be associated with medical profession. When Saturn is malefic in this house drinking wine, killing of snakes and laying the foundation of the house at night will give very bad results. Drinking milk in the night will also give bad results.

Remedies

1. Offering milk to snake and offering milk or rice to crow or buffalo.
2. Pouring milk in the well.
3. Pouring rum in running water.

Saturn in 5th House

This house belongs to Sun, which is inimical to Saturn. The native will be proud. He should not construct a house till 48 years, otherwise his son will suffer. He should live in the house bought or constructed by his son. He should keep articles of Jupiter and Mars in his ancestral house for welfare of his children. If the native has hairy body, he will be dishonest.

Remedies

1. Distributing salty things while celebrating son's birthday.
2. Offering almonds in the temple and bringing and keeping half of it in the house.

Saturn in 6th House

If the work related to Saturn is done at night it will always give beneficial results. When marriage takes place after 28 years it will produce good results. When Ketu is well placed the native will enjoy wealth, profitable journey and happiness from children. when Saturn is malefic bringing things associated with Saturn, like leather and things of iron, will give bad results, especially when Saturn is in 6th house in varshaphal

Remedies

1. Serving a black dog and offering meals to it.
2. Offering coconut and almonds in the running water.
3. Serving snakes will prove advantageous for the welfare of children.

Saturn in 7th House

This house is influenced by Mercury and Venus, both friends of Saturn. so this planet gives very good results in this house. The professions associated with Saturn, like machinery and iron, will be very profitable. If the native maintains good relation with his wife, he will be rich and prosperous, will enjoy a long life and good health. If Jupiter is in 1st house, there will be gain from government.

Saturn becomes malefic if the native commits adultery and drinks wine. If the native gets married after 22 years his

eyesight will be affected adversely.

Remedies

1. Bury a flute filled with sugar in a deserted place.
2. Serving black cow.

Saturn in 8th House

In 8th house no planet is considered auspicious. The native has a long life, but his father's life span is short and native's brothers turn out to be his foes. This house is considered headquarter of Saturn, but it will give bad result if Mercury, Rahu and Ketu are malefic in the native's horoscope.

Remedies

1. Keeping a square piece of silver.
2. Putting milk in water and sitting on a stone or wood while taking bath.

Saturn in 9th House

Native will have three houses. He will be a successful tour operator or civil engineer. He will enjoy a long and happy life and parents also will have a happy life. Maintaining three generations will protect from the bad effects of Saturn. if the native is helpful to others Saturn will always give good results. The native will have a son, though he will be born late.

Remedies

1. Offering rice or almonds in running water.
2. Work associated with Jupiter-gold, kiesar and Moon (silver cloth) will give good results.

Saturn in 10th House

This is Saturn's own house, where it will give good results. The native will enjoy wealth and property as long as he does not get a house constructed. Native will be ambitious and enjoy favours from government. The native should behave with shrewdness and should do his work while sitting at one place. only then he will enjoy the benefits of Saturn.

Remedies

1. Going to temple.
2. Abstinence from meat, wine and eggs.
3. Offering food to ten blind people.

Saturn in 11th House

Native's fate will be decided at the age of forty eight years. The native will never remain childless. Native will earn money by shrewdness and deceit.   Saturn will give good or bad results according to the position of Rahu and Ketu

Remedies

1. Before going for an important work place a vessel filled with water and drop oil or wine on earth for forty three days.
2. Abstinence from drinking and maintain good moral character.

Saturn in 12th House

Saturn gives good results in this house. Native will not have enemies. He will have many houses. His family and business will increase. He will be very rich. However Saturn will become malefic if the native starts drinking wine and becomes non- vegetarian, or if the dark room in the house is illuminated.

Remedies

1. Tying twelve almonds in a black cloth and placing it in a iron pot and keeping it in a dark room will give good results.

MICROSCOPY OF TRANSITING PLANETS SIMPLIFIED VOLUME-5

CHAPTER THIRTY ONE

REMEDIES OF PLANETS

REMEDY OF PLANET SATURN

SATURN'S SEVEN AND HALF YEAR'S CYCLE

"Shani's -Sade -Sati"

A horoscope is said to be under

"Sade-Sati" effect when the Saturn transits through the 12th, 1st and 2nd house from natal Moon. It is said to be under "Daiya" effect when Saturn Transits over the 4th and 8th house over the natal Moon.

The Effect of "Sade-Sati" remain for seven and a half years and that Of "Daiya" remains for two and a half years.

This generally affects health, mental peace and finance.

Generally "Sade-Sati" comes thrice in a horoscope in the lifetime. First in childhood, Second in youth and Third in old age.

First "Sade-Sati" has effect on education & parents. Second "Sade-Sati" has effect on profession finance & family. The last one affects health than anything else

.

Remedies of "Sade-Sati"

Generally the best remedy of "Sade-Sati" is to wear an iron ring made of a horse shoe or of a nail from a boat of a river or lake. There are many other remedies also according to the individual horoscope of a person. "Sade-Sati" is not malefic for all people it is benefic for those people for whom Saturn is a benefic.

After consultation with an astrologer a "Blue Sapphire or Neelam of can be worn to minimize the effect of Saturn

MICROSCOPY OF
TRANSITING PLANETS
SIMPLIFIED
VOLUME-5

CHAPTER THIRTY TWO

TRANSISTING MERCURY FROM MOON

Transit of Planet Mercury from 1st house of Natal Moon Sign

You may feel focused and even a bit radiant. You could find yourself in the limelight or able to really communicate and get yourself across to others Worries, headaches, injury to lips or tongue, sore throat, hoarseness of voice and tonsillitis, bad associations and accusations is expected during this transit.

Mercury will move through your first house from the Moon.

This may bring in some negative results in your life. You may lack any real sense of yourself today, or be unable to communicate or convey your ideas. You tend to feel that your personality lacks any vitality. This mostly brings in a situation where you may have to serve someone unwillingly. You are also susceptible to face oppression of some kind.

You should watch that you don't come on too strong today and attract conflict with others. You are also likely to befriend some bad personalities who may cause harm. Watch your words while dealing with your near and dear ones. Your insensitivity may create some unnecessary enemies within your circle. Avoid any kind of lawsuits and bad company. Be careful not to do anything that may make you lose your self-worth. You would always need your good fortune, so, save it. Take advantage of your education and experience to avoid any glitch in your life.

You could have problems relating to superiors, and your vitality may be on the low side. Be flexible during this period, as you may have to make some last minute changes in your plan, project or ideas due to pressure from different quarters or due to some anticipated fear. Obstructions may crop up related to your foreign residence if applicable. You may also find obstacles in performing any auspicious work at home. Take care of your family and yourself as you may become susceptible to deception particularly during this phase. Avoid travel if possible as you may not get the desired pleasure or expected result out of it.

2nd house: Transit of Mercury in the 2nd house from Natal Moon

You may appear very at ease and loose today. Everything seems to be working together, and you may find yourself expressive and able to communicate well. Recognition of merit, praise from friends and authorities, due. promotion, change for the better, study of new subjects, good income, success in undertaking's. During this period, Mercury will move through your second house from the Moon. This signifies pecuniary gain and growth of income especially to those who deal in precious gems.

You possess strong presence and generally feel confident about who you are and how others are receiving you now. Others may praise you or recognize some of your better qualities today. This period is also likely to bring in happiness to you in the form of success in learning and attainment of knowledge. This period also brings in the company of good people and gives you an opportunity to savor exotic culinary delights. However, for some, this particular period may bring in sufferings, bad name in the society and your enemy could also be more harmful than usual. This phase also indicates a probable loss of one of your relatives or a near friend.

3rd house: Transit of Mercury in the 3rd house from Natal Moon

You may experience opposition to the way you present yourself. Someone could challenge your sense of identity. Misunder-standing with relatives and co-workers, worries, expenditure, loss of a kin. During this period, Mercury will move through your third house from the Moon. This mostly indicates a rough phase with your superiors. You may have to be extra careful while dealing with your superiors and employer. Avoid any kind of argument that may lead to differences of opinion and misunderstandings. Stay away from your known enemies and be careful of unknown ones.

However, this period may also give you few new and worthy friends whom you would treasure for life. Expect significant encounters, meeting individuals who are or will be important players, at least for the moment. Handle your finances carefully as money needs extra attention during this period. Be cautious to avoid any loss of wealth. This journey of Mercury may make you suffer from depression, trouble in recollection of facts, mental stress and unexpected hassles in your endeavours.

4th house: Transit of Mercury in the 4th house from Natal Moon

There will be respect and honour from your circle of friends and relatives. You could be plagued by a feeling of not being good enough. Good name, good income, success in competitive examinations, study of new subjects popularity and enjoyment of luxuries. During this period, Mercury will move through your fourth house from the Moon. This signifies progress in every aspect of your life. On the personal front you are likely to be content with your life and you would succeed and gain in all your undertakings.

This is a time when others don't seem to notice your efforts, when progress appears to be minimal if at all, when nobody seems to extend their hand to you. Your status in the society will be heightened and you would be honoured. Financially this is a very good phase as this period indicates attainment of wealth in the form of money or property. You may also gain from your spouse or other members of the opposite sex. At home, this period indicates the arrival of a new member to the family. You are also likely to make your mother be proud of you. Your mere presence in the family may bring in success to the other members of the family. You may also make new friends who are highly educated and gentle people to be with.

5th house: Transit of Mercury in the 5th house from Natal Moon

You might have to face failures or inadequacies. As you face obstacles to your goals, you begin to see the tools you have to overcome them. Bad associations, bad name quarrels with co-workers, misunderstandings with family members, failure in examination. During this period, Mercury will move through your fifth house from the Moon.

This mostly indicates a troubled personal life. During this particular period you must try and avoid getting involved in any kind of arguments with your wife, children and other members of the family. This is not a conducive period for you to be headstrong and opinionated while dealing with friends as well. Be extra careful while handling your loved ones. A heavy dose of realism seems forced upon you during this influence, but your efforts to measure up to expectations can ultimately increase your confidence in your ability to be responsible for yourself. Health could also be a matter of concern at this particular point of time. Take care of your food, as you are likely to suffer from heat stroke or body heat during this time. Do not undertake any activity, which would put a risk to your life. Mentally you may feel agitated and all drained out. This period may also give you some bodily pain leading to much discomfort. There may also occur troublesome and difficult circumstances in the work front. If you are a student, you need to be more determined and focused in your studies to avoid any kind of distraction.

6th house: Transit of Mercury in the 6th house from Natal Moon

Good name, success in undertakings, income fair from business, fulfilment of desires, study of new subjects, good health. Today you will be able to tackle tasks that require real discipline or organization. You find yourself in a very practical mood and working with, instead of against, yourself. During this period, Mercury will move through your sixth house from the Moon. This indicates a mixed bag of positive and negative happenings. This particular period indicates success, stability and progress in your personal life. Your plans and projects will be successfully accomplished and you would also gain from the same. You are also likely to do better in the work front.

You may expect progress in all your undertakings. Your respect for authority is natural and helps superiors to look upon you favourably. This could be a good time to make a lasting investment if concurrent influences are favourable. This period also indicates your popularity in the society. Your status in the society is also likely to be heightened. Health should be fine and you would also have mental peace and contentment. However, for some, this movement of Mercury may bring in worries and troubles from enemies. You may have to be extra careful with your finances. Avoid any kind of arguments with your employer. It is better you stay away from activities involving risk to your health. However, body heat may trouble you during this particular period.

7th house: Transit of Mercury in the 7th house from Natal Moon

Ill heath, worries, false accusations trouble from servants and superiors, hill health of wife and children, disappointments. Obstacles to self-discipline or to your sense of organization may appear. You could be frustrated by someone in this regard, or external events might pile up and be thrust upon you During this period, Mercury will move through your seventh house from the Moon. This may bring in some trying time for you both mentally and physically. This period indicates illness. You may have to experience physical pain and bodily weakness during this phase. Mentally you might become restless and anguished.

A rise in mental perplexity and misunderstanding with the family is also indicated during this time. Your confidence may be undermined by feelings of doubt, pessimism, or feelings of guilt just now. Encountering obstacles to progress and inhibitions in your own attitude are prominent under this influence. You may have to be extra careful to avoid arguments and communication gaps while dealing with your spouse and children. Take care to avoid any situation where you may have to face humiliation. You could feel more hassled as you are likely to face hurdles in your endeavours. Travel plans, if any, may not yield the expected result and could be troublesome.

8th house: Transit of Mercury in the 8th house from Natal Moon

There will be respect and honour from your circle of friends and relatives. You could be plagued by a feeling of not being good enough. Good news, good income, success in official work, arrival of friends and relatives, enjoyment; of luxuries. During this period, Mercury will move through your eighth house from the Moon. This mostly signifies wealth and success. It indicates success in all your work and projects. During this period you may expect financial stability and gain in financial ventures. Socially you would see a rise in your status. People would respect you more and your popularity would increase. This period may also let you acquire a comfortable lifestyle. You are also likely to gain happiness from your children.

You are likely to receive happiness with a newborn member in the family. This is a time when you can expect a little boost, some sort of extra support or recognition from those around you. Your children would also remain happy and content during this particular period. This period sees a more alert and clever you. You would be able to use your intuition and intellect to make right decisions. Your enemies are likely to be defeated and will be mellowed down by your aura. Moreover, you may also expect help from all the sides. However, your health would require your attention, as you are susceptible to fall sick. Take care of your food intake and keep your spirits high to keep gloominess and unnecessary fears at bay.

9th house : Transit of Mercury in the 9th house from Natal Moon

Worries, increased expenditure, loss or wealth, sore throat, bad luck. During this period, Mercury will move through your ninth house from the Moon. This signifies sufferings from diseases. This particular phase may bring in obstruction and interruptions in your field of work. Take care to keep your respect and position in the workplace intact. Make sure you don't have to regret any of your actions done at this time. Watch out for probable hurdles before venturing into something new. Mentally you may feel hassled, overburdened, and unstable due to several reasons. Beware of your enemies as they could harm you more during this particular phase.

Avoid any arguments with your family and relatives as this may lead to unnecessary quarrels. During this period you are susceptible to become irritable and may try to find out faults in matters related to religion, common belief etc. This period may also demand more labour from you in order to accomplish any task undertaken. However, a feeling of lack of interest may stop you from working hard. Avoid undertaking any long distance travel, as it is likely to be troublesome and may not give you the desired result. Take care of your food habits and try and keep yourself in a positive frame of mind.

10th house: Transit of Mercury in the 10th house from Natal Moon

Good income, study of new subject, interest in religious matters and occult subjects, happy ceremonies, luxuries.

You could find yourself in the limelight or able to really communicate and get yourself across to others Shine brightly! This transit sometimes brings recognition for a personal achievement. During this period, Mercury will move through your tenth house from the Moon.

This denotes contentment and good times for you. You would be happy and successful in all your endeavours. Professionally a very good period could be expected as well. You would be able to finish off the work given to you successfully on time. Happiness at home is also indicated during this time. You could also expect to meet someone interesting during this time.

You may have real sense of yourself today, and would be able to communicate or convey your ideas. You tend to feel that your personality has rebound back. Possibility of gain from this person is also indicated during this particular time. Financially, this could be a good time for you. The success in your endeavours will be gainful for you and you may expect other monetary gain as well. This period may also bring in a rise in your status in the society.

You are likely to be honoured and may command more respect in the society. You may become socially more active and may get involved in social welfare work. Mentally peace and calmness is indicated. Your enemies are likely to be defeated with ease and you would find calmness in life during this particular time.

11th house: Transit of Mercury in the 11th house from Natal Moon

Others may praise you or recognize some of your better qualities today. Dealing with superiors is a breeze now, and you could win at a game or competition, if applicable. Gain of cattle, increase in income, happiness from friends & women, good name & fame and happiness. During this period, Mercury will move through your eleventh house from the Moon. This indicates achievement and monetary gain. This period is likely to bring in financial gains for you. You may expect to receive higher monetary gains from different sources. Your personal endeavours, businesses and investments are likely to bring in higher financial gains and more profits. If you are a professional or employed, you are likely to be more successful during this particular period.

Everything seems to be working together, and you may find yourself expressive and able to communicate well. You possess strong presence and generally feel confident about who you are and how others are receiving you now. You are likely to prosper in your field of activity especially during this time.

Health should be good. You are likely to be at peace with yourself. You may also expect to get some favourable news. You are likely to be surrounded by material comfort. Socially this is a good phase as well. You would be able to command more respect in the society. Pleasant company of the opposite sex would also surround you. Your wit and pleasant nature would also make people flock around you.

12th house: Transit of Mercury in the 12th house from Natal Moon

A new change is about to begin and you are more inclined to accept and appreciate all that is new, unusual, and of higher grade. You have an opportunity to shine for what makes you unique. Good income, general success, good name, happy ceremonies. During this period, Mercury will move through your twelfth house from the Moon. This denotes expenses for you. You may have to spend more than expected in order to live a comfortable life. Stay away from litigations as this may also cause some loss of money. Moreover, you may also have to work extra hard to accomplish any of the task undertaken by you.

You may experience opposition to the way you present yourself. Someone could challenge your sense of identity. Beware of your enemies and stay out of their way in order to avoid any humiliation. Hold on to your respect and try and keep your honour in the society. You could be mentally disturbed due to several reasons. You are susceptible to worries and restlessness during this particular time. You are also likely to be distressed and feel discontented during this phase. You are likely to lose interest in food and conjugal life. A feeling of sickness and suffering may trouble you during this particular point of time.

MICROSCOPY OF
TRANSITING PLANETS
SIMPLIFIED
VOLUME-5

TRANSITING PLANETS

CHAPTER THIRTY THREE

MERCURY TRANSITS URANUS NEPTUNE PLUTO

Transit Mercury Conjunct Uranus

You have tremendous nervous energy and may be more clumsy than usual, and need to take special care when driving to avoid speeding and the reckless actions of other people. Your communication is often rebellious, shocking or rather stubborn, and you'll find it more difficult to compromise or behave in a cooperative way.

Transit Mercury Opposition Uranus

Your nervous energy is high and your sense of adventure is stimulated. It will be very hard to sit still or endure mental concentration for a long period of time - or even a short period of time - and you should plan a day that allows you frequent movement or distraction. Your day is filled with sudden upsets or changes in plans, forcing you to be flexible and think on your feet. Your mind is extremely restless and you're looking for excitement, which you're likely to get, but it may be difficult to keep up with the hectic pace. This is not the best day to sit in one place or carry on long periods of concentration, as your body needs to keep moving.

Transit Mercury Sextile Uranus

The pace of business is fast and furious and you'll be exposed to new and stimulating ideas, although it may be difficult to keep up and process all the information. Be especially careful when operating machinery or electrical devices, and avoid speeding or impatience when traveling. The mind of business is fast and you enjoy variety in your schedule. You have more nervous energy than usual and may find it difficult to sit still for a long period of time.

Transit Mercury Square Uranus

Your thoughts are inventive and original and you love shocking other people with your outrageous opinions, all in the spirit of fun. You enjoy making connections and may find yourself in group activities or meetings that are stimulating and interesting. Your mind is extremely restless today and it will be more difficult to concentrate for long periods of time. Mundane chores are especially boring and you'd prefer more excitement in your routine.

Transit Mercury Trine Uranus

Other people irritate you easily and if you're not careful, you may find yourself blurting out comments that are inappropriate or even rude. Your mind is active and needing stimulation, and you'll look for excitement in your daily routine. You're exposed to information that's interesting, unusual or bizarre, and may meet new people or attend non-traditional gatherings. Your day is likely to be hectic and fast-paced, which will be more enjoyable to you than sitting in one place for very long, which you probably won't be able to do anyway. Stay as flexible as you can and expect plans to change you may get a nice surprise.

Transit Mercury Conjunct Neptune

Mental fatigue and confusion are more likely and you should put off critical thinking until tomorrow. You may have to contend with people who are confusing or dishonest, or be tempted to shade the truth to avoid a confrontation, but even little while lies will tend to be revealed. You may feel misunderstood or even paranoid today, but this will pass quickly and you should be back to your old self tomorrow.

Although there are better transits for personal magnetism than this one, you do tend to easily attract positive attention and circumstances now. Your urge to daydream and escape reality is very strong, and it will be difficult to concentrate on the more mundane issues of your everyday life. Misunderstandings are common today, as you find it difficult to say exactly what you think. You're very sensitive to the reactions of other people, which will influence the way you communicate.

Transit Mercury Opposition Neptune

Your sensitivity to what they need to hear will also make you more effective in sales, promotion or advertising. You may need a brief retreat from the pressures and hectic pace of business, and keeping up with details will prove more challenging. This makes communicating with others more difficult, as they're not likely to be on the same planet as you are; you need to clarify all agreements to avoid misunderstandings.

Transit Mercury Sextile Neptune

Today is not the best day for focused concentration or strictly logical thinking. Your imagination is stimulated and unless you're doing very creative work, it will be hard to avoid endless daydreaming. You have access to your creativity today and can translate subtle forms around you in clear and precise ways. You may enjoy photography, writing or music, or taking time to contemplate the spiritual issues in your life.

Transit Mercury Square Neptune

This is not the best day for doing work that calls for strictly logical or critical thinking, as you're more interested in exploring the recesses of your imagination. Your imagination is working overtime however, and this is a great day for any activity that allows you to fantasize, imagine or create. You're extremely sensitive to the comments of other people and may feel like they're picking on you, but avoid the tendency to be paranoid.

Transit Mercury Trine Neptune

Your mental energy is low and this is not the best day to handle details or projects that require logical thinking. You'll tend to drift off or daydream easily and would love escape from your normal routine. However, if you need to interpret or describe subtle images or abstract concepts, you have easy access to your intuitive mind and can give form to your vision. This is particularly good for photography, music or writing fiction. You're not terribly motivated to work or concentrate and should allow room in your day for frequent daydreaming or drifting off into pleasant fantasies.

Transit Mercury Conjunct Pluto

You may be a bit obsessive with your thoughts and the smallest detail may have you pondering all day, which will be helpful when involved in research, study or investigation. You may be a teacher or a student, and will be exposed to profound insights. When you focus and control this power, you'll have tremendous determination and perception for any kind of mental research or investigation, or writing, teaching, counselling or empowering other people with your words. You're not satisfied by superficial information and will explore the very core of the subject at hand. Secrets will be important; you may uncover secrets that have been kept from you, or keep secrets in order to gain power. In either situation, you need to stay very aware of the power of information.

Transit Mercury Opposition Pluto

Your communication is extremely powerful today and you may not be aware of the impact your words have on other people they'll tend to feel interrogated or challenged. You have a need to be honest, sometimes brutally, which may be your way of gaining some advantage or control over your associates. You won't be satisfied with superficial communication today and may tend to interrogate other people in order to get the whole picture. You may not realize how powerful you are in your approach, which is why other people are quick to defend themselves.

Transit Mercury Sextile Pluto

Other people seem to want to control what you're thinking or reform your opinions, which you won't tolerate, and you may become embroiled in heated arguments over things that aren't terribly important. You're highly intuitive and can see into their motives, and need to watch using this ability to take unnecessary advantage. You're thorough in your thinking and may enjoy research or investigation, or using your communication to elicit hidden information through interrogation or counselling. Be more aware of the power of your words and the impact you have on other people.

Transit Mercury Square Pluto

Your conversations will be serious, provocative or therapeutic, as you probe deeper into important issues. You may also have an enlightening experience when traveling. Your communication is fuelled by passion today, and you won't take no for an answer. You're extremely persuasive when dealing with other people and will look for common ground to effectively sway them to your side. Your mind seems more obsessive today, and you may spend an ordinate amount of time focused on one thought.

Transit Mercury Trine Pluto

You feel the need to thoroughly investigate every detail, which will be helpful in projects involving research or study, but may be more difficult when dealing with simple everyday chores. This may be a better day to explore your own feelings and thoughts, which will give you great insight into your own motives and how to direct your mental energy in productive ways. Today is a great day for any mental activity that involves research, investigation or concentration. You have a need to explore what's under the surface and won't be satisfied by superficial explanations.

MICROSCOPY OF TRANSITING PLANETS SIMPLIFIED VOLUME-5

CHAPTER THIRTY FOUR

TRANSITING MERCURY

Overview:

Your thoughts and ideas may not mesh with the plans and methods of someone you meet with today. This transit of mercury denotes good communication. You could be pleasantly busy now, conversing and socializing, writing or speaking, and handling details.

Mercury conjunct Sun

You find yourself talkative and quick-witted today. Ideas are clear and easy to come by. This could be a good time for thinking over your own affairs. You may have a conversation with an older person or someone in authority. You are especially sharp, communicative, and open at this time. This is because your wants are aligned with your thoughts. It's a favourable time for solving problems. What you say or write now has impact, for better or for worse! You are likely more interested in talking about yourself than in listening to others. This can be a very busy, communicative, or even hectic day.

Mercury sextile Sun

Opportunities a good time to move forward with long range plans that will bring future success. You are inclined to think positively and with growth in mind. Others tend to cooperate with you, and perhaps seek out your advice. You are at your mental best with sharp ideas and clear thoughts. This is an excellent time to make decisions and take care of mental work. Your ideas are especially intelligent and creative now, and come from the heart. Decision making comes easily now. You are expressing yourself with strength of character now, and others take note. Your confidence in what you have to say now helps you to be well-received.

Mercury square Sun

You may have a hard time being clearheaded right now. Thoughts and ideas that come may be inappropriate or misleading. Arguments are possible with an authority figure or someone older than you. Others' communications could frustrate you today or rub you the wrong way. Nervous tension is possible. Avoid letting your ego spoil your mood. Try not to read negativity into what others say now. However, it is more likely now than usual to hear criticism or news that makes you tense.

Mercury trine Sun

A time when you are no longer sure of the directions and choices you've taken to fulfil ambitions. Increased confidence in what you have to say means your audience receives your message. You are able to think quickly on your feet now, and you are communicating with authority. Alternatively, you could receive important information from a superior now. Your reasoning skills are especially strong now.

Mercury opposite Sun

Something you say or communicate may go against your own best interests. You could clash with an older person or one in authority. Someone may argue with you. You find it hard to clearly express yourself during this transit. You might unwittingly misrepresent yourself or your intentions through something you say or write. You might meet with people, or communicate with others, who don't share your perspective. You could also feel bogged down with details, tasks, or errands.

Mercury conjunct Moon

You may find yourself analysing your life situation and surroundings. Conversations of an inspiring kind may be in order with younger persons or others around you. Awareness of your emotions, as well as the need to verbalize them, comes with this transit. Verbalization can take the form of actual communication through speech or the written word with others, but it can also be an internal process.

There could be some tension or sense of opposition requiring compromise or negotiation on your part. Thinking about your past, feelings, and personal connections characterizes this influence. You might make a verbal connection with a female, your mother, or a person from your past now. This might be a good time to discuss domestic matters, as you are more likely to approach the topic with objectivity. It can also be a busy time with visits, conversations, and discoveries. Getting in touch with relatives, neighbours, and acquaintances can figure now.

Mercury sextile Moon

You have a natural sense for communicating with others, especially those younger than yourself. Clear thoughts about the past may also be flowing in today. News that you hear now is likely to be satisfying on an emotional level. Pleasing conversations with females, relatives, neighbours, or people from your past figure now. It's easy to ask for what you want and get it! Expressing your wants and needs is flowing, natural, and spontaneous right now.

Mercury square Moon

You may find that your ideas and thoughts run counter to what is going on around you, resulting in a lack of support or respect for what you think. There could be arguments, especially with younger persons. It can be challenging to get in touch with what you want and need now, yet you are inclined towards verbalizing your feelings nevertheless. You are easily distracted right now, and news you hear can be irritating as well. This is a time when you tend to misplace your keys, miss important phone calls, get stuck in traffic, forget appointments, and the like.

Mercury trine Moon

You have a natural sense for communicating with others, especially those younger than yourself. Clear thoughts about the past may also be flowing in today. News that you hear now is likely to be satisfying on an emotional level. Pleasing conversations with females, relatives, neighbours, or people from your past figure now. It's easy to ask for what you want and get it! Expressing your wants and needs is flowing, natural, and spontaneous right now.

Mercury opposite Moon

You may find yourself reflecting on your own youth or some event in the past. Communication with those around you, especially younger people, may be difficult or combative. You are likely to hear news that is in opposition to what makes you feel satisfied. Conversations can be frustrating now, and you could be hypersensitive to the opinions or statements of others. This is a time when you don't really want to hear truths or facts. It's also likely that plans are upset, keys misplaced, traffic prevents you from being timely, and so forth.

Mercury conjunct Mercury

You are just plain witty now, and the ideas roll off your tongue. A real time for communicate by phone, by letter or in person. The mind is clear. This is a time when you are bound to discover information that you need at just the right time. It's a strong period for objective observation and discussion. Your thinking is in line with current trends, and your ideas are received well.

Mercury sextile Mercury

This is a time when tensions with others can come from a lack of self-confidence or a sudden awareness of unfulfilled wishes and goals. Your mind could be quite clear and natural just now. Ideas are flowing and could come with ease. This is a time when you are bound to discover information that you need at just the right time. It's a strong period for objective observation and discussion.

Mercury square Mercury

During this transit, you find it easier than usual to rationalize your own behaviour and that of others. You will find that your mind and thoughts will be very intense just now. There could be a lot of pressure to make decisions that you will regret later. Disagree-ments on an intellectual level are quite possible. You are likely very busy processing information and thinking just now. You could be feeling quite restless now, and in the mood for new scenery.

Mercury trine Mercury

You can benefit now from a more confident manner and increased certainty about your goals in life. Your mind could be quite clear and natural just now. Ideas are flowing and could come with ease. This is a time when you are bound to discover information that you need at just the right time. It's a strong period for objective observation and discussion.

Mercury opposite Mercury

The only cautions are to try to avoid making decisions that are based on your emotions of the moment, and to avoid taking everything too personally. You could blurt out the wrong thing today or be unable to convey what you really intend to someone. Ideas and thoughts may not come with ease. Also, others may disagree with your ideas. You are likely to engage in a conversation with someone who has a different perspective on matters now. You can learn from the experience if you open your mind. You could be feeling quite restless now, and in the mood for new scenery.

Mercury conjunct Venus

It's easy to see what you value and care about. Your sense of appreciation is sharpened and in high focus. You find yourself more socially composed than usual now. Light-hearted conversations, sociability, humour, and cooperation characterize this period. It's a strong time for socializing and communicating with ease, telling others how you feel, and negotiating. Mentally, you are not as disciplined as usual, however, as you prefer to chat with others and to think about more pleasant things than work. You could receive a compliment or other pleasing communication. Alternatively, new information or knowledge learned now makes you feel good. This is a favourable transit for commerce and business transactions, all things equal.

Mercury sextile Venus

It's an excellent period for improving your skills and for opening up discussions on topics that you normally might sidestep. You could feel real support and harmony at this time for circumstances and those around you. You have a clear vision into your own inner sense of values, how you appreciate and love. You are currently able to handle opportunities well by focusing your energy on constructive activities and goals. It could be a time when promises and clarifications are made in love relationships.

Mercury square Venus

Your ideas and thoughts may run counter to accepted values, you're own or those of others. You may find yourself in a disapproving mood. Decisions made now may have to be re-thought later. You could find yourself tense. Hypersensitivity and lack of mental discipline could be issues in the circumstances you attract now. You could take offense at someone's ideas or communications, as it disagrees with your values.

Mercury trine Venus

You are more excitable than usual, and less inclined to make rational, thought-out decisions. Whims could take hold. You have a clear vision into your own inner sense of values; how you appreciate and love It's easy to make social connections under this influence. This transit favours diplomacy, charm, social graces, negotiations, presentation of ideas, romantic overtures, teaching, business deals, publishing, commerce, public relations, and joint ventures or partnerships. It could be a time when promises and clarifications are made in love relationships. Something you hear now, or new information that you learn, can give you pleasure. As well, you are more able to express your more charming or loving nature verbally.

Mercury opposite Venus

You may have difficult thoughts or conversations with someone you love or care for, or your ideas may go against the values of someone who confronts you. Something you hear, learn about, or the opinion of someone could bother you and disturb your sense of balance now. You might find it inappropriate, rude, or downright irritating! Superficiality in others could also be particularly irritating to you. A lover or friend might offer you information or advice that you don't want to hear. Others simply aren't pleasing you right now. It's not the best time for business transactions, beauty treatments, or purchases for the home.

Mercury conjunct Mars

There is a lot of energy behind what you say and think. You can make quick and sharp decisions. Also there is the possibility of sharp words. You communicate with feeling and strength. This is a time of quick wit and strong mental impulses. You are especially enthusiastic and productive. You are more inclined than usual to express your desires, and perhaps what gets your goat as well! Your observations are sharp, but you could be inclined towards mental pressures or impatience with others who don't seem to be getting your point right away. This is a time when plans are put into action.

Mercury sextile Mars

Your mind is quick and sharp, and your words are the only weapon you will need today. You have insight into your emotions and drive, and you can talk about your feelings with great insight and fluidity. Mental alertness, enthusiasm, and energetic communications figure now. Quick decisions can be made. You are productive and take "busy-ness" in stride. You are alert and aware, and can easily turn ideas into workable projects. You can talk your way out of practically anything now. Your conversations are animated and expressive now, and spontaneous impulses tend to work for rather than against you.

Mercury square Mars

Your mind is very sharp now, with the result that you may be a bit irritable or say too much. Quick-witted you are, but this could also result in arguments and hard words mental agitation. Although you are quick-witted now, you could also be ready to argue! Alternatively, you could be meeting with aggressive or critical people now. This could be a time when you are working under stressful or hectic conditions, as you feel pressure to get things done quickly.

If you are having problems on the domestic front, they are magnified now. Do your best not to force changes in your life. You are inclined to be snappy and irritable, and you might too easily interrupt others rather than listen. Conflicts of interest are likely to occur now. This is an unfavourable time for any kind of meeting, starting a new project, and business proposals. You can be irritable and say all the wrong things. Impulsive communications and hasty decision-making are things to watch for now.

Mercury trine Mars

This is a good time to uncover issues of emotional unrest that have been bubbling under the surface, and to take steps to take better care of your emotional needs. Enthusiasm and energetic communications occur during this transit. You are mentally alert and aware, and can easily turn ideas into workable projects. You can talk your way out of practically anything now. Your conversations are animated and expressive now, and spontaneous impulses tend to work for rather than against you.

Mercury opposite Mars

Steer clear of arguments and possible hard feelings. Your thoughts may not be in sync with your feelings, and this could result in a clash with someone today. Instead of listening to what others have to say, you could end up interrupting them and making assumptions. You could be quick on the trigger when it comes to verbal reactions to others, and you may seriously lack diplomacy at this time. You might find yourself doing the opposite of what you are told or what you normally think is best! Information that you receive now could lead you to take a wrong turn or action. This is not the best time to take a trip.

Mercury conjunct Jupiter

You are in a planning mood and are very clearheaded and able to view all the alternative paths. Go ahead and make those decisions. You can see the road ahead and will make the right choices. This could be a time when you have a strong desire to verbalize your own goals and ideals. You are optimistic, which can help you attract positive circumstances.

Mercury sextile Jupiter

You could feel real support and harmony at this time for circumstances and those around you. A clear-minded insight into your own plans and methods is available to you. This is a favourable influence for short trips, writing, teaching, studying, mailings, interviews, advertising and promotion, submitting applications and forms, and accurate observations. You are inclined to think positively and with growth in mind. Others tend to cooperate with you, and perhaps seek out your advice. You might receive some interesting offers now.

Mercury square Jupiter

You could find yourself mentally acute and in a problem-solving mood. However, there is a real possibility that the decisions you make today and the solutions you find may have to be re-done tomorrow Information overload. It is all too easy to miss or neglect important details under the influence of this transit. You may be tempted to exaggerate or overstate now, or you could have a hard time putting your ideas to practical use.

Mercury trine Jupiter

A clear-minded insight into your own plans and methods is available to you. This is a favourable influence for short trips, writing, teaching, studying, mailings, interviews, advertising and promotion, submitting applications and forms, and accurate observations. You are inclined to think positively and with growth in mind. Others tend to cooperate with you, and perhaps seek out your advice. You might receive some interesting offers now.

Mercury opposite Jupiter

Your thoughts and ideas may not mesh with the plans and methods of someone you meet with today. You could find yourself saying things against the way they do things. Your ideas may run counter to some plan of action. Avoid jumping into something without planning ahead, as important details are too easy to overlook right now. Also, avoid making promises you may not be able to fulfil, and be sure to read the fine print! In a search to attach greater meaning to your thoughts and ideas, you may exaggerate, overstate, or overestimate.

Mercury conjunct Saturn

It's an excellent time for taking tests or presenting your ideas. Your opinions and thought processes are generally well-received and appreciated now. This is a time when you handle opportunities that come your way very well. You are in a serious frame of mind and find yourself dealing with matters of much concern and responsibility. Your ability to concentrate and focus is enhanced now. You could experience an increased need for solitude in order to think or work. Travel for business purposes is possible. The possibility of some form of recognition or validation for what you do may come during this brief but effective period.

Mercury sextile Saturn

Put your mind to work and take care of any details that you may have, for mental discipline should come easily. Problems and obstacles that have heretofore been confounding should find easy explanations under your keen examination. This is a good time to get organized, do detail work, and prepare for the future. Decisions made now tend to be practical and well thought out. Work done now is likely to pay off in the future. Your thinking is clear and realistic under this influence. Conversations may be spare but to the point. Manifestation and achievement are what satisfy you.

Mercury square Saturn

It's a good time to mend relationship problems and to surround you with people. You may feel mentally depressed or restricted. Perhaps this is not the time to try to solve any serious problems or make important decisions. It could be hard to think. Getting from point A to point B can be a challenge during this transit due to obstacles. Communications may be blocked or delayed, and negative thinking could dominate at this time. Projects we thought were complete may need revision, and others could appear overly critical, insensitive, or sarcastic. Avoid signing on the dotted line at this time.

Mercury trine Saturn

New ways to communicate or an easy manner will make conversations and interactions go well today. You may find yourself more talkative and facile than otherwise. You may feel like talking a bit more than usual, exploring new ideas or getting happily lost in a conversation. You might find that you attract challenging situations simply because you are overreacting emotionally. There could be an emotional overtone to all of this that may require understanding and flexibility on your part.

Mercury opposite Saturn

Someone may tend to put the damper on what you say or think, or in some way manage to restrict your ability to communicate. You may have thoughts that differ with the establishment (the law).Communication challenges today make it hard to get a point across. Delays, red tape, and vague feelings of forgetting important details could figure now. Your thought patterns could take on a negative skew, as you think in pessimistic terms and communicate sparingly or reluctantly. It can be difficult to trust your instincts, and you might second-guess things automatically under this influence. You could also receive news or information that makes you tense or goes against your goals.

Mercury conjunct Ascendant

New ways to communicate or an easy manner will make conversations and interactions go well today. You may find yourself more talkative and facile than otherwise. You tend to say what you think now. Keep in mind that what you say or write now has impact, for better or for worse. Your communication skills are at a high-water mark. This is a period of heightened verbal ability or increased communications. You might be a little more assertive or more able to verbalize your ideas and thoughts. You could be thinking a lot about taking action on something important to you.

Mercury sextile Ascendant

It's an excellent period for improving your skills and for opening up discussions on topics that you normally might sidestep. What you say or write could be misinterpreted, or you could find it hard to verbalize what it is you want. Your thoughts could be all over the place, and it can be hard to concentrate on any one particular task. You can really get your thoughts and ideas across. Good communication. Your ideas are well-received, your mind is alert, and you can easily and quickly grasp information now.

Mercury square Ascendant

You could find yourself struggling to communicate or being easily misunderstood. Hard words are possible with an authority figure or an older person. You may have some difficulty speaking or getting your ideas and thoughts across to others. You might say the wrong thing. News or information you receive now could be frustrating, or conversations with others make you tense. You might be asked to do a favour that you don't want to do or you could feel overloaded with tasks and errands now. It's more likely than usual for you to make mental errors, and nervous tension is quite possible now.

Mercury trine Ascendant

New ways to communicate or an easy manner will make conversations and interactions go well today. Others tend to value your opinions and ideas under the influence of this transit. You can really get your thoughts and ideas across. Good communication. You could be pleasantly busy now, conversing and socializing, writing or speaking, and handling details. It's easier now than usual to verbalize exactly what you want. Others appreciate what you have to say and your ideas and opinions are received exactly as you intended them.

Mercury opposite Ascendant

You want to be the centre of attention right now, and you are feeling more vulnerable to how others receive you, so you may pay special attention to your charm and appearance or mannerisms. You may find yourself somewhat argumentative today. For instance, you could disagree with ideas or find communication with others difficult or fouled up. Reaching out to others on mental level figures now. Negotiations are in order, and you might feel a strong need for feedback from a significant other or special friend.

MICROSCOPY OF TRANSITING PLANETS SIMPLIFIED VOLUME-5

CHAPTER THIRTY FIVE

PLACEMENT OF PLANETS IN DIFFERENT HOUSES

MERCURY

In the First house. – Cheerful, humorous, well read, clever, many enemies, learned, fond of occult studies and astronomy, witty, influential, intellectual, respected, long-lived, love of literature and poetry.

Second house. – Learned in religious and philosophical lore, sweet speech, good conversationalist, humorous, clever many children, determined, fine manners, captivating look, self-acquisition, wealthy, careful, thrifty, and clever in earning money.

Third house. – Daughter, happy mother, clever, cruel, loved by fair sex, tactful, diplomatic, discretion, bold, sensible.

Fourth house. – Learned, agriculturist, good mother, unhappy, skilled in conjuring tricks, obliging, cultured, affectionate, popular, inclined to pursue literary activities.

Fifth house. – Showy, learned, quarrelsome, danger to maternal uncles, parents sickly, good administrative capacity, fond of good furniture and dress, respect from moneyed men, ministerial office, executive ability, speculative, scholar, vain, danger to father, combative.

Sixth house. – Respected, interrupted education, subordinate officer, executive capacity, quarrelsome, showy, dissimulation, losses in money peevish, bigoted, troubles in the feet and toes.

Seventh house. – Diplomatic, interesting literary ability early in life and success through it, early marriage, wife handsome, dutiful and short-tempered, breaks in education, learned in astrology, astronomy and mathematics, success in trade, successful, dashing, gay, skilful, religious, charitable, strong body.

Eighth house. – Long life, landed estate, easy access to anything desired, grief through domestics, obliging, few issues, many lands, famous, respected, ill-health.

Ninth house. – Highly educated, musician, many children, obliging, licentious, philosophical, lover of literature, creative mind, inquisitive, scientific-minded, popular, well known.

Tenth house. – Determined, fortunate, enjoyments in life, intelligent, bad sight, active, cheerful, charitable, able, philanthropic.

Eleventh house. – Wealthy, happy, mathematical faculty, good astrologer, many friends among famous men, many lands, logical and scientific, success in trade.

Twelfth house. – Philosophical, intelligent, worried, adulterous, obliging, capricious, wayward, narrow-minded, gifted, despondent, passionate, few children, lacking in opportunities, danger to mother.

MICROSCOPY OF TRANSITING PLANETS SIMPLIFIED VOLUME-5

CHAPTER THIRTY SIX

PLACEMENT OF PLANETS IN DIFFERENT SIGNS

MERCURY

In Aries. – Evil-minded, middle stature, obstinate, clever, social, great endurance, materialistic tendencies, unscrupulous, wavering mind, antagonistic, fond of speculation, impulsive, greedy, dangerous connections, deceitful, swerving from rectitude.

Taurus. – High position, well built, clever, logical, mental harmony, many children, liberal, persevering, opinionative, wealthy, practicable, friends among women of eminence, inclination to sensual pleasures, well read, showy.

Gemini. – Inclination to physical labour, boastful, sweet speech, tall, active, cultured, tactful, dexterous to mothers, indolent, inventive, taste in literature, arts and sciences, winning manners, liable to throat and bronchial troubles, musician, mirthful, studious.

Cancer. – Witty, likes music, disliked by relations, low stature, speculative, diplomatic, discreet, flexible, restless, sensual though religious, liable to consumption, strong parental love, dislike for chastity.

Leo. – Few children, wanderer, idiotic, proud, indolent, not fond of women, boastful, orator, good memory, two mothers, poor, early marriage, independent in thinking, impulsive, positive will, remunerative profession, likes travelling.

Virgo. – Learned, virtuous, liberal, fearless, ingenious, handsome, irritable, refined, subtle, intuitive, sociable, no self-control, morbid imaginations, dyspeptic, difficulties, eloquent, author, priest, astronomer.

Libra. – Fair complexion, sanguine disposition, inclination to excesses, perceptive faculties, material tendencies, frugal, agreeable, courteous, philosophical, faithful, ceremonial-minded, sociable, discreet.

Scorpio. – Short, curly hair, incentive to indulgence, liable to disease of the generative organ, general debility, crafty, malicious, selfish, subtle, indiscreet, bold, reckless.

Sagittarius. – Taste in sciences, respected by polished society, tall, well built, learned, rash, superstitious, vigorous, executive, diplomatic, cunning, just, and capable.

Capricorn. – Selfless, business tendencies, economical, debtor, inconsistent, low stature, cunning, inventive, active, restless, suspicious, drudging.

Aquarius. – Middle stature, licentious, proud, quarrelsome frank, sociable, rapid strides in life, famous, scholar, cowardly, weak constitution.

Pisces. – A dependent, serves others, dexterous, peevish, indolent, petty-minded, respect for goods, and Brahmins.

MICROSCOPY OF TRANSITING PLANETS SIMPLIFIED VOLUME-5

CHAPTER THIRTY SEVEN

REMEDIES OF PLANETS

Effects and Remedies

In astrological parlance Mercury has been understood as an externally variable, vacillating, convertible, neutral and dualistic planet. Mercury reflects the mentality of an individual, governs the reaction to our senses and impressions and rules over the central nervous system. As an intellectual planet it represents intelligence, genius, analytic power and reproducibility.

Mercury is the smallest planet of the solar system. The author of Lal Kitab has compared mercury with a bat, which keeps hanging upside down and pounces upon the face of a child at the first opportunity. The native fails to understand anything and meanwhile the mysterious and mischievous mercury turns the cycle of fortune in the reverse gear. Mercury produces the effects of the planet or planets it is associated with. Mercury is considered malefic in the 3rd, 8th, 9th and 12th houses. Rahu gives bad results in 1, 5, 7, 8 and 11th houses.

If mercury and Rahu both are in their auspicious houses then Mercury causes havoc in the natives houses and produces disastrous result like putting the native behind the bars or creating troubles of the same sort. Mercury is considered auspicious in the 1, 2, 4, 5, 6 and the 7th houses and gives bad results when placed in the 3, 8, 9, 10, 11 and

12th. Its colour is green and moon is its enemy. Sun Venus and Rahu are friends, whereas mars, Saturn, and Ketu are neutral to him. 7th house is the Pukka Ghar of mercury. It stands exalted in the 6th house and gets debilitated in the 12th house. Affected Venus causes diseases of tooth and nervous system. If mercury is placed alone in any house the native keeps running and wasting time here and there.

Mercury in 1st House

Mercury in 1st house makes the native kind, humorous and diplomatic with administrative skill. Such a native generally lives long and becomes selfish and mischievous by nature having special attraction for non-vegetarian dishes and drinks. He receives favour from the government and his daughters have royal and luxurious lives. The relatives represented by the house in which sun is placed gain wealth and riches within a little time and he himself will be having many sources of income. If Sun is placed along with Mercury in the 1st house or if the Mercury is expected by Sun the wife of native will come from a rich and noble family and will be good natured. Such a native will be affected by the evil effects of Mars but Sun will never give bad effects.

Rahu and Ketu will have evil effects, which suggest that the in laws and the offspring of the native will be adverse. If mercury is in the 1st house, the native will be adept in the art of influencing others and he will live like a king. Malefic Mercury in the 1st house along with Moon in the 7th house destroy the native because of intoxication.

Remedies

1. Keep away from the things of green colour and sisters in law.

2. Avoid consumption of meat, eggs and liquor.

3. Business that requires your sitting at one place would be more beneficial than the one that requires running around.

Mercury in 2nd House

Mercury in the 2nd house makes the native intelligent self-centred, destroyer of enemies and cheats. He may be able to provide sufficient happiness to his father. he will be rich. The things represented by mars and Venus will prove beneficial to him.

Remedies

1. Abstain from eggs meat and liquor.
2. Association with your sisters in law is harmful.
3. Keeping sheep, goat and parrots as pets is strictly Prohibited.

Mercury in 3rd House

Mercury in the 3rd house is not considered good. Mercury is inimical to Mars. But Mars does not have enmity with mercury. therefore the native could receive benefits from his brother, but he will not be beneficial to his brother or others. By virtue of its aspects of 9th and 11th houses Mercury affects the income and the condition of the father very adversely.

Remedies

1. Clean your teeth with alum everyday.
2. Feed birds and donate a goat.
3. Don't live in a south facing house.
4. Distribute medicines of asthma.

Mercury in 4th House

The native in the 4th house is considered fortunate, very dear to his mother, good trader and receives favours from the government. However mercury in this house affects the income and health of another person adversely.

Remedies

1. Putting on silver chain for mental peace and golden chain for gaining wealth and property.
2. Putting kesar tilak regularly for 43 days on fore -head.
3. Serving monkeys by offering jaggery.

Mercury in 5th house

Mercury in this house makes the native happy, wealthy and wise. Spontaneous utterances from the mouth of the native will certainly prove true.

It gives very good results if the moon or any male planet is placed in 3rd, 5th, 9th and 11th houses, but if moon and Jupiter are not placed in good houses mercury would provide malefic effects.

Remedies

1. Wear a copper coin in white thread for obtaining riches.
2. Serving cows for the happiness of wife and good luck.
3. A Gomukhi house (narrow at the front and wider at the end) would prove highly auspicious where as Shermukhi house (wider at the front and narrower at the end) would prove highly disastrous.

Mercury in 6th House

Mercury becomes exalted in the 6th house. The native will be self-made man and will receive benefits from agricultural land, stationery, printing press and trade. Good or evil words from his mouth will never go waste. north facing house will give bad results. Daughter's marriage in the north direction will make her unhappy in every way.

Remedies

1. Burying a bottle filled with Ganga water into the Agricultural land.
2. Putting on a silver ring in the left hand of one's wife.
3. Starting any important work in the presence of a girl or Daughters or with flowers in hand proves auspicious.

Mercury in 7th House

In a male horoscope, mercury in the 7th house proves highly beneficial for others for whom the native wishes well. in a female horoscope it produces good result. The pen of the native wields more power than the sword. The sister of the native's wife will prove highly helpful in every matter. If a Moon is placed in the 1st house, overseas journey will be advantageous. Saturn in the 3rd house will make the wife's family very rich.

Remedies

1. Avoid any business in partnership.
2. Avoid speculation.
3. Do not keep relationship with sister in law of spoilt Character.

Mercury in 8th House

Mercury gives very bad results in 8th house, but if it is placed along with a male planet it will give good effects of the associated planet. The native lives a hard life, victimized by diseases and during the age 32-34 his income goes down by half. It is more harmful if some planet is placed in the 2nd house. If Rahu is also placed in the same house the native may have to go to jail, may have to be hospitalized or may have to wander from place to place. Bad results accrue if mars is also placed therein. Mercury here causes disfavour from the government and diseases like blood disorder, eye problem, tooth and vein troubles, as well as big loss in business.

Remedies

1. Get an earthen pot filled with honey and bury it in the cremation ground or deserted area.
2. Place milk or rain water in a container on the roof of the house.
3. Put a ring in the nose of your daughter.

Mercury in 9th House

Mercury provides very bad results in the 9th house also, because this house belongs to Jupiter and Mercury remains inimical to it. It causes continuous mental restlessness and defamation of various types. If moon, Ketu and Jupiter are placed in 1, 3, 6, 7, 9 and 11th houses, mercury does not give very advantageous results.

Remedies

1. Avoid the use of green color.
2. Get your nose pricked.
3. Offer mushroom filled in an earthen pot to a religious place.

4. Do not accept any tabeez from any sadhoo or faqir.

Mercury in 10th House

Mercury in the 10th house provides favour from the government. Gives good sources of livelihood. he manages to get his work done in every way. The business of such a native flourishes in a shermukhi house, but residency in such a house gives very bad result and can be disastrous.

Remedies

1. Consumption of eggs, meat and liquor are strictly Prohibited.
2. Offer rice and milk in religious places.

Mercury in 11th House

Mercury in this house gives bad results, because of enmity to Jupiter. At the age of 34 the native undertakes works of extreme foolishness. here mercury causes loss of wealth, loss of mental peace and loss of reputation. Even hard work is not awarded. however the children of native will be well educated and get married in very rich and noble families.

Remedies

1. Wear copper coin in neck in a white thread or silver chain.
2. Do not keep a widowed sister or father's sister in your house.
3. Avoid green colour and emerald.
4. Do not accept any Tabeez from a sadhoo or faqir.

Mercury in 12th House

Mercury here destroys night's sleep of the native and causes troubles of many sorts. He loses peace of mind and very often suffers from headache. he has a long life but suffers from mercury, although, however, if mercury is accompanied by Saturn in this house very good results follow. Saturn along with sun and Mercury in 12th house also gives good result. Daughters, sisters, father's sister and niece will be unhappy as long as they are living in the native's house. Such persons are generally self-praising and of irritable nature. If something right or wrong goes into his mind, he will ensure to stick to it in every manner. If such a native is fond of taking liquor he will be of pretentious nature. Speculation in business will prove harmful. Marriage in the 25th year will prove harmful for the native's wife and father.

Remedies

1. Throwing new empty pitcher in a river.
2. Putting on a ring of stainless steel.
3. Putting kesar tilak on face, head and visiting religious places of worship.
4. Taking advice of another person before starting any new or important work.

MICROSCOPY OF TRANSITING PLANETS SIMPLIFIED VOLUME-5

CHAPTER THIIRTY EIGHT

TRANSISTING VENUS FROM NATAL MOON

Transit of Planet Venus from First House of Natal Moon Sign

Venus takes about a month to transit a sign. A craving for sweetness and comfort in the form of loving affection or food is strong now. This is a good time to baby yourself and also to spend time with the people who love and appreciate you the most. The following are the effects of Venus transit, as per the moon sign, they can vary quite a bit based on your own individual horoscope.

1st house: Transit of Venus in the 1st house from Natal Moon

You are more likely to be received well today than on other days. This is a good time to enhance the beauty and grace of your home. A good time for surrounding yourself with friends and younger people and for having a good time. Take this opportunity to express your feelings to people close to you. During this period, Venus will move through your first house from the Moon. This mostly signifies material and sensual comfort for you.

You may expect a lot of happenings on the personal front. A passive approach to life works best now. This transit is a cosmic nudge to slow down and enjoy quiet and nurturing activities. If eligible, you are likely to find your perfect match during this time. Some of you may also expect the arrival of a new member in the family. Socially, this is a good period to meet new people and enjoy the company of the opposite sex. You would be honoured and your status is also likely to be heightened in the society. You would also get plenty of opportunity to enjoy and would also indulge in exotic culinary dishes.

This period would also let you acquire sensuous material and accessories to enrich your life. You are likely to indulge in clothes, perfumes, cosmetics and vehicles as well. This is a good time to enhance the beauty and grace of your home, as well as to attain some level of harmony in your domestic affairs. Financially, you would sail through smoothly during this period. Your economic condition would also improve during this particular time. If you are a student, this could prove to be a very good period for you to succeed in your field of learning. You may also expect the annihilation of your enemies during this time. Stay away from any influence that might create a negative outburst in you.

2nd house: Transit of Venus in the 2nd house from Natal Moon

You may find yourself with a different set of values and at odds with younger people or with your surroundings. Success in love affairs and matters connected with females, good income, arrival of relations and friends, happy ceremonies, purchase of articles of comfort. During this period, Venus will move through your second house from the Moon. This mostly denotes pecuniary gain for you. Moreover, this period also sees you having a great time with your spouse and other family members. If applicable, you can also expect a baby in your family.

Financially you would be comfortable and the prosperity of your family in general is expected to be on the upward move. This transit stimulates your affections but can lead to excessive emotionality. Personally, you are likely to acquire great attire and accessories including precious gems for yourself. Your interest in art and music would increase. You may also expect some favour from the higher authorities or the government. Health is expected to be fine and you may consider improving your present look as well.

3rd house: Transit of Venus in the 3rd house from Natal Moon

Happy ceremonies in the offing. A good time for surrounding yourself with friends and younger people and for having a good time. You appreciate your particular situation and enjoy support from those around you. Visit of brothers and sisters, welcome friends, gain, success its social undertakings. During this period, Venus will move through your third house from the Moon. This denotes happiness and contentment for you. You may expect an upward move in your financial condition giving you financial security. This could also be a professionally good period for you and you may also expect a rise in position. You may also expect a gain in authority. Your ventures are likely to earn profits as well.

Your best bet for personal success is expressing yourself sincerely and warmly. Your personal popularity gets a boost now. Socially this should be a good time for you, as you are likely to overcome all your fears and worries. Your colleagues and acquaintances would be cooperative and helpful towards you. You are also likely to widen your circle of friends and win over your enemies during this particular time. Your rapport with your immediate family would be cordial and your siblings are also likely to enjoy good times with you.

Moreover, you may also indulge in good clothes and great food during this time. Your interest towards religion would rise and an auspicious happening may cheer you up as well. Health is likely to be in good shape. If eligible, you may also consider marriage, as this seems to be a good time to find the perfect match. Some of you may also expect a new member in your family. This is a good time for socializing and for communicating with ease, telling others how you feel, and negotiating.

4th house: Transit of Venus in the 4th house from Natal Moon

This influence is generally favourable for commerce, and it sometimes indicates a business related and social function. Good income from property, good name, social success, happiness in family, good health, enjoyment of articles of comfort and conveyances. During this period, Venus will move through your fourth house from the Moon.

This mostly denotes financial growth for you. You could also expect a rise in your prosperity. If you deal in agriculture, this could prove to be a good time bringing you profit in your agricultural venture. At home, you are likely to spend quality time with your spouse and children discussing matters of importance. Moreover, you would also enjoy good food, gorgeous attire and perfumes. The social aspect of your life would be full of happenings.

You may find yourself enjoying a long conversation. You come across as gracious and diplomatic. Your popularity would increase and you are most likely to acquire new friends. The company of your old and new friends would give you much happiness and you may even consider staying away from home having fun. This period is also likely to see you enjoying the company of the opposite sex. Health should remain fine and you would feel more energetic than ever. Acquisition of material comfort could also become a priority for you during this particular period.

5th house Transit of Venus in the 5th house from Natal Moon

You could receive a compliment today, or hear of someone's affection for you, particularly someone younger than yourself. Good name, enjoyment of articles of comforts, happy relations with other sex, social success, success in gambling etc. During this period, Venus will move through your fifth house from the Moon. This signifies a time mostly spent being entertained. This period also denotes a good time financially, as you would be able to increase your funds. If you are taking any examination under any government department during this time, you are most likely to be successful. If employed you are also likely to get promoted during this time. Moreover, you may also expect a rise in position in the society.

You could receive a compliment today, or hear of someone's affection for you, particularly someone younger than yourself. Your friends, elders and teachers are also expected to be good to you during this particular period. Relationships are expected to go smoothly and you may expect intense and sensuous times with your beloved. You may also enjoy conjugal bliss or the physical company of someone special of the opposite sex. You may also expect to meet someone new in your family or may even bring in someone new into the family. Health should be fine during this time. This period also sees you enjoying delicious food and gain of wealth and objects that you desire.

6th house: Transit of Venus in the 6th house from Natal Moon

This is a period when you are more inclined to be immature. This transit fires up your feelings and stirs up your need for action, activity, and challenges. You are more inclined to act on impulse now, and you could be quite temperamental. Quarrel with wife and other females of household, misunderstandings in social circles, bad name, trouble from females, loss in lottery, bad health. During this period, Venus will move through your sixth house from the Moon. This may bring some trying times for you. This period sees you going through a lot of trouble in your endeavour.

You could be feeling less vigorous than usual or more stressed. It could also be a rather passionate time, simply because, for the time being, you tend to be ruled by your passions. You may have to compromise with your enemies against your will as well. Avoid any kind of arguments with your wife and children particularly during this phase. It is advised that you avoid travelling long distance, as you are susceptible to face with an accident during this time. Health would require your extra attention, as you are likely to suffer from ill health, mental unrest, anxiety, fear and an untimely rise in sexual desires. Hold on to your respect in the society and your honour at workplace as these could be at risk during this particular time. Otherwise you may have to face humiliation, useless discussions and litigations.

7th house: Transit of Venus in the 7th house from Natal Moon

There could be an emotional overtone to all of this that may require understanding and flexibility on your part. Quarrel with wife and other sex, trouble through females, worries, expenditure, and disappointment in love. During this period, Venus will move through your seventh house from the Moon. This mostly indicates a troublesome period caused mostly by women. Stay away from any litigation involving women and try and maintain a good rapport with your wife. Moreover, this phase also indicates ill health of the female whose birth chart is housing Venus in the seventh house. Your wife may suffer from various gynaecological diseases, bodily pain, and mental anxiety and so on.

The dynamic energy of this transit could give you just the right kick in the pants to push you out of a bad situation. You may also realise that you have some wicked friends who would try to harm you. This period may also see you suffer from mental agitation, distress and anger. Take care of your health, as you are likely to suffer from venereal diseases, urinary tract disorder and other minor diseases. Professionally this period could not be regarded as conducivc. Avoid wicked colleagues as they might create obstacles in your progress. However, you are likely to get honour from the higher authority in your field of work or the government.

8th house: Transit of Venus in the 8th house from Natal Moon

This transit boosts your self-confidence and ability to assert yourself without ruffling the feathers of people around you. During this period, Venus will move through your eighth house from the Moon. This signifies good times. During this particular period you may expect to gain physical comforts and overcome all your previous miseries. You may consider acquiring landed property or a house as well. If an eligible bachelor or maiden lady, you may also expect to get a good match who could also bring in good fortune. During this period, Venus will move through your first house from the Moon.

Your desire nature and your emotions are cooperating beautifully just now, which increases your resourcefulness and independence. This may also expect the company of pleasant and beautiful women during this particular time. Health is expected to remain good at this time. If a student, you would be more progressive. Your brilliance will be noticed and you would command more respect and honour in your social circle. Professionally it is a good time. Trade and business is expected to flourish with the help of well-wishers and friends. There is a possibility of meeting a higher government authority.

9th house: Transit of Venus in the 9th house from Natal Moon

This influence heightens your feelings, awakens your impulses, and stirs your passions, mostly in a positive way. During this period, Venus will move through your ninth house from the Moon. This mostly signifies the onset of a new wardrobe. Moreover, it also denotes bodily or material comfort and happiness. Financial gain and indulgence in precious jewellery is also indicated during this period. Businessmen will find this period to be a smooth one with satisfactory profits. Success in education is also indicated during this time. Health would remain in good shape.

Passionate liaisons sometimes begin under this transit. Do something that breaks the routine or that you've always wanted to do but have been hesitating to do due to shyness or fear. Some auspicious deeds are likely to be performed at your home and you may also decide on your own marriage if eligible. During this time you are likely to get a match of your choice, who would also bring in fortune for you. Your good qualities and virtuous deeds would be noticed and would bring in good reputation in the society. This time could see your desires fulfilled and enemies defeated. If you get involved in any kind of discussion, you are likely to be winning the same. You may even consider going on a long journey during this period.

10th house: Transit of Venus in the 10th house from Natal Moon

You might find that you attract challenging situations simply because you are overreacting emotionally. During this period, Venus will move through your tenth house from the Moon. This brings in mental anguish, agitation and restlessness. Physical health also suffers during this particular time. You may have to be extra careful with your finances and try to avoid any kind of loans, as you are likely to be under debts during this particular phase.

Beware of your enemies and avoid unnecessary and useless, discussions, as it might lead to quarrels increasing the number of your enemies. Be careful to avoid defamation and humiliation in the society. Be cautious while handling your relatives and women folks as a silly misunderstanding may add on to the number of your enemies. Avoid all kinds of arguments with your spouse to maintain the healthy equilibrium in the marriage. You are likely to face trouble caused by higher authority of your chosen field or by the government. You may have to put in extra hard work to meet with success in all your endeavours.

11th house: Transit of Venus in the 1th house from Natal Moon

A new connection with a man, or problems with males, may feature. You could get caught up in a domestic squabble. Success in love, happy domestic affairs, good relations with other sex, social success. During this period, Venus will move through your eleventh house from the Moon. This mostly signifies financial security and relief from debts. You may also expect solutions to your other economic problems as well. This period also brings in success in your endeavours. Your popularity increases and your reputation would also see an upward move during this period.

This is a lucky expansive, happy, and prosperous period. Some sort of emotional relief is likely, particularly with regards to your personal life. You are likely concentrate on acquisition of material comfort, means of pleasure, good food, clothing, jewels and other exotic accessories. You may consider owning a house as well. Socially a bright period could be predicted. You could expect a rise in your status and prestige in the society and cooperation of your friends. You may also expect good times with the members of the opposite sex. If married you are likely to savour conjugal bliss with your spouse.

12th house: Transit of Venus in the 12th house from Natal Moon

You are especially sharp, communicative, and open at this time, as your wants are aligned with your thoughts.

You may enjoy opportunities to do any of these things now. Success in society, fair income success in love affairs, good name, articles of enjoyment, short journeys. During this period, Venus will move through your twelfth house from the Moon. This indicates a mixed bag of positive and negative happenings. On one hand this period signifies financial gain and on the other, it also denotes some unforeseen losses of wealth and clothing. This period also indicates unnecessary expenditure and wastage of money on a trip to a foreign country.

Your personal popularity increases, in direct proportion to your own elevated, positive mood, and some kind of recognition or honour may come your way. At home you would enjoy conjugal bliss. If unmarried, you may expect to savour some sensual pleasure with member of the opposite sex. Friends would be good to you and would be cooperative and helpful towards you. Try to stay away from sharp weapons and doubtful people. If you are involved with agriculture, you may have to take extra care to avoid any loss during this particular time.

MICROSCOPY OF TRANSITING PLANETS SIMPLIFIED VOLUME-5

TRANSITING PLANETS

CHAPTER THIRTY NINE

VENUS TRANSITS URANUS NEPTUNE PLUTO

Venus conjunct Uranus

You will develop a more direct method of communication, getting to the very heart of things. Independence, as well as anything unusual or different, is valued. You may enjoy getting away from routine and doing something completely different for a change. What makes you unique is more attractive to others under this influence, so emphasize what makes you special. Excitement and newness is valued over permanence in social relationships. You lose your fear of taking risks in love and social situations. Romantic infatuations, gossip, unanticipated opportunities socially or financially are all possibilities.

This is a positive time when you express your deepest feelings openly and intensely. This is a favourable influence for social meetings and events, and for situations that call for treating others with equality and respect. You are itching for a change now on a social or romantic level. You have a greater need for self-expression, personal freedom, and social excitement. Independence, as well as anything unusual or different, is valued. Excitement and newness is valued over permanence in social relationships. You have a greater need for self-expression, personal freedom, and social excitement.

Venus sextile Uranus

You may enjoy getting away from routine and doing something completely different for a change. You are itching for a change now on a social or romantic level. What makes you unique is more attractive to others under this influence, so emphasize what makes you special. Sometimes this correlates with an unexpected income boost, a surprise visit or social event, a transient or sudden romantic attraction, or unpredictable experiences in matters of the heart. You, or a loved one, may struggle with freedom versus intimacy issues at this time.

Venus square Uranus

This signals an emotionally upbeat period when you enjoy your family, friends, and social life. You may be in the mood for deep and penetrating conversations or thoughts. You are able to get to the bottom of things. It's a favourable time to work on improving your skills. You tend to say what you think now. This is a fortunate, albeit brief, period for achievement and recognition in business. Independence, as well as anything unusual or different, is valued. You are ready to experiment, but not necessarily ready to commit.

Venus trine Uranus

A very nice time, perhaps filled with some renewed appreciation for all that is beautiful and fine. A sense of value and valuing that may find you lavishing affection on those near you. You may not value something extraordinary or unusual. Instead, you find yourself appreciating what is quite normal or ordinary. Values and tastes may clash, and group activities that you are involved in may suffer as a result. Impulsive attractions to both people and material goods can lead you astray. People are more willing to socialize with you.

Venus opposite Uranus

Someone unexpected may confront you or you may not like their independence or eccentricity. You may not appreciate their very different perspective or attitude. Unusual attractions (to people and things) can have you acting on a whim. You, or a close partner, may be dealing with freedom versus closeness issues in your relationships. Breaking the unspoken (or spoken) rules in a friendship or love relationship is tempting now, perhaps in an attempt to stir up trouble or excitement.

Venus conjunct Neptune

This is a positive time when you express your deepest feelings openly and intensely. You may enjoy a good movie or book or feel like escaping from day-to-day realities for a while. You can appreciate an imaginative approach and may value communal or futuristic ideas. Heightened sensitivity to, and awareness of, beauty and spirituality is the order of the day. You are easily influenced, seducible and seductive, and given to strong powers of imagination. You are more attuned to the world of beauty and romance today. Psychic openness and compassion characterize this period.

Venus sextile Neptune

You may enjoy a good movie or book or feel like escaping from day-to-day realities for a while. You can appreciate an imaginative approach and may value communal or futuristic ideas. You are more imaginative and attuned to the world of beauty and romance today. Gentleness with others is the best way to harness this energy. This could point to a magical time on a romantic and social level. You appreciate the subtleties of human interactions now, and you could notice some interesting synchronicities occurring in your own relationships or with your personal finances.

Venus square Neptune

You express great intensity and passion in the way you appear and express yourself to others. You prefer the simple, ordinary virtues and don't appreciate any form of other-worldliness or escapism. Not the best time to read a book or take in a movie. Unclear desires. Imagination and fantasy fog judgment and create romantic confusion. Relationship ups and downs characterize this transit time when romantic mirages are more than likely. You see what you hope to see, rather than what really is. Be careful not to set yourself up for disappointment. The same goes for finances what appears to be a great buy is likely to turn out to be a financial drain or money pit.

Venus trinc Neptune

A good time to consolidate and organize your affairs or rearrange your living situation. You could be seen by others as just the person to be put in charge of some project requiring a conservative mind. New ways to communicate or an easy manner will make conversations and interactions go well today. Your positive state of mind can attract others, as well as favourable circumstances, to you. Gentleness with others is the best way to harness this energy. The pleasures of life are experienced fully. You see the very best in people now, and this eases your interactions and takes the pressure off in personal relationships.

Venus opposite Neptune

Situations that require you to keep a cool head will work out well under this transit. You are not easily swept away by your feelings now, enabling you to effectively tend to appreciate someone's unrealistic approach to a situation. Their general fogginess and impractical attitude may find you at odds with them. Happiness is addictive under this influence. Your tendency to see what you want to see and gloss over the more realistic points, details, and flaws provides you with instant gratification. However, it's wise to hold off on making important purchases, or nasalizing a relationship until the veil lifts.

Venus conjunct Pluto

This is a very positive aspect for starting a money-making endeavour or a new project all things equal. You stand to gain some personal power or influence. You might uncover information or material items that help further your goals. You may enjoy probing into your inner workings or some good solid gossip. You value your darker, more secretive areas and don't mind working through some sensitive problems. Your own inner need for change and growth may be threatened by someone older or by circumstances. There could be some underhanded or devious goings-on behind the scenes as well. You have the power of attraction at your disposal. Your social presence may be larger than life, so a little charm goes a long way now.

Venus sextile Pluto

You almost transfix those who meet you with your fixedness and sense of power. You may enjoy probing into your inner workings or some good solid gossip. You value your darker, more secretive areas and don't mind working through some sensitive problems. If you seize the opportunity, this is a good time for either or finances and relationships. Your feelings are impassioned, but not in an offensive or unpleasant way. You are focused and confident, and you appreciate depth of feeling and authenticity in your dealings with others. Enjoying an especially intimate moment may be part of the picture now.

Venus square Pluto

You feel as though you have been drifting along with the tide and following the crowd for too long, and your inner needs and motivations must assert themselves more strongly. You value what is above-board and straightforward and have a particular aversion to what is secret, intense, and private. You will develop a more direct method of communication, getting to the very heart of things. You may enjoy probing into your inner workings or some good solid gossip. You value your darker, more secretive areas and don't mind working through some sensitive problems.

Venus trine Pluto

You may find yourself being put to good use by your friends, or it could be that circumstances force you to reorganize and be more conservative. Motions and issues in a close relationship that have been brewing beneath the surface for quite a while come to the surface at this time, possibly in a very disruptive way. You might feel relationships are threatened.

Venus opposite Pluto

There is an inner drama taking place now, and a feeling that external circumstances are undermining your own feeling of powerfulness. You don't appreciate the secretive and overly private approach of someone you encounter. You may not care to work through their inner goings-on just at the moment. This is a sensual transit a time when a little charm goes a long way.

MICROSCOPY OF
TRANSITING PLANETS
SIMPLIFIED
VOLUME-5

CHAPTER FORTY

TRANSITING VENUS

Venus Transits

A very nice day, perhaps filled with some renewed appreciation for all that is beautiful and fine. The transits of Venus brief influences to planets and points in the natal chart are lasting nearly a day. This is a good day for relationships or other pursuits expressing you creatively through.

Venus conjunct Sun

You may be unable to appreciate or value people and things now. You are in a perhaps rare mood of self-enjoyment and can appreciate your own better qualities. You may see value in or feel love for an older person or someone in authority. This is a day for sentimentality and tenderness. You are especially charming today, however, so you might not want to isolate yourself. At this time, you desire to please and to be pleased; to treat and to be treated.

You might be particularly irritated by others' behaviour now, but consider that problems encountered now could be a reflection of your own inner discontent. This is the day to start new projects or push forward with those already in motion. You may enjoy a sense of creating your own opportunities. You are more sensitive to imbalances in your environment, and you seek to find harmony in whatever you do. You are motivated by the desire to strike a balance in your relationships and in your environment.

Venus sextile Sun

You are in a (perhaps) rare mood of self-enjoyment and can appreciate your own better qualities. You may see value in or feel love for an older person or someone in authority. You are more willing, yielding, and compromising than you are typically. The aura around you is tender and caring, and others take notice.

This transit rids you of inhibitions, at least for the time being. This is a time of much enthusiasm. You are more interested in being around loved ones. This easy energy can also cause you to temporarily lose interest in work. It's not an ambitious energy, and some laziness or a tendency to procrastinate is possible. Sometimes, first dates occur during this transit. Relationships in general improve. This is a good time to ask for a raise or the support you need, and you might see some success on a financial level.

Venus square Sun

You are able to creatively solve problems and to instinctively take action when necessary under the influence of this transit. You may find some of your values at odds with your own best interests. You may not appreciate tradition or someone older or in authority. This is a period when you are less motivated or driven than usual. Lazy appreciation for the good life comes now. You are distracted when it comes to work, and you are more likely to overeat, overspend, and avoid anything that makes you feel unbalanced or uncomfortable. Irritations that seem to stem from others could be the reflection of your own inner uneasiness. Do your best to control yearnings for more than what you have and search for a creative solution for your inner dissatisfaction.

Venus trine Sun

You are in a perhaps rare mood of self-enjoyment and can appreciate your own better qualities. You may see value in or feel love for an older person or someone in authority. Love is in the air, and your relationships are harmonious and rewarding. Others find you attractive and enjoyable to be with. Social functions and artistic endeavours go well. You may be interested in purchasing objects of beauty or adornment. Efforts to improve your appearance run well. Gifts or increased income may be part of the picture.

Venus opposite Sun

You may find yourself at odds with someone you care about or someone in authority over questions of values. You may not appreciate what they represent. This is a time when laziness and self-indulgence are more likely. You're simply not in any mood for hard work. You could be looking for an easy way out. Delaying spending might be wise now. Relationships could prove expensive.

You are more able to assert yourself without rubbing people the wrong way just now. You might find that you stand up for yourself or your principles. You may find yourself at odds with someone you care about or someone in authority over a question of values. Your own values or way of expressing love and affection may differ from someone you interact with now. Your ego may be a bit inflated right now. As long as you don't think with your ego, you could learn a whole lot about a person you love.

Venus conjunct Moon

This is an excellent time to begin a self-improvement program. This is not an especially sexual energy you are more inclined to philosophize and seek out bigger and better experiences. A good time for surrounding yourself with friends and younger people and for having a good time. You appreciate your particular situation and enjoy support from those around you Feeling sentimental. Your mood is especially romantic and sensual. Let it guide you, and you might just find yourself in a very fortunate situation.

This transit represents hopefulness, good will, and increased influence. This energy is excellent for any behind-the-scenes or domestic activities. It's an opportune time to make domestic purchases, and to buy or wear new clothing for the first time. Beauty treatments are favoured. This is a time when praise or compliments naturally come your way, when you receive friendly greetings, and when you might extend a hand to others you care about. Aiding someone financially or spiritually is bound to boost your own spirits.

Venus sextile Moon

A good time for surrounding yourself with friends and younger people and for having a good time. You appreciate your particular situation and enjoy support from those around you. Your best bet for personal success is expressing yourself sincerely and warmly. Your personal popularity gets a boost now. Others could lean on you for a little support, and you are more than willing to give it. Tensions on the home front ease, and a partner is more attentive to you. Mental peace satisfies an instinctive need now, and your focus should be on ways to improve or maintain a state of balance in your personal life.

Venus square Moon

You may not appreciate your surroundings, or someone younger than you does not measure up. Your values may be at odds just for the moment with those around you. A sweet tooth for pleasure. A craving for sweetness and comfort in the form of loving affection or food is strong now. This is a good time to baby yourself and also to spend time with the people who love and appreciate you the most. You could be emotionally and financially irresponsible now, however, and the tendency to bicker with others over emotional and domestic matters is high. Someone whose values are different from yours could easily rub you the wrong way. Watch for over-sensitive reactions.

Venus trine Moon

A good time for surrounding yourself with friends and younger people and for having a good time. Take this opportunity to express your feelings to people close to you. You are more likely to be received well today than on other days. This is a good time to enhance the beauty and grace of your home, as well as to attain some level of harmony in your domestic affairs. You may not feel like working or pushing yourself too much now, but that's just fine. A passive approach to life works best now. This transit is a cosmic nudge to slow down and enjoy quiet and nurturing activities.

Venus opposite Moon

You may find yourself with a different set of values and at odds with younger people or with your surroundings. You may not like the way they are or what they represent Emotionality. This transit stimulates your affections but can lead to excessive emotionality. Avoid falling head over heels into relationships just for the sake of having company. The tendency to bicker over emotional, domestic, or social matters runs high now. Your feelings are easily hurt now, and you could feel underappreciated. This is not the most personally popular time for you, but thankfully this transit is brief.

Venus conjunct Mercury

Perhaps a time to think and study, for you have a real appreciation for ideas and thoughts. You may find yourself enjoying a long conversation, writing a letter, or making a special phone call. Light-hearted conversations, sociability, humour, and cooperation are hallmarks of this transit. This is a good time for socializing and for communicating with ease, telling others how you feel, and negotiating. Mentally, you may not be as disciplined as usual, as you prefer to chat with others and to think about more pleasant things than work. This influence is generally favourable for commerce, and it sometimes indicates a job-related social function.

Venus sextile Mercury

Perhaps a time to think and study, for you have a real appreciation for ideas and thoughts. You may find yourself enjoying a long conversation, writing a letter, or making a special phone call. Self-expression is enhanced by a touch of the romantic and the poetic. You come across as gracious and diplomatic. Some laziness on a mental level is possible now. Business opportunities or proposals are favoured today. Also, job-related social functions may be part of the picture. Measured and balanced agreements can more easily be drawn up. You could receive a compliment today, or hear of someone's affection for you, particularly someone younger than yourself.

Venus square Mercury

You may not place much value on ideas and thoughts. Something that someone says or communicates to you may be unappreciated or taken the wrong way. You could find that you are socially active but others rub you the wrong way. Something is a little off right now, and social blunders are more likely now than usual. Difficulties in social or romantic communication are possible today. Hypersensitivity and lack of mental discipline are other negative manifestations of this energy. Your mind tends to wander, and working effectively may suffer as a result. It would be best to make an extra effort to be polite and diplomatic.

Venus trine Mercury

Perhaps a time to think and study, for you have a real appreciation for ideas and thoughts. You may find yourself enjoying a long conversation, writing a letter, or making a special phone call. Self-expression is enhanced by a touch of the romantic and the poetic. You come across as gracious and diplomatic. Some laziness on a mental level is possible now. Business opportunities or proposals are favoured today. Also, job-related social functions may be part of the picture. Measured and balanced agreements can more easily be drawn up. You could receive a compliment today, or hear of someone's affection for you, particularly someone younger than yourself.

Venus opposite Mercury

You may not like the ideas or thoughts of someone who confronts you. What they say may seem inappropriate or be unappreciated. You could find that you are socially active but others rub you the wrong way or vice versa. Something is a little off right now, and social blunders are more likely now than usual. Difficulties in social or romantic communication are possible today. Hypersensitivity and lack of mental discipline are other negative manifestations of this energy. Your mind tends to wander, and working effectively may suffer as a result. It would be best to make an extra effort to be polite and diplomatic.

Venus conjunct Venus

You may be especially sociable, tolerant, and generous. Confidence comes from a stronger sense of who you are and the principles you represent. Your taste in art and appreciation in general are heightened. Beauty and art are especially appealing now. Feelings are affectionate. Your desire for love, companion-ship, and affection predominates at this time. A new friendship or romance could begin, or an established relationship can be revitalized and enhanced. If there is someone you have wanted to reach out to, doing so now is likely to create warm feelings between you, and may be the start of something beautiful. A shift or change in your attitude towards money and personal possessions is also possible now.

Venus sextile Venus

Your taste in art and appreciation in general are heightened. Perhaps a good time to select furnishings, colours, and so on the finer things of life. Your sense of value is to the fore. A great time to just sit back and enjoy what you have, to live life socially smooth. Harmonious interactions with others are favoured at this time, likely because you are projecting the more charming, cooperative, and agreeable side of your nature! Smoother negotiations are the result, and love is easier than usual to enjoy -- and to find -- today. This could be a prosperous time for your financial affairs or investments. Pleasing contact with females is probable.

Venus square Venus

Someone older or in authority may disapprove of your actions or decisions. You may feel vague restlessness and discontent with life as it is. You may experience dissatisfaction with what you have or find around you. You could feel unloved or be unloving. Although this influence is subtle, you might notice an imbalance in your relationships. Someone is giving more or feeling more than the other. Differences in personal style, tastes, and ways of expressing affection may emerge or become glaringly apparent. Compromise requires some effort. Touchiness could be coming from you or from those close to you, and you might be feeling underappreciated.

Venus trine Venus

Your taste in art and appreciation in general are heightened. Perhaps a good time to select furnishings, colours, and soon the finer things of life. Your sense of value is to the fore. Let your feelings and affections flow.

This is a time when the rest of the world seems to be appreciating your romantic style. You are unlikely to be coming on strong and trying to make things happen, but instead are inclined to flow along with people and situations, attracting what you need and letting the world come to you.

Venus opposite Venus

Someone with a different set of values than your own may confront you. That person's taste may run counter to yours. There could be a mutual lack of appreciation. Differences in values or ways of expressing affection in your personal relationships are made very noticeable to you now. Whether or not you are with someone romantically, you could be feeling underappreciated or even unloved. Rather, it's likely to take the form of pouting, distancing, and side-stepping the real issue. Inner unrest could lead you on a shopping spree or some other attempt to reward yourself, when what you really need is to work on establishing a deeper connection with the people you love--or to get in touch with your own true needs.

Venus conjunct Mars

You may find yourself looking for a little romance today or at least enjoying some emotional release. You can appreciate feelings and movement. You may want to just get out and walk or exercise. Cooperating with others is easy. If an existing relationship needs a boost, now is the time to put the extra effort forth. Venus acts to soothe and soften whatever it contacts. In this case, it's your raw, instinctual nature, so your aggressive nature is toned down. Your powers of attraction are heightened, and you are more likely to be the one who's pursued. Any new relationship begun under this transit is likely to be especially passionate.

Venus sextile Mars

You may find yourself looking for a little romance today or at least enjoying some emotional release. You can appreciate feelings and movement. You may want to just get out and walk or exercise. This is a good day to begin or develop a project, to meet new people, or to smooth over problems in existing relationships. Sexual and romantic activities are favoured today. Romantic activity, sexual attraction, creative action and self-expression in business and the arts, active participation in social functions, and creative initiative are favoured under this influence.

Venus square Mars

You may not feel like being very emotional and might tend to ignore any emotional needs that you might have. Your sense of values may be in conflict with your feelings. Although this can be a sexy transit, tensions in relationships are likely. There is an air of competitiveness under this influence, which need not be difficult. In fact, it can be stimulating, creative, and invigorating. Passions run high under this influence. Sexual tensions and competitiveness are possible, and there can be conflicts that arise from differences between romantic and sexual needs. Social blunders are a possibility now. Be wary of making impulse purchases. You could stir up problems in order to fulfil a need for excitement.

Venus trine Mars

Your mood may be elevated, but somewhat unstable as the source of your enthusiasm may not be based on reality. You can appreciate feelings and movement. You may want to just get out and walk or exercise. This transit points to success and ease in close personal interactions. You are feeling passionate, warm, expressive, lively, and sexy. It is a good time for financial ventures, your social life, artistic pursuits, romance, and pleasure. You are now able to take the initiative and to achieve harmony and sexual fulfilment. This influence brings satisfaction to the feelings.

Venus opposite Mars

You may not appreciate the emotional energy of someone you meet. They could appear aggressive or pushy. You don't like the way a situation feels at the gut level. When you try to be friendly, you seem to miss the mark. Attempting to satisfy romantic needs and assertive/sexual needs simultaneously can be challenging. Your romantic sensibilities and your desires are at odds with one another, and problems (especially misunderstandings) in romantic and sexual relationships may result. Passions run high. Jealousies are possible. Impulsive decisions affect your finances and/or your established relationships. You could stir up problems in order to fulfil a need for excitement.

Venus conjunct Jupiter

You may find yourself very appreciative of your career and practical skills. You might enjoy solving puzzles and problems, finding solutions, and so on. A renewed appreciation for your work may be apparent to your superiors -- in fact, to everybody. This is a magical transit when you are especially generous and giving, optimistic, and kind towards others. This is an excellent influence under which to begin a new relationship or financial undertaking. Love brings happiness and optimistic feelings. If you need to make amends with someone, now is the best time to do so.

Venus sextile Jupiter

The good life, and all that is fine and luxurious, may be what you value just now. You could enjoy making your own way and finding solutions to whatever problems you have. This is a cooperative, happy influence. Consideration for others, cheerfulness, and a positive attitude towards relationships are themes now. Financial endeavours are generally successful now, as long as they are reasonable. You are more open and trusting of friends and lovers, and they of you.

Venus square Jupiter

Correct choices the best path for you may be at odds with your sense of values. You may not appreciate the easy way or clear-cut option, and may choose instead a more difficult path. This is a time when you could take great strides to get noticed. Avoid impulsive buying. Problems in your personal life likely won't get resolved under this influence. Avoid hasty decisions. You might overstate your feelings or promise more than you can deliver. Feelings of elation in love or with regards to the pleasures of life can lead you to overdo, overindulge, overspend, and overstate your feelings. You may also feel lazy and you are inclined to procrastinate.

Venus trine Jupiter

The good life, and all that is fine and luxurious, may be what you value just now. You could enjoy making your own way and finding solutions to whatever problems you have. Friendliness and optimism characterize this transit. You are big-hearted and your feelings are expansive. Your outlook is cheerful and hopeful and the atmosphere around you is cooperative. This is a sociable, perhaps lazy and self-indulgent, time. This is a period when you easily find meaning in your social connections. You are more open and trusting of friends and lovers. Integrity and loyalty are favoured. This is an especially favourable influence for winning people's trust. Speculation, advertising, publishing, and travel are also favoured. Don't pass up a social opportunity now.

Venus opposite Jupiter

Avoid promising more than you can deliver, as you are unlikely to be able to follow through on your promises. You may not appreciate someone's methods, the way they get things done. Someone in authority may have very different values from yours. Challenges in relationships now are likely due to overblown expectations. It can be hard to find a balance between responsibilities and the desire for self-gratification. Your love nature is strong, but given to extremes.

Venus conjunct Saturn

You feel a love of order and law an appreciation for responsibilities and duty. Problems are valued for the lessons they represent, rather than perceived as obstacles. You are attracted to people with maturity, worldly wisdom, and a solid sense of values perhaps an advisor, elder, or teacher, and are disinclined to frivolous activities or wasting your time. In fact you may be pleased and happy to be alone or perhaps with just one other person that you know well. On the other hand, you may feel quite cool or withdrawn in a crowd. You are also restrained and careful about spending money at this point, and that's as it should be. It is a good time to reflect, set priorities, enjoy simple pleasures, and appreciate quality time with yourself or with your chosen companion.

Venus sextile Saturn

You feel a love of order and law -- an appreciation for responsibilities and duty. Problems are valued for the lessons they represent, rather than perceived as obstacles. Your affections stabilize and mature. Relationships are reinforced and steady, although feelings are expressed reservedly, formally, or sparingly. A new sense of realism in existing partnerships comes now. Small advances can be made in business and in partnerships. Support from older people or authority figures may come by way of solid advice or tangible help.

Venus square Saturn

The need to make changes in your life that will further your psychological development arise. Impatience with rules and compulsiveness are shadow energies of this transit. Your values may run counter to established tradition. There may be difficulties relating to others under this influence. People may appear cool with their affections and emotionally distant. There may be anxiety or troubles with regards to matters concerned with the feelings. Gaining what you want is challenging under this influence, due to negative attitudes and the tendency to need more than what is possible. Difficulties socializing with others stem from an increased sensitivity to rejection. This transit is best used for reflection.

Venus trine Saturn

You feel a love of order and law an appreciation for responsibilities and duty. Problems are valued for the lessons they represent, rather than perceived as obstacles. Affections stabilize and mature now. Small advances can be made in business and in partnerships. Support from older people or authority figures may come by way of solid advice or more tangible help. Renewed ties to old friends are possible, or a new sense of responsibility in existing friendships. A commitment could be solidified now. The simple pleasures of a relationship or friendship are appreciated now.

Venus opposite Saturn

Someone important or in authority may oppose your values and put a damper on your desires. You may be unable to appreciate their attitude or understand their problems Dissatisfaction. Anxiety may overcome you when you wish to express your affections or social urges, and this hesitation can express itself through inhibitions and emotional distancing. You keep others at arm's length, unsure of whether you are loved or not. This is a somewhat inhibiting influence when it appears that others value utility over true love. An element of seriousness permeates your love relationships. You may feel criticized and inhibited, unloved and unsatisfied, but your worst enemy may be yourself and your own fears of getting close to others. A serious matter on your mind could sap fun out of your day.

Venus conjunct Ascendant

You appear perhaps more charming and refined than usual. Now could be the time to make that date, apply for the job, or otherwise make you known. Today you exude personal magnetism; you express your love and affection to others easily, and they do to you. Others more openly express their affection for you right now.

This is a very favourable time for doing something to enhance your appearance, such as getting a haircut or purchasing new clothing.

Venus sextile Ascendant

You appear perhaps more charming and refined than usual. Now could be the time to make that date, apply for the job, or otherwise make you known.It's easy for you to receive warm responses from others right now. You are charming, personable, and reasonable. This influence sometimes brings new romantic or social relationship opportunities. This is a good time to purchase property, art objects, or to use new methods to increase your personal finances. Doors open that may have previously been closed or undiscovered.

Venus square Ascendant

Your manner may not be warm or loving at the moment. Perhaps not the best time to present you to others or take a job interview. Be aware that you are far more sensitive than usual, which can complicate partnerships, romantic relationships, and/or dealings with women in general. Guard against impulsive spending. You're more inclined to buy items on emotional whims rather than based on clear thinking. If circumstances call for an aggressive or forthright approach, you are more inclined to shy away or to fumble. In fact, you may be procrastinating with your work now, preferring to enjoy or simply pamper yourself.

Venus trine Ascendant

You appear perhaps more charming and refined than usual. Now could be the time to make that date, apply for the job, or otherwise make yourself known. This is a good time to go on first dates, schedule appointments, ask for a favour, make presentations, or apply for jobs, simply because you are coming across well. You portray the more reasonable, refined, and likable side of your personality now, and others tend to respond warmly. You are more willing than usual to bend and compromise. Remember that you get what you want by the forces of attraction during this period, rather than coming on strong. This is a good time to purchase property, art objects, or to use new methods to increase your personal finances.

Venus opposite Ascendant

The urge to get to the bottom of matters is with you, but you could be too insistent. Avoid beating a dead horse and attempting to force matters that should naturally take time to unfold. You may find yourself caring too much about what others think of you. If there are problems now, employing tact and diplomacy can help offset them. You are more sensitive than usual to subtleties in your personal environment, and all the more vulnerable as a result.

MICROSCOPY OF
TRANSITING PLANETS
SIMPLIFIED
VOLUME-5

CHAPTER FORTY ONE

TRANSITING VENUS TRANSITING PLANETS

PLACEMENT OF PLANETS IN DIFFERENT
HOUSES

VENUS

In the Ascendant. – Expert mathematician, very fortunate, ambitious, bold, long life, pioneering, fond of wife, strenuous, skilled in sexual science, successful, practical, scents, flowers, women skilled in fine arts, pleasing, vivacious, astrologer, much magnetic power, leader of people.

Second house. – Large family, happy, delicious drinks, luxurious meals, handsome, large fair eyes, charming wife, witty, brilliant, polite, educated, hating women, obliging, rapid in mind, clever in speech, agreeable, creative author, conservative, composer, economical, wealthy, logical, able.

Third house. – Lover of fine arts, prosperity to mother wealthy, miserly, obliging, well placed, travelling, original.

Fourth house. – Intelligent, happy, affectionate, learned, affectionate mother, agriculturist, educated, scientific methods, peaceful life, protector of cattle, endeared by relations, fond of milk, famous, literary, successful, popular.

Fifth house. – Clever, intelligent, states manly ability, good counsel, danger to mother, commander, educated, able, sociable, kind-hearted, affable, good-natured, many daughters and few sons, affable manners.

Sixth house. – Licentious, loose habits, anger, low minded, well informed, destruction to enemies, fond of other women.

Seventh house. – Passionate, unhealthy habits, happy marriage, sensual, inclined towards sex pleasure.

Eighth house. – Danger to mother, happy, given to bad habits, short-lived, famous, celebrated, unexpected legacies, trouble in mind, disappointment in love affairs, pious later in life.

Ninth house. – Selfish, religious, respect for preceptors, able, successful, commander, lover of fine arts, generous.

Tenth house. – Respect for divine people and parents, carriage, broken education, successful as a lawyer, popular, social, moderate eater.

Eleventh house. – Influential, learned, wealthy, good conveyances, successful, many friends, much popularity.

Twelfth house. – Mean-minded, find of low women, miserly, obscure, licentious, unprincipled, weak eyes, fond of sexual pleasures, clever, liar, pretentious, unhappy love affairs.

MICROSCOPY OF TRANSITING PLANETS SIMPLIFIED VOLUME-5

CHAPTER FORTY TWO

PLACEMENT OF PLANETS IN DIFFERENT SIGNS

VENUS

In Aries. – Extravagant, active, mutable, artistic, dreamy, idealist, proficient in fine arts, licentious, sorrowful, fickle-minded, prudent, unhappy, irreligious, easy going, loss of wealth due to loose life.

Taurus. – Well built, handsome, pleasing countenance, independent, sensual, love of nature, fond of pleasure, elegant, taste in dancing and music, voluptuous.

Gemini. – Rich, gentle, kind, generous, eloquent, proud, respected, gullible, love of fine arts, learned, intelligent, good logician, just, dual marriage, tendencies towards materialism.

Cancer. – Melancholy, emotional, timid, more than one wife, haughty, sorrowful, light character, inconsistent, unhappy, many children, sensitive, learned.

Leo. – Money through women, pretty wife, wayward, conceited, passionate, fair complexion, emotional, zealous, licentious, attracted by the fair sex, premature in conclusions, superior airs, unvanquished by enemies.

Virgo. – Petty-minded, licentious, unscrupulous, unhappy, illicit love, agile, loquacious, rich, learned.

Libra. – Statesman, poet, intelligent, generous, philosophical, handsome, matrimonial felicity, successful marriage, passionate, proud, respected, intuitive, sensual, wide travels.

Scorpio. – Broad features, quarrelsome, medium height, independent, artistic, unjust, proud, disappointed in love, haughty, not rich.

Sagittarius. – Medium height, powerful, wealthy, respected, impertinent, generous, frank, happy domestic life, high position, philosophical.

Capricorn. – Fond of low class women, imprudent, ambitious, unprincipled, licentious, boastful, subtle, learned, weak body.

Aquarius. – Liked by all, middle stature, handsome, affable, persuasive, witty, timid, chaste, calm, helpful and humanitarian.

Pisces. – Witty, tactful, learned, popular, just, ingenious, caricaturist, modest, refined, powerful, exalted, respected, pleasure seeking.

MICROSCOPY OF TRANSITING PLANETS SIMPLIFIED VOLUME-5

CHAPTER FORTY THREE

REMEDIES OF PLANETS

REMEDY OF PLANET VENUS

Effects and Remedies

As a feminine planet, Venus has been regarded as the goddess of love, marriage, beauty and all worldly comforts. Venus represents that power of love which leads to the merger of two individual selves into one and rules the gentle and refined attributes of human life.

As a preceptor of demons, Venus stands for the husband in the horoscope of a female and represents the wife in the horoscope of a male. Venus offers good results if placed alone in the birth chart. the 2nd and 7th houses are owned by Venus who gets exalted in the 12th house. Saturn, Mercury and Ketu are friends of Venus, whereas Sun, Moon and Rahu act as enemies.

Venus offers very good results if posited in the 2nd, 3rd, 4th, 7th and 12th houses, but the Ist, 6th and 9th houses are considered bad for Venus. Accordingly, Venus offers very good results in the houses of Mercury, Saturn and Ketu, whereas evil effects will follow if posited in the houses of Sun, Rahu and Moon. When Rahu aspects Venus or vice versa, or when both are placed together in a house, the good results of Venus will be nullified and the native will get deprived of money, wealth and family comforts altogether. The eyes of the native's, mother will become severely defective if Moon and Venus are placed just opposite to each other.

Afflicted Venus causes trouble in the eyes, diseases of the ovaries, gout, anaemia and other complications due to over indulgence in amusements and sex, including gonorrhoea and syphilis. An afflicted Venus may cause vehicular accidents, faithlessness in love and marriage and will deprive the native of the comforts of vehicles, conveyance etc.

Venus in 1st House

Venus in Ist house makes the native highly handsome, long lived, sweet tongued and popular among the opposite sex. wife of the native remains ill. Religion, caste or creed is never a bar for having sexual relations with anyone. Such a native is generally highly romantic by nature and longs for love and sex with other women. He gets married before he starts earning his living. Such a native becomes a leader of persons of his age group, but leadership of the family members causes several family troubles. Such a native earns great profits through the trade of clothes. Such a native is generally deprived of interest in religious pursuits. When Venus comes in 7th house in Varsha phal, it causes chronic fever and blood cough.

Remedies

1. Do not marry at the age of 25 years.
2. Always act according to the advice of others.
3. Serving a black cow.
4. Avoid sex during day time.

5. Take bath with curd.
6. Intake of cow's urine is very useful.

Venus in 2nd House

Doing bad or evil towards others would prove harmful to the native. Money, wealth and property would continue to grow up to sixty years. Shermukhi house (wider at the front than the rear portion) would prove disastrous for the native. Business or trade associated with gold and jewelry will be extremely harmful. Business associated with earthen goods, agriculture and animal will prove highly beneficial. Venus in 2nd second house in a female horoscope renders the native barren or infertile and in a male 's horoscope makes the wife incapable of producing a son.

Remedies

1. For getting a son, intake of things associated with mars like honey, Saunf or deshi Khand will be highly effective.
2. Feed two kgs of potatoes colored by yellow turmeric to cows.
3. Offer two kgs. cow's ghee in a temple.
4. Avoid adultery.

Venus in 3rd House

Here Venus blesses the native with a charming personality and every woman would get attracted to him. He is generally loved by all.

If the native gets involved with other women he will have to live in subservience to his wife, otherwise his wife will always be dominated by him, though she may be dominating everyone else coming into contact with her.

She would be courageous, supportive and helpful to the native like second bullock of the cart. He will be saved from deceit, theft and harm from others. Contacts with other women would prove harmful and affect the longevity adversely. If planets placed in 9th and 11th houses are inimical to Venus, highly adverse results will follow. He will have many daughters.

Remedies

1. Respect your wife and never insult her.
2. Avoid flirting with other women.

Venus in 4th House

Venus in 4th house strongly establishes the possibility of two wives and makes the native rich, too, If Jupiter is posited in 10th house and Venus is placed in 4th, the native will face adverse results from all sides if he tries to be religious. Venus in 4th house destroys the possibility of a son to the native if he covers a well by a roof and constructs a room or house over it. The business associated with mercury will also prove harmful. Saturn will give disastrous effects if the native consumes liquor. The business or trade associated with mars will prove advantageous to such a native. Venus in 4th and Jupiter in Ist house will create frequent quarrels with the mother-in-law.

Remedies

1. Change the name of your wife and remarry her formally.
2. Throwing rice, silver and milk in the running water or feeding Kheer or milk to mother like women will ward

off the quarrels between mother-in-law and daughter-in-law.

3. Keep the roof of the house clean and well-maintained for the health of your wife.

4. Drop things of Jupiter, like gram, pulses and Kesar, in the river.

Venus in 5th house

5th house is the Pukka ghar of the sun, where Venus will get burnt with the heat of the Sun. Consequently the native is a flirt and amorous by nature. he will face big misfortunes in life. However, if the native maintains a good character he will steer through the hardships of life and obtain great riches and promotions in service after five years of his marriage. Such a native is generally learned and destroyer of enemies.

Remedies

1. One should not marry against the wishes of his parents.

2. Serving cows and mother like women.

3. Avoid relationship will other women.

4. Native's wife should wash her private parts with curd or milk.

Venus in 6th House

This house belongs to mercury and Ketu, who are inimical to each other, but Venus is friendly to both. Venus stands, debilitated in this house. However, if the native keeps the opposite sex happy and provides her with all the comforts, his money and wealth will continue to grow. The wife of the native should not get dressed like a male and should not get her hair cut like a male, otherwise poverty will crop up. Such a native must marry a person who has got a brother or brothers. Further, the native should not leave any work in the midway, i.e., before completion.

Remedies

1. Ensure that your wife puts gold clips in her hair.
2. Your spouse must not remain barefooted.
3. The private parts should be washed with red medicine.

Venus in 7th House

This house belongs to Venus, so Venus gives very good results if it is placed in this house. The planet of Ist house offers the effects of 7th house in such a manner as if it is placed in 7th house itself. If a planet inimical to Venus is placed in Ist house e.g. Rahu, the wife and the household affairs of the native will be adversely affected. The native spends his money largely on women. The native should take up the trade or business which is associated will marriage ceremony, like tent house and beauty parlor. Association with one eyed and black woman will prove useful.

Remedies

1. Domestication of white cows prohibited.
2. Serving red cows.
3. Donate Jawar equal to the weight of your spouse to a temple.
4. Throwing blue flowers in a dirty canal for 43 days.

Venus in 8th House

No planet is considered benefic in this house Even Venus in this house becomes rotten and poisonous. The wife of such a native becomes highly irritable and short tempered. Evil utterances from her mouth will certainly prove to be true. The native will be suffering from the feeling of self-pity. Taking guarantee or surety for someone will prove disastrous. If there is no planet in 2nd house, do not marry before 25 years of age, otherwise the wife will certainly die.

Remedies

1. The native should not accept daan.
2. Bowing head in the place of worship and temples.
3. Copper coin or blue flower to be thrown in gutter or dirty Nullah continuously for ten days.
4. Wash your private parts with curd.

Venus in 9th House

Venus in this house does not offer good results. The native may have riches, but he will get his bread only after hard labour. His efforts are not properly rewarded. There will be dearth of male members, money, wealth and property. If Venus is accompanied by Mercury or any malefic planet the native will be a victim of intoxication and disease from seventeen years of age.

Remedies

1. In the foundation of the house silver and honey should be buried.
2. Silver bangles to be worn after putting some red colour on them.
3. Bury a silver piece under a Neem tree for 43 days.

Venus in 10th House

Venus in this house makes native greedy, suspicious and interested in handicraft. The native would act under the control and guidance of his spouse. as long as the spouse is with the native all sorts of troubles will remain warded off. If in a motor car no accident will take place or even if it takes place the native cannot be harmed in any manner. The business and things associated with Saturn will prove advantageous.

Remedies

1. Washing private parts with curd.
2. Western wall of the house should be of mud.
3. Abstinence from wine and non-vegetarian food.
4. At the time of illness, the native should donate a black cow.

Venus in 11th House

Venus in this house is influenced by Saturn and Jupiter, because this house belongs to Jupiter and Saturn. This house is aspected by 3rd house which is influenced by Mars and Mercury. Native's wife, through her brothers, will prove very beneficial.

Remedies

1. Remedies of Mercury will be useful.
2. Oil to be given on Saturday.
3. The native usually suffers from low sperm count in his semen. Native should drink milk in which hot piece of gold has been dipped.

Venus in 12th House

Exalted Venus gives very beneficial results in this house. The native will have a wife, who will act as a shield in the time of trouble. Taking help from women will prove highly advantageous for the native, who receives all favours from the government.

Venus being inimical to Jupiter causes health problems to the wife. Mercury in 2nd or 6th houses makes the native diseased, but bestows literary and poetic talent to the native. Such a native gains high spiritual powers at the age of 59 and generally lives up to about 96 years.

Remedies

1. Blue flowers to be buried by the wife at the time of sunset, for good health.
2. The wife will act as a defence wall for the husband, if she gives things in charity to people.
3. Domesticating and giving cows in charity.
4. Offer love, respect and honour to your wife.

MICROSCOPY OF
TRANSITING PLANETS
SIMPLIFIED
VOLUME-5

TRANSITING PLANETS

CHAPTER FORTY FOUR

URANUS NEPTUNE PLUTO

TRANSITING URANUS

Uranus the planet in the orbit takes approximately eight four years to come full circle. This slow-moving planet's transits are long-lasting, and each transit takes its time to unfold. As the planet Uranus transits a point in our chart, and retrogrades back over it, and then hits it again in direct motion, it imparts its own special wisdom upon the point in question the sensitive areas of lives and parts of our bodies ruled by at point.

Uranus the planet of independence, liberation, and enlightenment influences our lives depends very much on whether we resist its effects or we try to work with. While the slow moving planet Saturn delays our inner cycle in order to reckon us to face facts, Moreover planet Uranus speeds up the speed in order to consider taking risks and making changes in us.

Uranus-Sun Transits

You feel the need to pursue the things that you love. This can be an exciting period of your life that is filled with change and stimulation. Your ego is awakened, and you feel compelled to express yourself in unique and perhaps unusual or unconventional ways. With increased openness to all that is new and different, you may encounter opportunities that appear to come out of the blue. Your consciousness expands to the point where you are receptive to new ways of thinking and patterns of living. Especially if you are female, you may begin a relationship with a male, and this association leads you into undiscovered territory or some kind of break from your past.

Uranus transits conjunct Sun

Your work may take on some higher purpose, or you may find yourself feeling more community-oriented. The transit is offering, nudging, and opening doors to permit you to express yourself more spontaneously and creatively, or to take a risk you have been contemplating. Fortunately, the heart and brain is lively but not hectic. In fact, this is an enjoyable time when you meet interesting and entertaining people, and you share enthusiastic and lively ideas and interests with others. Freedom, independence, and individuality are the key issues for this time period.

You could feel much more intuitive and psychic than heretofore possible. You may sense and feel things that others do not. Not a time when you are at your most practical; you lose yourself in home and family. The pace of your life is accelerating, and some changes may be forced upon you. Patterns of behaviour that worked for you in the past are questioned, and change is in order. Arming yourself with the awareness that you may be over-confident and hasty in your decisions is essential for the best handling of this transit.

Uranus transits sextile Sun

New means of self-expression and communication are possible. You may find yourself changing your appearance, moving toward the more unconventional and less traditional. Eccentricities and a different manner of presenting yourself may be in order. You may receive unexpected aid from someone older or from authority figures. Clear yourself to the fact that something must change, rather than resisting or fearing it. You tend to idealize others in particular, your partners and relationships during this time period . Resistance will only attract circumstances that leave you feeling out of control.

Uranus transits square Sun

New means of self-expression and communication are possible. You may find yourself changing your appearance, moving toward the more unconventional and less traditional. Creative impulses are strong; your magnetism helps you make rapid strides, if you are controlling the purely self-cantered and self-indulgent urges which are powerful. You may have to control an urge to rebel and be different that could set your ambitions and goals back a step. An inner struggle between your sense of purpose or direction and a need for independence and freedom makes this a possibly tense time. Create daily rituals or do small acts that anchor and stabilize you in the midst of the changes you are going through.

Uranus transits trine Sun

There is little that could be negative or difficult now, other than allowing inertia or conservatism to prevent you from taking the opportunities presented to you. It is dawning on you that a spirit of community and togetherness is preferable to personal differences. You could receive unexpected help from someone older or from authority figures. To create, experiment, or plunge into new territory, now is the time. You may branch out in an entirely new direction. If you are involved in work that is creative, innovative, unusual, or unconventional, you experience an influx of inspiration as well as support for what you are doing.

Uranus transits square Sun

After this time, you will find it much easier to express and communicate your inner dreams and ideals to others. A sense of imagination and unity previously limited to your mind becomes a reality for you and is carried through to your person. Whatever you consider to be liberating for you, you will seek to achieve it now. This is a period of sudden awakenings that can lead to greater independence and personal freedom, more authentic self-expression, and living your life more on your own terms. You may well have to take a stand, in a way that is controversial or sets you apart from the crowd.

Uranus-Moon Transits

You could disagree with ideas or find communication with others difficult or fouled up. During this time period, you cast off some of your old roles and adopt new ones. Uranus transits to the Moon directly affect the feelings, the public image, and personal popularity. Other people and things affected by Uranus are the mother, important women in the native's life, domestic life, and the home.

Uranus transits conjunct Moon

You tend to idealize others, in particular your partners and relationships, during this time period. It is dawning on you that a spirit of community and togetherness is preferable to personal differences. Discontent with things as they are leads to rebellious and irregular actions, for the satisfaction of the ego and of self-indulgent urges is stronger than the desire to find the good.

Your courage, confidence and communication skills will be at their best and you will have success in the existing assignments and also in new ones. This is a time of tremendous change that can be liberating, electrifying, exhilarating, and tumultuous all at once.. Impulses to do or be something completely different from anything you've done or been before are quite likely. You're also apt to find yourself much more discontented and impatient than normal, without quite knowing what would feel better or what you really want instead.

Uranus transits sextile Moon

A dreamy manner or appearance, plus the ability to enchant others, finds this a time when mysticism and idealism seem to really be living in you. Time to have new thoughts and sudden insights and to get an unexpected boost in the way you think, speak, or write. Communications are facilitated, connections of all kinds, news, and so on, are furthered, often at the expense of tradition, established order. Your emotions are highly stimulated by this transit, and you will allow yourself to look at the world very subjectively.

You could feel slighted as a result of others misunderstanding what you communicate or get offended over a difference of opinion. If your current relationships cannot adjust to your increased emotional needs, you will not hesitate to find others that do. You have to be able to exercise total freedom in your emotional self-expression. Anyone who tries to limit you in this area will meet with great resistance. You want your home to be stimulating and exciting and will not settle for safety and security alone in your domestic life now. Now is also a great time to entertain guests in your home. This is an excellent time to plan lively get-togethers and parties, especially with close friends or family.

Uranus transits square Moon

This is a good day for expressing yourself creatively through relationships or other pursuits. You tend to kick over the traces and run wild with whatever ideas you have been suppressing up until now. You can see your complexes and your subconscious in the cold light of day if you are sufficiently in possession of yourself to look for them. During this time period you periodically become overwhelmed with the feeling that you need to make changes and make them now. In this case, your tendency to rebel acts at cross-purposes to those who care for you.

Uranus transits trine Moon

You can see your complexes and your subconscious in the cold light of day if you are sufficiently in possession of yourself to look for them. You are more spontaneous, free, and uninhibited in your expression of feelings now. Your sense of humour is very good, and you can expect a lot of good times, laughter, and joking throughout this period. You might make some social contacts that benefit your career or life direction. A time when you may get insights into your living situation or support system. New ideas about your past history, new approaches to established facts.

Uranus transits opposite Moon

A dreamy manner or appearance, plus the ability to enchant others, finds this a time when mysticism and idealism seem to really be living in you. Exposure to new ideas and learning is emphasized now. Your mind will be flooded with new information and ideas, and you will feel enthusiastic and excited by these fresh ideas and insights. You tend to kick over the traces and run wild with whatever ideas you have been suppressing up until now.

Watch out for over-spending, as you may feel a greater than average need to please or pamper yourself. This is a time to explore scientific and technological ideas and inventive, progressive, innovative perspectives in any area. You could achieve real breakthroughs in the form of ideas, communications, and the mind in general. To be, or become, your best self as a result of this transit is to harness your magnetism, your originality and your creative talents for all time. You could feel much more intuitive and psychic than heretofore possible. You may sense and feel things that others do not.

Uranus-Mercury Transits

A sense of value and valuing that may find you lavishing affection on those near you. Your career could take a turn toward the idealistic, or you could find yourself developing a practical sense for making your dreams a reality. Uplifting of your career. Uranus transits to Mercury directly affect your curiosity, learning, communication skills, self-promotion, the formulation of ideas, and your ability to rationalize and think logically.

Uranus transits conjunct Mercury

A very nice day, perhaps filled with some renewed appreciation for all that is beautiful and fine. Uplifting for the career Computers and electronics may suddenly become important. Your career could take a turn toward the idealistic, or you could find yourself developing a practical sense for making your dreams a reality.

Uranus transits sextile Mercury

You tend to idealize others in particular, your partners and relationships during this time period. It is dawning on you that a spirit of community and togetherness is preferable to personal differences. You are mentally alert, sharp, and on your toes during this time period. You will perform superbly in a debate or other mental task that requires quick thinking, fast response, and fluent expression of ideas. Writing comes easily now, so if you have some writing you need to do, now is a good time to do it.

Uranus transits square Mercury

You are unlikely to feel on top of your game now, so don't push matters. Instead, take time for rest and relaxation. You could feel much more intuitive and psychic than heretofore possible. You may sense and feel things that others do not. Not a time when you are at your most practical; you lose yourself in home and family. Be extremely careful in all practical affairs at this time. You tend to overlook details, forget to consider some aspect of a problem, and make silly mistakes.

Uranus transits trine Mercury

Your goals and ideals are uplifted during this period and take on a more spiritual or mystical dimension than heretofore. Your work may take on some higher purpose, or you may find yourself feeling more community-oriented. Creative thinking and innovative ideas are key issues now. You are mentally alert and keen, able to absorb new ideas very quickly, and less resistant to new information than usual. A time to have new thoughts and sudden insights and to get an unexpected boost in the way you think, speak, or write. Communications are facilitated, connections of all kinds, news.

Uranus transits opposite Mercury

Your career could take a turn toward the idealistic, or you could find yourself developing a practical sense for making your dreams a reality. The tempo of your life is very fast at this time. If you live in an urban area or are involved in activities that are fast-paced and dynamic, then this time period may become too intense for you. You could be under considerable mental tension or feel hemmed in by an overly conservative mental atmosphere. You may feel compelled to change your mind now and have new thoughts and forms of expression. Bucking other people's ideas may be in order

Uranus-Venus Transits

It's an excellent period for negotiations and smoothing over of differences .Upsets and unexpected changes in relationships are extremely likely at this time. A free-spirited, independent streak arises in you, making you more selfish, independent, and unwilling to tolerate being stifled by another. If your job is tedious, boring, and unexciting, there is a strong possibility that you will quit your job now. Because the need for freedom and excitement is very strong, you are more willing to be innovative and daring. Breakthroughs in personal relations, perhaps through unconventional behaviour and appearance, may occur.

Disagreements that may crop up now tend to be about differences in principles or matters of personal style and for personal magnetism than this one, you do tend to easily attract positive attention and circumstances now. New means of self-expression and communication are possible. You may be unable to appreciate or value people and things now. Eccentricities and a different manner of presenting yourself may be in order, spending more time away from it, engrossed in your personal and domestic scene.

Uranus transits conjunct Venus

Your initiative to find individuality now sets a new course and brings redirection in life goals. If there is room in your existing relationships for this type of change, it can be a time of exhilaration and growth for both partners. If not, you may feel the need to end some of your present relationships and seek this new freedom elsewhere. If you are not currently involved in a love affair, this transit could bring a new love into your life that would be more exciting and unconventional than your prior relationships.

Go with the flow and once transit passes avoid aggressive behaviour or dangerous places . Venus also rules money, and you may encounter sudden changes in your financial condition. Whether or not this turns out to be a successful long-term relationship depends on your ability to maintain this sense of excitement after the newness has worn off. Wait until this transit passes before making any long-term commitments to a new love. Again, whether this is a positive or negative change depends on your ability to accept necessary changes in your life.

Remember its' best to make changes as smoothly as possible while adjusting to new conditions and status in life. Don't hang on stubbornly to an old familiar situation just for the sake of security. This is the time to strike out on new, innovative projects. Parties, celebrations, social gatherings, music, dance, and vacations are very high on your priority list now. You are in a swinging mood and you seek fun and excitement.

Uranus transits sextile Venus

A very nice day, perhaps filled with some renewed appreciation for all that is beautiful and fine. Freedom and independence are critically important to you at this time. A certain amount of mental tension can be expected, so bear with it. New means of self-expression and communication are possible. You may find yourself changing your appearance, moving toward the more unconventional and less traditional.

You can benefit now from a more confident manner and increased certainty about your goals in life. New attachments or projects may be formed now. A time for discovering others or for finding yourself able to respond to friends or lovers and enter into relationships with a renewed sense of love and compassion. Real breakthroughs, willingness to try new and different approaches to relationships. A kind of mini-revolution may find you altering your value system, allowing you to like new things.

Uranus transits square Venus

This is a pleasing influence for harmonious contact with others and for prosperity in general. A strong streak of you now to have the courage to make some needed changes in your life for overly rebellious behaviour and insensitivity towards others independently can overcome you during this time, upsetting the status quo in your life, and particularly in your relationships. You should not force anyone to do anything, and it's better to give others freedom if they are looking for it .You have creatively value system may receive a challenge from a new independent streak that wants to break away and try new things.

Expressing yourself creatively through relationships or other pleasurable pursuits is favoured now. Sometimes this energy is experienced in such a way that changes in a relationship seem forced upon you. Keep in mind that this leads to tension. Upsets and change in your love relationships is the key issue now. A shift in your romantic and sexual energies at this time causes changes in love relationships. You may not appreciate the urge to upset and change things that is trying to assert itself.

Uranus transits trine Venus

Your personal charm is natural and well-received now, making this a good time to be amongst people. You are in a loving, generous, helpful you discover new and different reasons or ways to enjoy and appreciate life. Your values are more altruistic, and you are less concerned with personal gain than you are with making important contributions to life and helping others. A time during which A kind of mini-revolution may find you altering your value system, allowing you to like new things.

Uranus transits opposition Venus

Whatever you consider to be liberating for you, you will seek to achieve it now. Solid friendships and marriages will survive the challenges of this transit. You are likely to meet people of many various walks of life, and discover new perspectives and interesting ideas from your interactions with others. You are less inhibited, more open and spontaneous than usual. Positively, you now have the courage to make. Have in mind that you cannot force anyone to do anything. Happy relationships at this time go through a lot of changes. It is uneasy to say how things will end up when this astrological influence is over, but they are guaranteed to be different.

Uranus-Mars Transits

You are currently able to handle opportunities well by focusing your energy on constructive activities and goals. This is a good period for dealing with others in general, but particularly on professional levels or with those in charge. Uranus transits to Mars means of self-expression and communication are possible. You may find it very easy to overdo or work at cross purposes to yourself just now You are not easily satisfied with things now; even if everything seems to be going along fine, even during this time period, you are very impatient, energetic, obstinate, and self-willed.

Uranus transits conjunct Mars

You also are able to manage and motivate others very effectively, even if there is no specific deadline for a task, you work as if it must be completed with lightning speed. You may feel emotions of a religious nature. You love physical activity and adventure now. If you vacating at this time, skydiving or white water rafting would suit you much better than lying on the beach. You may find that you have intuitive and psychic abilities that have never surfaced before. An urge may exist to be more devoted to high ideals and to making your dreams real.

Uranus transits sextile Mars

You might find you have to push a little harder during this transit than you normally would .This is an upbeat, refreshing time period. Progressive changes in your life and relationships make this an enjoyable, exciting time. You may have to resist attempts to sway your energy level; your work may find yourself involved in a successful and productive team effort. You feel the need to stir things up. You would almost rather have an upset or crisis just for the excitement. Uranus urges us to let go and express ourselves in the areas of life it touches.

Uranus transits square Mars

Obstacles in your path tend to arrive now, although you are capable of turning them into positive energy. With a transiting square from Uranus to Mars, we begin to get things off our chest whether we wanted to or not. Passions and anger that you may not even know you had emerged during this transit. They do come from somewhere, from deep within you, but Uranus awakens them in such a dramatic manner. You have spurts of energy, and you can be temperamental with your productivity or output.

This is not an ideal time for new enterprises or undertakings. Inner restlessness may take you out of your typical routine. You may have a sense of circumstances working against you or feel a lack of support and love from those around you. Periodic fits of restlessness and impatience overcome you throughout this period, and others will wonder what is disturbing you. You are very demanding and difficult to please now. You tend to feel like progress is too slow, and you are tired of waiting for the things you want.

Uranus transits trine Mars

This is a period when ego-gratifying circumstances are highlighted. The changes are not likely to be extraordinary in scope, but a definite enlivening of your relationship to others and the world in general is evident .With confidence and courage, you assert yourself boldly. There could be some tension or sense of opposition requiring compromise or negotiation on your part.

Uranus transits opposite Mars

This is a time of great personal change. You feel as though you have been drifting along with the tide and following the crowd for too long, and your inner needs and motivations must assert themselves more strongly. Courageous and undaunted, you step boldly forth, assert yourself, and charge ahead. If you are normally shy and receding, you will burst out of your shell now. If you are a strong and aggressive person, then you will try to take full command of every aspect of your life, and force weaker personalities to submit to you and support you.

You may find yourself becoming intensely personal and passionate in the way you appear or come on to others.

You will develop a more direct method of communication, getting to the very heart of things. Unexpected behaviour and an urge to be independent could find you ignoring your feelings and much of what has motivated you up to now, taking you off in a different direction. Your unusual behaviour could provoke others, cause emotional confrontation.

Uranus-Jupiter Transits

Uranus Transits Conjunct Jupiter

An opportunity for understanding and even growth. Tensions with others can come from a lack of self-confidence or a sudden awareness of unfulfilled wishes and goals. You may find yourself becoming intensely personal and passionate in the way you appear or come on to others. You will develop a more direct method of communication, getting to the very heart of things Underlying motives come to the surface and relationships become deeper and more meaningful. This is a positive time when you express your deepest feelings openly and intensely.

You seek intensity in your life and in your relationships, and you become more aware of hidden sides of your personality, untapped talents and interests, and also emotional blocks or confusions. This is the time to spread your wings and explore imaginative new possibilities. You express great intensity and passion in the way you appear and express yourself to others. Career insight and breakthroughs are possible.

Uranus Transits Sextile Jupiter

You almost transfix those who meet you with your fixedness and sense of power. Enthusiasm and progress are the key issues for this time period. You will find that others who normally resist your suggestions are now more receptive and supportive. Organizations, businesses, and government agencies also respond favourably to your suggestions and proposals. During this time period you reach a critical point in your life and relationships. Breakthroughs in your career could open up during this time, making it possible for you to solve problems and reach new levels of accomplishment. Improved solutions, insights, and approaches make this an opportunity not to be passed over.

Uranus Transits Square Jupiter

A need for excitement, adventure, and fun pervades this time period. Exciting outdoor activities appeal to you now. Ski trips, canoe rides, softball, tennis, swimming, or camping appeal to you now, depending on your tastes and the season. You almost transfix those who meet you with your fixedness and sense of power .An urge on your part to rebel or break away could affect your career direction or vocation. Your wish to be independent, to try new things, and so on comes at an inappropriate time and could cause real tensions at work.

Uranus Transits Trine Jupiter

During this time period you reach a critical point in your life and relationships. You want greater intensity and intimacy in your relationships, and you are also inclined to have power struggles with others. The astrological influence at work now is so positive and beneficial that you are almost guaranteed of having some major improvements in your overall life during this time period.

You want closeness but you do not want to be dominated or restricted by the other person. Breakthroughs in your career could open up during this time, making it possible for you to solve problems and reach new levels of accomplishment. Improved solutions, insights, and approaches make this an opportunity not to be passed over.

Uranus Transits Opposition Jupiter

This is a positive time when you express your deepest feelings openly and intensely. Daily concerns and worries fade during this time period, and you become motivated by the need to become free of restrictions, obligations, and responsibilities. A restless time, which could find you trying new and unexpected ideas at the expense of the status quo, especially your career.

MICROSCOPY OF TRANSITING PLANETS SIMPLIFIED VOLUME-5

CHAPTER FORTY FIVE

TRANSITING NEPTUNE OVER OTHER PLANETS

Neptune Trine Natal Neptune

You can benefit now from a more confident manner and increased certainty about your goals in life. New attachments or projects may be formed now. You could feel real support and harmony at this time for circumstances and those around you. Well grounded, idealizations, compassion and wellness at home.

Squares:

The possibility of some form of recognition or validation for what you do may come during this brief but effective period. They can bring on confrontational energy that allows breaking free of confining situations. A Transiting Square to a Natal Planet placement occurs when two planets are 90 degrees apart and within a one to three degree orbit of each other. This indicates challenges. This makes the Natal planet feel confined and brings challenges to some more than others depending on the two Planets involved..

Neptune Square Natal Neptune

During this time period you reach a critical point in your life and relationships. A generational aspect where your same age group becomes disillusioned with society.

Withdrawal from society. Individually evasive actions to avoid others. Desire to escape and get away from it all. Make no permanent commit-ments now.

Neptune conjunct Sun

You want closeness but you do not want to be dominated or restricted by the other person. A time during which you bring imagination and new ideals to your ambitions and life direction. You could get carried away and lose sight of the practical, day-to-day realities in your quest for religious, philosophical, and mystical understanding.

Neptune opposite Sun

You want closeness but you do not want to be dominated or restricted by the other person. This marks a time when you could easily get carried away or even deluded with respect to your own goals and ambitions. A tendency to over-imagining and dreaming. If you spend all of your time at the sideshow, the main tent will be gone.

Neptune square Sun

You want greater intensity and intimacy in your relationships, and you are also inclined to have power struggles with others. Your idealism and the dreams you dream right now may end up costing you in terms of lost ambitions and setbacks in your life goals. Escape could be at the expense of a reality that you have planned and worked for. Delusion is in the air.

Neptune sextile Sun

This is a time of conscious striving knowing what you want and working towards getting it. You find that you are able to bring more imagination to bear on your goals and ambitions now. You might find your ideals taking a more spiritual turn, thus involving you more in community and religious projects.

Neptune trine Sun

Underlying motives come to the surface and relationships become deeper and more meaningful. You find that you are able to bring more imagination to bear on your goals and ambitions now. You might find your ideals taking a more spiritual turn, thus involving you more in community and religious projects.

Neptune conjunct Moon

Very important people come into your life now. You meet someone who becomes a strong influence on you. A time during which you may be able to carry your ideals and dreams into reality to make your home and environment reflect your inner desires and become as you dreamed it could be. You may find that you can escape with your friends, those who support you.

Neptune opposite Moon

Your vitality gets a little boost and your recuperative powers are better than normal. Relations with others tend to flow smoothly now. A time of real inner growth through other people, the social life. A tendency to escape or withdraw into your imagination at the expense of your friends and supporters. You may be unrealistic, taken with dreams, psychic matters, and the like. Your living situation or a younger person may challenge your dreaminess.

Neptune square Moon

Your career and overall direction in life reach a critical turning point now. You could get the wrong idea, develop false ideals, and let your imagination carry you away to the point that those who support and care for you are neglected or hurt. Walk a careful line when it comes to dreams versus realities. The dreams can be bad.

Neptune sextile Moon

A positive frame of mind does wonders now. Familiarity and comfort are dominant motivators for you during this period. You feel the need to pursue the things that you love and instinctively find appealing rather than do what is practical. An opportunity to use your imagination to improve your living environment or beautify your surroundings. You may feel very idealistic about your friends, especially someone who is younger or who could use your help. Others give you ideal support.

Neptune trine Moon

You are likely to receive some benefits, raises, promotions, or increased stature and recognition in your work. An opportunity to use your imagination, to improve your living environment or beautify your surroundings. You may feel very idealistic about your friends, especially someone who is younger or who could use your help. Others give you ideal support.

Neptune conjunct Mercury

This is a positive time for your career. There will definitely be changes: you may change jobs, receive additional training or education that will help you reach your goals, or develop a fresh, new approach to your work. Your goals and ideals are uplifted during this period and take on a more spiritual or mystical dimension than heretofore. Great aspirations and goals. You are able to put your dreams and ideals into words.

Neptune opposite Mercury

This is a positive time when you express your deepest feelings openly and intensely. It could be easy to get carried away and to ignore facts or think in a fuzzy or deluded manner. Your ideals (what you imagine for yourself) may be challenged by the ideas and thoughts of others. Communications could become blurred.

Neptune square Mercury

There will definitely be changes: you may change jobs, receive additional training or education that will help you reach your goals, or develop a fresh, new approach to your work. A long dreamy time when you find it easy to lose yourself in one flight of fancy or another, often at the expense of rational thinking and good judgment. Normally clear ideas are fuzzy now, and it is hard to be logical or consistent.

Neptune sextile Mercury

You seek intensity in your life and in your relationships, and you become more aware of hidden sides of your personality, untapped talents and interests, and also emotional blocks or confusions. It is dawning on you that a spirit of community and togetherness is preferable to personal differences. You tend to idealize others in particular, your partners and relationships during this time period. Not a time when you are at your most practical; you lose yourself in home and family. You could feel much more intuitive and psychic than heretofore possible.

Neptune trine Mercury

You express great intensity and passion in the way you appear and express yourself to others. You almost transfix those who meet you with your fixedness and sense of power. You are at your most poets, able to put your dreams and ideals into words and communicate them through speaking and writing. Your whole mental environment takes on an almost other-worldly hue during this time. Your muse wakes.

Neptune conjunct Venus

You want closeness but you do not want to be dominated or restricted by the other person. A time to appreciate philosophy, religion, and all that is mystical. Your value system and the way you care for others may shoot up a notch to a higher plane. Imaginative purchases and acquisitions are at an all-time high. Not a very practical time.

Neptune opposite Venus

You seek intensity in your life and in your relationships, and you become more aware of hidden sides of your personality, untapped talents and interests, and also emotional blocks or confusions Others may not appreciate your expressed ideals and goals or may challenge them. You could find it easy to get carried away and be indiscriminate or lose hold of your sense of values. You could do something that goes against your own sense of good taste.

Neptune square Venus

A time of real inner growth through other people, the social life. Your career and overall direction in life reach a critical turning point now. Your current bout of idealism may carry you away to the point of damaging or obscuring your true life values. Probably not the best time to make aesthetic or value judgments, since your ability to appreciate may be blurred or unrealistic.

Neptune sextile Venus

You feel the need to pursue the things that you love and instinctively find appealing rather than do what is practical, marketable, secure, and logically correct. An appreciation for ideas and thoughts that are quite other-worldly is upon you. It is easy for you to love and be compassionate and to value what life offers. You have a sense of unity and brotherhood that will stay with you.

Neptune trine Venus

An important relationship, perhaps a younger person or someone in your near environment, may come into focus. You seek intensity in your life and in your relationships, and you become more aware of hidden sides of your personality, untapped talents and interests, and also emotional blocks or confusions. Not a time when you are at your most practical; you lose yourself in home and family. You have a sense of unity and brotherhood that will stay with you.

Neptune conjunct Mars

You take things more personally now, and issues that have been stewing beneath the surface reveal themselves now. This is a time when you handle opportunities that come your way very well. Achievement is smooth. Recuperative powers are increased. You may have a sense of circumstances working against you or feel a lack of support and love from those around you. You express great intensity and passion in the way you appear and express yourself to others. You may find that you have intuitive and psychic abilities that have never surfaced before.

Neptune opposite Mars

You meet someone who becomes a strong influence on you. This other person may be a kind of idol, a teacher, or a friend. Your imagination and fancied ideals may mislead you to the point of motivating you in a wrong direction. Your real feelings could be obscured by some supposed spiritual or humanitarian ideal. Later you may feel you did the wrong thing.

Neptune square Mars

The new people you attract now will be very different from your norm, as friends go. Your current crop of dreams and ideals may not feel right to you or may seem to go against all that normally motivates you. It may be easy to be misled and to find yourself pouring energy and effort into directions that will bring no return.

Neptune sextile Mars

You almost transfix those who meet you with your fixedness and sense of power. Moody, even dreamy, during this period of time. Your emotions and feelings could reach heights that are close to ecstatic. It is easy for you to find the proper motivation to fulfil your ideals or make your dreams into reality.

Neptune trine Mars

Positive new connections may be made now. The possibility of some form of recognition or validation for what you do may come during this brief but effective period. This is a positive time when you express your deepest feelings. You want greater intensity and intimacy in your relationships, and you are also inclined to have power struggles with others. You want closeness but you do not want to be dominated or restricted by the other person.

Neptune conjunct Jupiter

Underlying motives come to the surface and relationships become deeper and more meaningful. You could find yourself pursuing more spiritual directions or finding someone who can guide you to realizing your inner dreams and ideals. Your path is toward cooperation and union with others, even at the expense of the practical and selfish.

Neptune opposite Jupiter

There could be an emotional overtone to all of this that may require understanding and flexibility on your part Very important people come into your life now. You meet someone who becomes a strong influence on you. It could be easy for high-sounding ideas and false ideals to mislead you into making career or vocational decisions that are wrong for you. Be careful that you don't involve yourself in some plan to misguide or deceive another.

Neptune square Jupiter

You take things more personally now, and issues that have been stewing beneath the surface reveal themselves now. A time of real inner growth through other people, the social life. It could be easy to make career moves now that are the result of deception, yours or somebody else's. Your imagination carries you in a wrong direction.

Neptune sextile Jupiter

This is a period when you are more inclined to be immature or childish if you have not been managing or acknowledging your emotions in a healthy manner to date. Your career and overall direction in life reach a critical turning point now .

Your career could become almost ideal, or you could find yourself taking an interest in more spiritual and mystical matters. The direction of your life could turn more to questions of religion and world unity. Occult and esoteric subjects may concern you.

Neptune trine Jupiter

You feel the need to pursue the things that you love and instinctively find appealing rather than do what is practical, marketable, secure, and logically correct . Your career could become almost ideal, or you could find yourself taking an interest in more spiritual and mystical matters. The direction of your life could turn more to questions of religion and world unity. Occult and esoteric subjects may concern you.

Neptune conjunct Saturn

Managed well, this can be a time in which you arrive at increased self-understanding of your innermost needs and wants. You are likely to receive some benefits, raises, promotions, or increased stature and recognition in your work. You might have a sense of living in a dream world or of being awake in your own dream. The spirit world seems real and possible.

Neptune opposite Saturn

Your relationships are now very intense and ever so personal. In fact, they are capable of transforming you at the most basic level. Misguided idealism and false spirituality could find you ignoring responsibilities in favour of a lot of high-sounding talk. You might find yourself losing your resolve or determination to take care of business and get things accomplished.

Neptune square Saturn

There will definitely be changes: that will help you reach your goals, or develop a fresh, new approach to your work. There could be a tendency to view your accomplishments as having almost no substance during this time. A false set of ideals may mislead you and cause you to neglect your responsibilities and get lost in what will amount to a bunch of nothing.

Neptune sextile Saturn

A day for thinking and ideas. You may feel like talking a bit more than usual, exploring new ideas or getting happily lost in a conversation. Your goals and ideals are uplifted during this period and take on a more spiritual or mystical dimension than heretofore. The problems and responsibilities of life may be seen in a new light, as part of a larger drama you are living .You are able to handle difficulties more easily, seeing them as part of a larger story.

Neptune trine Saturn

You are at a peak of physical energy now. Your enthusiasm runs high, and so does your courage. It's a time of decisiveness, taking the initiative, handling problems directly and straightforwardly. You seek intensity in your life and in your relationships, and you become more aware of hidden sides of your personality, untapped talents and interests, and also emotional blocks or confusions Your work may take on some higher purpose, or you may find yourself feeling more community-oriented. You are able to handle difficulties more easily, seeing them as part of a larger story.

Neptune conjunct Uranus

This is a positive time when you express your deepest feelings openly and intensely. A time when insights and ideas flow together and add up to form a larger reality. A sense of unity and connection as everything merges together and works. It is almost like a big dream, like being out of the body.

Neptune opposite Uranus

You feel as though you have been drifting along with the tide and following the crowd for too long, and your inner needs and motivations must assert themselves more strongly. Ideals and dreams conflict with your need to be different and perhaps unconventional. Being slavish to established ideals could result in a loss of freedom and insight. Be aware that lofty ideals do not automatically guarantee honesty.

Neptune square Uranus

You seek intensity in your life and in your relationships, and you become more aware of hidden sides of your personality, untapped talents and interests, and also emotional blocks or confusions. A rugged time when it is easy for you to get lost in the clouds and lose sight of your own intrinsic originality and independence. You could deceive yourself in matters concerning personal freedom and real insight.

Neptune sextile Uranus

Underlying motives come to the surface and relationships become deeper and more meaningful Insights into your deeper, more spiritual nature are available to you during this period of time. You may be able to discover whole new areas of your psyche or mind that have been closed up to now. Insights into dreams and ideals.

Neptune trine Uranus

You will develop a more direct method of communication, getting to the very heart of things. Insights into your deeper, more spiritual nature are available to you during this period of time. You may be able to discover whole new areas of your psyche or mind that have been closed up to now. Insights into dreams and ideals.

Neptune conjunct Neptune

This is a time of great personal change. You become tired of your role in life, and you are very sensitive to habits, customs, and social requirements. A dream world where ideals are real and reality is as we always dreamed it would be. The dewdrop slips into the shining sea. A sense of unity and world communion.

Neptune opposite Neptune

This other person may be a kind of idol, a teacher, or a friend. A time of real change when many give up or accept life on new terms. There is the possibility of taking a more active part consciously in life, a sense of sharing the creative force, the experience of becoming one with the creative force, the creator.

Neptune square Neptune

You feel the need to express yourself now, and any person or situation that has restricted your freedom of expression will have to go. You could take a turn toward the idealistic, or you could find yourself developing a practical sense for making your dreams a reality is dawning on you that a spirit of community and togetherness is preferable to personal differences .A time when dreams, fantasies, and the urge to be free of this hard world could themselves be a fantasy that deceives and misleads you. Your own goals and ideals may be stressed and challenged.

Neptune sextile Neptune

Your close personal relationships will be tested now, and persons who are unable to accept the newly-emerging you will have no place in your new circle of friends . A time to reach beyond the physical into the realm of myths and dreams. You may have the sensation of being awake within your own dream, and reality may be like you dreamed it could be.

Neptune trine Neptune

You have a tremendous need for liberation now, and many long-time friends of yours will be surprised at the radical changes you will initiate in your life during this time . A time to reach beyond the physical into the realm of myths and dreams. You may have the sensation of being awake within your own dream, and reality may be like you dreamed it could be. This is a time for visions and seeing the unity beyond differences.

Neptune conjunct Pluto

This search for information beyond what you can readily see is part of the overall liberation that you are seeking. A sense of devotion and the spiritual. A time to explore your own inner resources and psychic sensitivities. The psychological world takes on the qualities of a living dream. A journey to the essence or beginnings of life.

Neptune opposite Pluto

People will share with you new and revolutionary perspectives on life that you have previously rejected Your dreams and ideals may conspire to ignore and push aside the need in you for real inner growth and transformation. If you get too carried away or lost in the dream world, you can expect to be hauled back by some very personal inner confrontations.

Neptune square Pluto

Whatever you consider to be liberating for you, you will seek to achieve it now. A tendency to become unrealistic and over-imaginative may lead you to ignore and deny your own need for inner growth and personal change. Your current ideals may tell you that analysis and sensitivity are not where it's at.

Neptune sextile Pluto

During this time period, you cast off some of your old roles and adopt new ones. You take a fresh approach to life and your personality undergoes major changes. Your own inner psychology and vulnerabilities are open to you now, almost as if in a waking dream. A renewed interest in exploring the realm of dreams and imagination finds you getting to the heart of your secrets and sensitive areas.

Neptune trine Pluto

A time that can mean great change for you personally, during which you break away from the past and try new and different ways of presenting yourself. Your own inner psychology and vulnerabilities are open to you now, almost as if in a waking dream. A renewed interest in exploring the realm of dreams and imagination finds you getting to the heart of your secrets and sensitive areas.

MICROSCOPY OF TRANSITING PLANETS SIMPLIFIED VOLUME-5

CHAPTER FORTY SIX

TRANSITING PLUTO

Pluto takes almost two hundred and forty years to come full circle. This slow-moving planet transit is long-lasting, takes its time to unfold. As Pluto transits a point it retrogrades back over it, and then hits it again in direct motion, it imparts its own special wisdom upon the point in mark the areas of our lives and the parts of our markings ruled by that point.

You are also likely to establish a good rapport with some important influential people through whom you are likely to be benefited .Pluto probes much deeper, shining light on our darkness. Transiting Pluto offers us the chance to evolve and to rebirth. Pluto affects our lives depends very much on whether we resist its influences or we try to work with the planet of rebirth and destiny. Whatever part of our lives and of our psyches that Pluto touches, especially by hard transit, is an area that Pluto compels us to explore more deeply. Superficiality is not acceptable for Pluto.

You are also likely to get involved in some sinful activities, which is unacceptable in your religion. Transiting Pluto brings intensity and focus to our lives. Pluto breaks through illusions, in search of the utter truth. Pluto acts to strip away what is unnecessary or superficial in our lives. Pluto wants deep experience, of the transformational kind. Things that are not working for us, whether they are thought processes or lifestyles, undergo a transformation.

Keep your spirits high as due to unsuccessful or suspended endeavours, you are likely to suffer from deep mental anguish during this particular phase. Pluto transits bring about rebirths of sorts in the areas of life affected. Pluto transits are about letting go of things that are holding us back from deep and meaningful experience. Fear sometimes intense fear can reveal itself at the beginning of a challenging Pluto transit.

Some of you may also suffer from temporary loss of memory during this time. Work might ask for some more dedication, lack of which may make you suffer in your field of work or business. This acquaintance may encourage you to meditate and be more spiritual in nature. If we do this, Pluto's energy has to go somewhere, so we end up meeting Pluto in our lives in the guise of events and people. If we are attracting jealous, manipulative, and controlling people or situations, we can ask ourselves why this is happening. Transiting Pluto is often associated with such things as separation and deaths, it is important to note that Pluto's action is to revolutionary.

Pluto-Sun Transits

You are likely to develop sleep disorders, which could also be a result of your constant worries. Intense focus on your career can find you mercilessly cutting back and getting down to the bare essentials regarding the path or direction you are taking with your life. You will have a sense of being almost driven to pursue your course and succeed. We discover our own power and strength, and we re-work our very sense of identity, which invariably affects our life path.

Pluto conjunct Sun

This mostly denotes pecuniary gain for you. Moreover, this period also sees you having a great time. This transit of the Sun brings about the need to understand yourself on a deep, inner level, much deeper than the image you normally show to the world. There is also a need to get to root causes. An ultra-intense time, during which you may eliminate a lot that, is superficial and unessential in your life. A deep and lasting change in your ambition and life goals could evolve.

Pluto brings about drastic, revolutionary changes, but ones which are necessary to halt the process of stagnation and instigate continued growth. You could be feeling less vigorous than usual or more stressed. You might find that you attract challenging situations simply because you are overreacting emotionally. One of the lessons you will learn is that change is necessary - all things which have lapsed into a cult routine or become meaningless will be cleared away to make room for more progressive attitudes and creative activities.

Pluto transits sextile Sun

Socially this should be a good time for you, as you are likely to overcome all your fears and worries .You could receive some help in the form of a real drive towards realizing your inner self and your life ambitions. You are able to cut through a lot that is unessential and get on with the real work. Subtle but profound changes within you will have a tremendous effect upon your relationships, quite possibly totally altering significant relationships in your life.

Your enemies may also create problem for you during this time. Stay away from all kinds of arguments and misunderstandings. A new spirit of self-respect, personal empowerment, and deeper honesty arises. It is a time of births and deaths, and these will have a powerful impact upon you and your decisions. Group work is very powerful and positive for you now, especially if the focus is on conscious awareness, deeper learning, healing, or combining energies to create positive changes in the collective (media, education system.

Pluto square Sun

This mostly denotes financial growth for you. You could also expect a rise in your prosperity. A time when your basic life direction and sense of purpose may be tested by sensitive and very personal matters. Questions of vulnerability and insecurity may hound you, trying to force you off your slated path. You may have to tread with care.

Pluto opposite Sun

Quarrel misunderstandings in social circles, bad name, trouble from females, loss in lottery, bad health during this period. Power struggles, with authorities in particular, can be one sign of this aspect. Your need for constant inner change and growth may end up setting you back as much as it helps. Your ambitions and basic life direction could be challenged. This transit marks a major growth period in your life in which you struggle with the buried elements of your personality and ego as you learn to accept, transform, or face them. You may be acting in a controlling, jealous, or overbearing manner which can alienate others or even push them away.

You may have to compromise with your enemies against your will as well. This comes from a deep fear of letting go and surrendering to the idea that some things cannot be directed or controlled. As this fear surfaces, your behaviour may be compulsive or obsessive; or you may experience these traits through someone close to you, especially a male. However, the process can be lengthy and challenging. You may feel threatened in some way, and you might feel somewhat paranoid. This can be something you experience on a subconscious or emotional level in that you are unlikely to feel physically threatened. Instead, you might fear the loss of a significant other, a lifestyle, a job, or other significant part of your life.

Pluto trine Sun

At this time you come across in an appealing, charming, openly affectionate manner that is likely to win you new friends. You could receive some help in the form of a real drive towards realizing your inner self and your life ambitions. You are able to cut through a lot that is unessential and get on with the real work. This is a potentially empowering time in your life when your personality is more vibrant, magnetic, focused, and resolute. You might take up a pleasantly consuming new hobby, line of work, or interest now.

Pluto-Moon Transits

Vitality increases now as your confidence in your effectiveness builds. You feel more generous, optimistic, and sociable under this influence. This can be a time in which you arrive at increased self-understanding of your innermost needs and wants. Pluto transits to the Moon directly affect the feelings, the public image, and personal popularity. Other people and things affected by Pluto are the mother, important women in the native's life, domestic life, and the home. Our early experiences often cause us to build a life script that incorporate our expectations from the world, and this process is ruled by the Moon.

You appear perhaps more charming and refined than usual. In some cases, men live this transit through key female figures in their lives. Sometimes the relationship with the mother or other important female figures come into focus. Look to the house of your natal chart with Cancer on the cusp for areas of your life where Pluto is stimulating. Look to planets in Cancer in your chart to see other parts of your personality that Pluto is now infusing with intensity.

Pluto conjunct Moon

It's easy for you to receive warm responses from others right now. A time of great change and evolution, in particular regarding your home life and surroundings your support system. You may draw a whole new environment around you after boiling down the current situation to the bare essentials.

Pluto opposite Moon

This influence sometimes brings new romantic or social relationship opportunities. Your tendency to analyses, to probe, and generally to get at the heart of things finds itself at loggerheads with your living and support system.

Others may resent your persistent prying and digging, and confrontations can be expected.

Pluto square Moon

Your manner may not be warm or loving at the moment. Perhaps not the best time to present yourself to others. Social upsets are possible, or you may find that you are unable to do something pleasurable even though you would really like to. You could be unable to share all the changes you may be experiencing with those around you. Someone may be unable or unwilling to support your feelings.

Pluto sextile Moon

You're more inclined to buy items on emotional whims rather than based on clear thinking .Your support system becomes more secure. You are able to dispense with some of the unessential and develop what is most basic and true in your environment. You encourage better support.

Pluto trine Moon

You may be procrastinating with your work now, preferring to enjoy or simply pamper yourself. During this time period relationships deepen and grow, and penetrate to a very personal level. This process is sometimes initiated by you and sometimes initiated by the other person, but in either case it leads to a much deeper understanding and bond between you. Your support system family, home, those who give you nourishment become more secure.

You appear perhaps more charming and refined than usual. These transits bring intensity and passion to the feelings, a tendency to act on impulse, some irrational or compulsive behaviour, and likely a stronger awareness of your deeper emotional needs. Habits that spring from deeply ingrained fears are brought to the fore, and Pluto challenges you to face them, as well as to examine your deepest attachments--to people, things, conditions, and attitudes.

You portray the more reasonable, refined, and likable side of your personality now, and others tend to respond warmly Emotions that you may have never been in touch with, particularly of a darker, obsessive, or primal quality, come bursting forth. There is always some level of paranoia associated with hard Pluto transits, and the things you are paranoid about generally are the very fears that you are called upon to face. With the Moon involved, these fears have to do with significant women in your life, personal habits, emotional patterns, and the home and domestic life. Your attachments to these things may be challenged now.

You are more willing than usual to bend and compromise. Remember that you get what you want by the forces of attraction during this period, rather than coming on strong. You portray the more reasonable, refined, and likable side of your person-ality now and others tend to respond warmly .You get what you want by the forces of attraction during this period, rather than coming on strong. Your relationships may be intense, complicated, or entangled at this time. You can experience obsessive desires to uncover secrets, and levels of suspicion run high, as you may be living in fear that significant people in your life are not as attached to you as you are to them.

You are more willing than usual to bend and compromise. Remember that you get what you want by the forces of attraction during this period, rather than coming on strong. You will be learning that self-control is the only path to fulfilment. You might fear their loss and attempt to control or manipulate the people around you in an attempt to. You are learning that in so doing, you will eventually learn what is really yours, who truly loves you, and which habits and patterns serve your own growth. Your fears now have to do with the feeling of helplessness in the face of changes in the people and circumstances around you.

Pluto-Mercury Transits

Doors open that may have previously been closed or undiscovered. You look, sound, and feel good, so take advantage. Pluto transits to Mercury directly affect your curiosity, learning, communication skills, self-promotion, the formulation of ideas, and your ability to rationalize and think logically. Look to the houses of your natal chart with Gemini and Virgo on the cusp for areas of your life where Pluto is stimulating.

Pluto transits conjunct Mercury

Other people may not appreciate the way you come on or present yourself. You may find yourself caring too much about what others think of you. However, you will be intensely examining ideas, thoughts, and concepts with an eye to getting rid of unwanted dross. You are more sensitive than usual to subtleties in your personal environment, and all the more vulnerable as a result.

Search for information beyond what you can readily see is part of the overall liberation that you are seeking The new people you attract now will be very different from your norm, as friends go. They will share with you revolutionary perspectives on life that you have previously rejected. Your communications with others take on a new level of depth and intensity at this time. Secrets come out into the open, and conversations have a greater sincerity and depth than usual.

Pluto transits square Mercury

During this time period, you cast off some of your old roles and adopt new ones. During this time period your thinking is intense and penetrating. You tend to become impassioned about your ideas, and you are inclined to feel very strongly about your ideas. You tend to have a one-track mind now, and you talk to others about your interests whether they are interested or not. A crazy time when you may feel under a lot of mental pressure. You may be unable to put some of your insecurity and sense of change into words, to communicate them. A tendency to probe and analyse may not fit in with your normal way of thinking.

Pluto transits trine Mercury

A time that can mean great change for you personally, during which you break away from the past and try new and different ways of presenting yourself. You take a fresh approach to life and your personality undergoes major changes. This time period is excellent for any kind of research or in-depth study. You are motivated and interested in probing beneath the surface and learning the underlying causes behind any event or behaviour. The nature of your studies depends on your personal interests, but whatever area you pursue, you pursue with intensity.

Pluto transits opposite Mercury

Breakthroughs in personal relations, perhaps through unconventional behaviour and appearance, may occur. Whatever you consider to be liberating for you, you will seek to achieve it now. You pursue ideas with intensity now. You have a questioning, almost cynical attitude now, that probes beneath the surface of any issue. This is an excellent time for any kind of research or in-depth study.

Pluto-Venus Transits

A day for thinking and ideas. You may feel like talking a bit more than usual, exploring new ideas or getting happily lost in a conversation. You feel the need to express yourself now, and any person or situation that has restricted your freedom of expression will have to go. Your close personal relationships will be tested now, and persons who are unable to accept the newly-emerging you will have no place in your new circle of friends.

Pluto transits conjunct Venus

This sometimes triggers an attraction to someone who is simply not right for you, or minor problems in existing love affairs. Solid friendships and marriages will survive the challenges of this transit by expanding to allow greater freedom of expression for both partners Your romantic life, social life, and value system are undergoing a complete transformation with Pluto transiting conjunct natal Venus. You are seeking depth of experience in your social and love relationships with Pluto transiting conjunct your natal Venus; or, this kind of experience comes into your life now.

Pluto transits sextile or trine Venus

You are especially sharp, communicative, and open at this time, as your wants are aligned with your thoughts. This should be an especially fruitful and rewarding period in your life, when you experience new depths of intimacy with an existing or new partner, when you learn to appreciate the important people in your life, and when your value system transforms and evolves. This is likely an excellent period for finances as well. Work you've done might pay off, and you are able to manage your finances better, with more attention to planning and strategy, as well as the elimination of frivolous expenditures.

Your erotic life might get a real boost now as you delve deeper into the spirit behind sexual acts. You might find yourself strongly attracted to someone, almost to the point of obsession. This can also be an especially creative transit. It's an excellent time during which to refine artistic skills or to work on creative projects with new or renewed focus and commitment.

Pluto transits square or opposition Venus

You might hunger for increased recognition and respect, and, with your generous attitude and concern for others' well-being, you might just get them. This transit can be very difficult on marriages, especially if one partner is playing a submissive role. Men may decide they want more out of life than a house in the suburbs and two cars in the garage. Women may decide they're tired of being limited to a domestic or clerical role and demand more control over their lives. This major transit challenges you to find meaning in your life through romantic connections and partnerships.

It's an excellent time for taking tests or presenting your ideas. Your opinions and thought processes are generally well-received and appreciated now. Sometimes this transit is associated with divorce or separation, and sometimes new relationships begin. There may be some problems with money during this transit. By the end of the transit, you should have a renewed sense of worth, although getting to that point may not be entirely pleasant.

Pluto transits trine Venus

You may sense and feel things that others do not. Not a time when you are at your most practical; you lose yourself in home and family. The process is rich, eye-opening, and rewarding, but it can also be confusing and intense while it lasts. You are acting on impulse more than you are listening to reason, and you should keep a close eye on this. New relationships formed now seem fateful and, at the very least, timely. New attitudes towards spending are possible at this time. Cutting off some of your frivolous expenditures may be easier than ever during this transit.

Pluto-Mars Transits

Your career could take a turn toward the idealistic, or you could find yourself developing a practical sense for making your dreams a reality. Uplifting for the career A very emotional time during which you can find your basic drive and energy ramming up against questions of security, power, and deep insecurity. Pluto transits to Mars affect your drive and desire nature, strength, stamina, as well as your ability to assert yourself.

Pluto transits conjunct Mars

Your emotions intensify and you instinctively desire change and adventure. It would be wise to keep your cool and avoid confrontations. Very important people come into your life now. You meet someone who becomes a strong influence on you. You might discover possessive, jealous, and controlling aspects of your personality that surprise you. You can apply yourself to specific projects, competitive or individual sports, and other activities with much determination, focus, and concentration now. You may be dealing with so much beneath the surface of things that you are not as available to others as you were previously.

Pluto transits sextile Mars

During this period you may expect financial stability and gain in financial ventures. Your vitality and energy level are at a high point. You are in an ambitious and dynamic phase of your life. You have an especially good ability to motivate others. You have little patience with bureaucratic obstacles, inefficiency and evasiveness, and you boldly challenge these inadequacies. A time when you may feel very passionate, or during which your feelings, emotions, and basic life urges undergo change and possibly transformation. You feel more personal and direct and find that you waste less time with hurt feelings than before.

Pluto transits square Mars

It is better you stay away from activities involving risk to your health. Your ambition and drive to succeed are incredibly strong now. You will go to any lengths to achieve your goals, and you have the energy to do it now.

You are driven by a compulsive need to achieve, and you often find it difficult to stop. Power struggle may well be the keyword here. You could find yourself pushing against a need for greater sensitivity and inner growth. Push could come to shove, and you may end up driving against your own inadequacies and vulnerability.

Pluto transits trine Mars

You may have a hard time concentrating on any one subject. Either you are easily distracted or a whole slew of information and demands are thrown upon you at once. Your vitality and energy level are at a high point. You are in an ambitious and dynamic phase of your life. Your inner powers are excellent and your health is robust. Many people are inspired to strength up their physical strength during this astrological influence, and this is a good idea; you can develop greater endurance and vitality now, which will rejuvenate your body.

Pluto transits opposite Mars

You may expect progress in all your undertakings. This period also indicates your popularity in the society. Your ambition and drive to succeed are incredibly strong now. You will go to any lengths to achieve your goals, and you have the energy to do it now. You are driven by a compulsive need to achieve, and you often find it difficult to stop. You don't feel like dealing with some of the very hot psychological issues that keep springing up.

Pluto Transits Conjunct Jupiter

Avoid any kind of argument that may lead to differences of opinion and misunderstandings. Stay away from your known enemies and be careful of unknown ones. Your perspective on what you want from life, what you are willing to do to get it and the values that you want to express undergoes a change. If you have been working in a direction that is compatible with your standards and your philosophical or religious views, you are likely to be effective. If you have been working along lines that are in conflict with your religious and philosophical views, this could be a time of tension.

It may be challenging to get in touch with what you truly want to do as you tend to live in your brain rather than your heart for the time being. Your situation seems too limiting and confining and you want to break free from the obstacles and responsibilities that keep you tied to your current life style. A change either in the direction of your life or in your values will thus be necessary to deal with your growing sense of frustration. Whether this religious growth is along institutional or personal lines depends on what you feel is missing from your life. You feel hemmed in by surroundings and people that are too simplistic, narrowly focused, and petty.

Pluto Transits Sextile Jupiter

This period is also likely to bring in happiness to you in the form of success in learning and attainment of knowledge. This time period is a positive one of broadening horizons and expansion. This expansion can take many forms. You are likely to travel more now, and have more exposure to other cultures, life styles, and ethnic groups than usual. You find yourself uninterested in side tracks what is not essential.

Pluto Transits Square Jupiter

You are also susceptible to face oppression of some kind. Take care to avoid facing a haul over the coals and the lashes of unsympathetic words from others. Your perspective on what you want from life, what you are willing to do to get it and the values that you want to express undergoes a change. If you have been working in a direction that is compatible with your standards and your philosophical or religious views, you are likely to be effective. This thus becomes a time when your past faith and hard work are rewarded, bolstering your confidence and helping you to make even bigger plans for your future plans that are based on a realistic and solid foundation.

Others appreciate what you have to say and your ideas and opinions are received exactly as you intended them. If you have been working along lines that are in conflict with your religious and philosophical views, this could be a time of tension. A change either in the direction of your life or in your values will thus be necessary to deal with your growing sense of frustration. At this point in your life your current situation seems too restrictive and confining.

New ways to communicate or an easy manner will make conversations and interactions go well today. You may find yourself more talkative and facile than otherwise. Your main effort now should be in trying to live up to the best in you, rather than lowering your standards to achieve a more transient worldly success. You feel claustrophobic now. You certainly need to spread your wings now, but be wary of taking major risks and gambling on a venture that promises you prosperity, freedom, and adventure. Your career can end up at right angles to your own inner sensitivities and need for growth and change.

Pluto Transits Trine Jupiter

What you say or write could be misinterpreted, or you could find it hard to verbalize what it is you want. This time period is a positive one of broadening horizons and expansion. This expansion can take many forms. You are likely to travel more now, and have more exposure to other cultures, life styles, and ethnic groups than usual. You find yourself uninterested in side-tracks what is not essential. You can really home in on how to solve problems and get where you want to go.

Pluto Transits Opposition Jupiter

Your ideas are well-received, your mind is alert, and you can easily and quickly grasp information now. Your perspective on what you want from life, what you are willing to do to get it and the values that you want to express undergoes a change. If you have been working in a direction that is compatible with your standards and your philosophical or religious views, you are likely to be effective. You can translate your thoughts into actions readily now decisiveness helps you to say what you think and think what you say. Improving your skills also comes naturally and easily. This thus becomes a time when your past faith and hard work are rewarded, bolstering your confidence and helping you to make even bigger plans for your future - plans that are based on a realistic and solid foundation.

If you have been working along lines that are in conflict with your religious and philosophical views, this could be a time of tension. You are less cautious, more adventurous and confident, and more willing to spread your wings to explore new possibilities than usual. You are attracted to power and wealth, and may engage in a power struggle or go out on a limb to achieve your goals.

Pluto conjunct Saturn

Taking tests, making plans, presenting your work or ideas, and communications of all kinds are favoured. Others tend to value your opinions and ideas under the influence of this transit. You could be thinking a lot about taking action on something important to you. But your perspective is narrowed now, so you aren't able to look at changes as opportunities. The high premium you place on security may prove detrimental to your growth, since you tend to equate what you have with what you are. Such things may have more symbolic than actual value and could be holding you back from working toward what is really important to you.

Pluto Transits Sextile Saturn

Your mind is especially alert and you could be particularly busy running errands, taking short trips, networking, negotiating, or corresponding. Discipline, concentration, and determination are the key issues now. You are likely to adopt a rather austere and intense routine during this time period. You stubbornly pursue your interests, and you are willing to work long hours without complaint. You can dispense with all that is unsound or superficial, leaving only that which has been properly determined or solid.

Pluto Transits Square Saturn

You might be asked to do a favour that you don't want to do or you could feel overloaded with tasks and errands now. New obstacles arise and increasing responsibilities make it difficult for you to expand and grow. New obligations are likely to arise both in your personal life and your work. Your sense of responsibility and sheer determination may not allow you to admit any feelings of vulnerability and sensitivity that may be coming to your attention. A power struggle could result, and a careful compromise may have to be found.

Pluto Transits Trine Saturn

It's easier now than usual to verbalize exactly what you want. Your thoughts could be all over the place, and it can be hard to concentrate on any one particular task. You stubbornly pursue your interests. This is an excellent time for any form of training or laborious and painstaking work. You can dispense with all that is unsound or superficial, leaving only that which has been properly determined or solid.

Pluto Transits Opposition Saturn

This is a good influence for scheduling dates and for love in general. You are somewhat vulnerable, wearing your feelings on your sleeve. New obligations are likely to arise both in your personal life and your work. Inner searching and a sense of being vulnerable and exposed could tempt you to drop your responsibilities and spend more time on personal growth. It may be difficult to concentrate on your duties during this time of psychological sensitivity.

MICROSCOPY OF TRANSITING PLANETS SIMPLIFIED VOLUME-5

CHAPTER FORTY SEVEN

TRANSIT OF DRAGON'S HEAD

FROM OTHER PLANETS

Transit of Planet Dragon's Head from natal Moon

This transit also favours legal, educational, religious, and cultural endeavours. You seek a larger range of experience. The following are their transit effects as per your Moon Sign. Here are the general effects as given in the classical astrology. However they can vary quite a bit based on individual horoscope.

Dragon's Head transit from your Moon

Transit of Dragon's Head in the 1st house from Natal Moon

There could be a noticeable discrepancy between the demands of your personal life and what is expected of you at work. During this period, Dragon's Head will move through your first house from the Moon. This mostly denotes several negative effects in your life. This position of Rahu signifies loss of financial resources or wastage of money on unnecessary expenditure. You may have to be extra careful to avoid trouble from enemies. Moreover, you are also likely to be humiliated and some unseen problems might crop up in your field of activity.

Be careful of an ill-willed person and avoid suspicious activities like indulging in black magic etc.

You could have a restless sleep. Examining bad dreams can help you understand what is bothering you. Health would require your constant attention. You may even develop some unknown ailment, which might take more than usual time to recover. The health of your parents would also require attention during this period. The physical suffering is likely to cause much worry for you mentally. You may feel worried constantly and may suffer from deep mental misery. You may even become nervous, mentally troubled and restless during this particular phase

Transit of Dragon's Head in the 2nd house from Natal Moon

Perhaps a sense of challenge or blockage just now. You may not find the support you flowing to you. Some sort of temporary obstacle may appear. You may feel frustrated. During this period, Dragon's Head will move through your second house from the Moon. This signifies a troubled time financially, physically and socially for you. During this period, keep an eye on your expenditures and beware of thieves or any unforescen expenses.

Take care of your health and your food habits particularly at this time of the year. Avoid indulging in unknown food or untimely eating as you may develop stomach disorders very easily. You may become aware of a conflict between what you want and what you need. Even if you are not aware of this inner imbalance, it could cause some tensions or feelings of being unsupported by others or by circumstances in your life.

This is the time when you must stay away from all the litigations or issues related to the judiciary; chances are, you may even lose in such cases especially during this particular time. Avoid any kind of arguments and confusions with your near and dear ones as well. This time may also see you go through a rough phase with your spouse. Stay away from any kind of situations where you smell foul play, as this or some scandals related to a person of the opposite sex may damage your image in the society

Transit of Dragon's Head in the 3rd from natal moon.

General good feeling and a sense of support and harmony make this happy times. It's easy to put your best face forward and to cooperate with others because you are not conflicted on the inside. During this period, Dragon's Head will move through your third house from the Moon. You may expect to gain money from various known and unknown sources and you may even get financial benefits from your enemies. If employed you may expect a raise in your salary and those who are involved in trade may also expect added profit during this particular time.

You are expressing yourself more genuinely, and you are received well as a result. Progress at work could also be expected. Your efficiency at work and in your field of learning would be noticed as well. Health should remain fine and you would face any problem with much courage and vitality. Socially also, this could be regarded as a good time. You may even expect a raise in your social status and in your fame in the society. Comfort would define your life at home. You are most likely to enjoy a soothing atmosphere at home. This time could also prove to be great as it also brings in opportunities to satisfy your taste buds.

Transit of Dragon's Head in the 4th house from Natal Moon

You possess strong presence and generally feel confident about who you are and how others are receiving you now. During this period, Dragon's Head will move through your fourth house from the Moon. This would see you going through a troubled time. You will have to be extra careful in matters related to your landed property as this journey of Rahu denotes loss of the same.

You may also have to change your place of residence at this time. It would be a good idea to avoid any kind of property related litigations during this phase. Your health may require some extra care, as you are susceptible to developing diseases during this time. Take good care of your spouse and children's health as well. Expect significant encounters, meeting individuals who are or will be important players, at least for the moment.

Emotions that you may have never been in touch with, particularly of a darker, obsessive, or primal quality, come bursting forth. This brings along considerable good times along. Financially this period is expected to be very good. Avoid travelling during this time. Travel of any kind may lead to an accident where you may lose your vehicle or your valuables. At home, you would have to make that extra effort to keep the atmosphere conducive for peaceful living. Beware of your enemies during this time, as they are likely to add some more trouble in your life.

Transit of Dragon's Head in the 5th house from Natal Moon

During this period, Dragon's Head will move through your fifth house from the natal Moon. You express great intensity and passion in the way you appear and express yourself to others. You will develop a more direct method of communication, getting to the very heart of things. This signifies grief, especially due to matters related to your children. Financially this may not be regarded as a good time for you. Hold tight to your finances, as it is likely to be spent on unnecessary purchases. Health of your parents and spouse may become a cause of concern, as they are susceptible to developing diseases.

Your motives come to the surface and relationships become deeper and more meaningful Matters related to your children may worry you more during this particular phase which is termed as the period of Son Affliction meaning sorrow related to your son. Attend to any health problem of your children that may come up during this time. Some of you may even find your children going astray or developing some serious ailments. Mentally you may suffer from increased agony and confusion. Your decision-making skill may go haywire making you get carried away to make the wrong decision.

Transit of Dragon's Head in the 6th house from Natal Moon

During this period, Dragon's Head will move through your sixth house from the Moon. You may find yourself becoming intensely personal and passionate in the way you appear or come on to others. This brings in wealth from various sources for you. You may expect smooth sailing on your work front during this time. If you are into trade or business, agriculture or poultry farming you may expect a considerable profit in your respective fields of work. You may even expect some monetary gain from your opponents during this time.

You seek intensity in your life and in your relationships, and you become more aware of hidden sides of your personality, untapped talents and interests, and also emotional blocks or confusions. This is a positive time when you express your deepest feelings openly and intensely. Chances are that you would also be benefited by your maternal uncle. However, if attended on time, you can be cured of all your ailments and regain your sound health. Socially you would be in a great shape. Your respect and honour in the society would see an upward move during this time.

Transit of Dragon's Head in the 7th house from Natal Moon

You tend to feel that your personality lacks any vitality. An authority figure could be hard to connect with now. During this period, Dragon's Head will move through your seventh house from the Moon. This brings in fatigue and worry for you. This is the time when you need to keep away from any kind of property related litigations and trade, as you are likely to lose your property at this time. However, some of you may even gain profit or suddenly progress in your field of trade. At home, avoid any kind of argument with your spouse as this might lead to quarrels. Try and maintain a cordial relationship with your friends and relatives to avoid being deserted by them.

You should watch that you don't come on too strong today and attract conflict with others. Feeling slighted, overlooked, or misunderstood could lead you to seek out attention now. Avoid this kind of relationship during this time as this might end up ruining your name in the society. Pay attention to your health as you may catch some venereal diseases. This transit suggests you now have a stronger sense of who you are and the principles you represent. The realization of a long-term goal may come now. You may also develop some bile and wind related diseases.

The health of your spouse may also cause worry during this particular time. Keep an eye on your behaviour and avoid any kind of arguments with your enemies. You also tend to get involved in unnecessary litigations during this time. Keep away from all kinds of litigations to avoid humiliation and defamation. Some of you may also have to go to a distant place, which could also prove to be troublesome for you.

Transit of Dragon's Head in the 8th house from Natal Moon

It will be difficult for you to recover pending dues hence avoid unnecessary expenses and wasteful spending. During this period, Dragon's Head will move through your eighth house from the Moon. This mostly denotes physical ailments for you. This is the time when you must give top priority to your health. This period may make you suffer from diseases of the reproductive organs, small pox, and various sexually transmitted diseases. Do not take any health related complications for granted as it might prove to be life risking for you. You may also suffer from mental anxiety and unnecessary fear from everything. Those who are also going through the maraka period in your Birth Sign must avoid taking risks with their lives.

There may be some false charges against you. Avoid any tricky situation during this time. Keep away from corruption and malpractices as you may end up with the judiciary. You may also have to face humiliation and defamation during this particular phase. Utmost care should be taken for the success of all your endeavours as your enemies or ill-wishers may conspire against you. Secure your landed property and jewellers, as you are likely to lose some during this phase. Be calculative enough to avoid any losses in your business, trade or profession.

Transit of Dragon's Head in the 9th house from Natal Moon

It will be difficult for you to recover pending dues hence avoid unnecessary expenses and wasteful spending. During this period, Dragon's Head will move through your ninth house from the Moon. This mostly signifies loss of wealth and your involvement in malicious activities. Most of you are likely to invest your hard earned money in lottery, whereas, you are likely to lose money in speculation and unnecessary expenses. Hold on tight to your finances, as you may have to embrace poverty during this particular phase. You are also likely to break the code of your religious conduct and practice black magic. Your professional life is likely to go on a bumpy ride with several ups and downs.

Your bosses and employers will not be happy with your work and you will face blame and you face some humiliation. Avoid any kind of arguments with your siblings. Handle your friends and acquaintances carefully to avoid being forsaken by them. Moreover, due to your cosmic graph, this could be a trying time for your parents and siblings. Avoid bad company to keep yourself away from more trouble particularly during this time. Health would also require your attention as you may suffer from a few minor ailments at this time.

Transit of Dragon's Head in the 10th house from Natal Moon

There will be misunderstandings and clash of opinion with your spouse and family members. During this period, Dragon's Head will move through your tenth house from the Moon. Avoid taxing yourself physically as you will be prone to pains in the hips, knees and spine. You will feel tired and mentally depressed. This brings in mixed results for you. Hence, if you see a great time during the first half of this period you may have to experience some negative results in the second half of this phase.

The progress of work will be excellent and your seniors will appreciate and honour your efforts. This is a very happy and fruitful period for you and your family. There will be merrymaking, good food and sweets at home during this time and you will have a great time with spouse and children. You may even expect some gain from your cordial relationship with people of distinction.

A good period for making plans or decisions and finding your way through just about any problem you may discover. You are also likely to get new opportunities in your work front, which would give you higher responsibilities and more rights. Health of your parents would require attention as well. Be extra careful with your finances during this period and avoid impulsive buying and waste.

Avoid all risky investments as this is a period of losses. Some of you may also be affected by black magic. At home, you are likely to get involved in fights with your spouse. You are also likely to be transferred to a place that doesn't interest you much. Your food habits may also suffer due to several reasons. Some auspicious deed may be performed at your home

Transit of Dragon's Head in the 11th house from Natal Moon

This is a time when you can expect a little boost, some sort of extra support or recognition from those around you. This period, Dragon's Head will transit your eleventh house from the Moon. This brings in good times for you. This period could be regarded as particularly favourable for matters related to your finances. You may feel that you are in touch and in harmony with others; the lines of communication are open. The support you need is there. You may even acquire some landed property and buy some jewellery during this particular time. Domestic life would be good. You are likely to enjoy exotic dishes at home.

There is a chance to understand those around you and to have a special time with someone you love. General good feeling and a sense of support and harmony make this a happy time. There could be a mutual lack of appreciation. Differences in values or ways of expressing affection in your personal relationships are made very noticeable to you now. This could be regarded as a socially good time as well, as you would be able to command more respect and honour in the society. Your interest in religious and spiritual field would increase and you may also get providential help from these disciplines

Transit of Dragon's Head in the 12th house from Natal Moon

This transit offers you increased clarity derived from a feeling that what you want and what you need are in harmony. During this period, Dragon's Head will move through your twelfth house from the Moon. This denotes trouble for you. There could be loss in business and in your professional field. Your projects and endeavours may not bring in the desired result. You may even face difficulty in completing your previous tasks on time.

You would need to hold on to your courage and confidence as these may also be shaken due to these hurdles at work. Your intentions and actions harmonize, which improves your relationships with others and with your own body and spirit. Take note of all your expenses and practice stinginess, as you are likely to embrace indebtedness. You may even lose your landed property during this phase.

MICROSCOPY OF
TRANSITING PLANETS
SIMPLIFIED
VOLUME-5

CHAPTER FORTY EIGHT

TRANSITING RAHU

Planets in Different HOUSES

DRAGON'S HEAD (RAHU)

In the Ascendant. – Obliging, sympathetic, abortion, courageous, sickly wife or husband.

Second house. – Poor and more than one wife if afflicted, dark complexion, diseased face, peevish, luxurious dinners.

Third house. – Few children, wealthy, bold, adventurous, courageous, good gymnastic, many relations.

Fourth house. – Liaison with women of easy virtue, subordinate, proficient in European languages.

Fifth house. – Childless, flatulent, tyrannical, polite, narrow-minded and hard-hearted.

Sixth house. – Enjoyment, venereal complaints, no enemies, many cousins.

Seventh house. – Wife suffering from menstrual disorders, widow or divorcee connection, diabetes, luxurious food, unhappy.

Eighth house. – Vicious, degraded, quarrelsome, narrow-mined, immoral, adulterous.

Ninth house. – A puppet in the hands of the wife, impolite, uncharitable, emaciated waist, loose morals.

Tenth house. – Intimacy with widows, taste in poetry and literature, good artist, traveller, learned.

Eleventh house. – Wealthy, influential among lower castes, many children, and good agriculturist.

Twelfth house. – Deformed, few children, defective sight, very many losses, saintly.

MICROSCOPY OF TRANSITING PLANETS SIMPLIFIED VOLUME-5

CHAPTER FORTY NINE

REMEDIES OF PLANETS

REMEDIES OF PLANET   RAHU

(DRAGON'S HEAD)

Effects and Remedies

Unlike other planets of the solar system Rahu and Ketu are not observable, substantial heavenly bodies, with shape or mass content. Rightly termed as shadowy planets, their movement is interrelated and as parts of one body they are at all times just opposite to each other. Greater significance has been attached to the role of Rahu influencing human affairs in various dimensions, especially in Kaliyug

The author of Lal Kitab describes Saturn as a serpent and Rahu and Ketu as its head and tail respectively. As a node of moon, Rahu shall not provide adverse results so long as 4th house or moon is not afflicted. He gives good results when Mars occupies houses 3 and 12, or when Sun and Mercury are in house 3, or when he himself is posited in 4th house. Rahu further provides good results if placed together with Mercury or expected by him.

Rahu offers highly beneficial effects if placed in houses earlier than Saturn. But if it is otherwise, Saturn becomes stronger and Rahu acts as his agent. Sun provides very good results when Rahu is expected by Saturn, but Rahu gives the effects of a debilitated planet when Saturn is expected by Rahu.

Rahu gets exalted in houses 3 and 6, whereas he gets debilitated in houses 8, 9 and 11. 12th house is his SOLID HOUSE and he proves highly auspicious in houses 3,4 and 6. Saturn, Mercury and Ketu are his friends, whereas Sun, Mars and Venus are his enemies. Jupiter and moon are neutral to him.

If Sun and Venus are placed together in a horoscope, Rahu will generally provide adverse results. Similarly, Rahu will provide bad results if Saturn and Sun are also combined in a horoscope.

Here Mars will also become Mars negative. If Ketu is placed in houses earlier than Rahu, Rahu will provide adverse results, whereas Ketu's effect would be zeroed.

Rahu in 1st House

1st house is influenced by Mars and Sun, which is like a throne. The planet in 1st house is considered to be the king of all planets.

The native will achieve a position higher than indicated by his qualification and will obtain good results from government. Rahu in this house would give the result of exalted Sun, but it will spoil the fruits of the house in which Sun is placed. If Mars, Saturn and Ketu are weak only then Rahu would give bad results, otherwise it will give good results in 1st house.

If Rahu is malefic the native should never take any electric equipment's or blue/black clothes from his in-laws, else his son could be affected adversely. Its malefic result too could last till the age of 42 years.

Remedies

1. Offer 400 gm lead in running water.
2. Wear silver in the neck.
3. Mix barley in milk in ratio of 1:4 and offer in running water.
4. Offer coconut in running water.

Rahu in 2nd House

If Rahu is in benefic form in 2nd house one gets money, prestige and lives like a king. He will have a long life. 2nd house is influenced by Jupiter and Venus. If Jupiter is benefic then the native will live the early years of his life in wealth and comfort. If Rahu is malefic the native will be poor and have a bad family life, suffer from intestinal disorders. The native is killed by a weapon and is unable to save money. In the 10th, 21st to 42nd years of his life, he loses wealth by theft etc.

Remedies

1. Keep a solid silver ball in the pocket.
2. Wear things associated with Jupiter, like gold, yellow cloth, saffron etc.
3. Keep cordial relations with ones mother.
4. After marriage do not take any electric equipment from in-laws.

Rahu in 3rd House

It is the 'Pukka Ghar' of Rahu. 3rd house belongs to Mercury and is influenced by Mars. When Rahu is benefic the native will enjoy great wealth and a long life. He will be fearless and a loyal friend. He would be a clairvoyant for seeing future in his dreams. He will never be issueless. He will be victorious over his enemies; can never be a debtor. He would leave behind property. 22nd year of his life would be of progress. However if Rahu is malefic in 3rd house then his brothers and relatives would waste his money. His money once borrowed would never be returned. He would have defective speech and would be an atheist. If Sun and Mercury are also there (in 3rd house) with Rahu then his sister would become a widow in 22nd or 32nd year of his life.

Remedies

1. Never keep ivory or things of ivory in the house.

Rahu in 4th House

This house belongs to moon, which is an enemy of Rahu. When Rahu is benefic in this house the native would be intelligent, wealthy and will spend money on good things. Going on pilgrimage would be beneficial for him. If Venus is also benefice then after marriage the native's in-laws could also become rich and the native would also benefit from them.

When Moon is exalted the native would become very rich and would benefit from the works or relatives associated with Mercury. If Rahu is malefic and the Moon is also weak then the native will suffer from poverty and native's mother would also suffer. Collecting charcoal, altering toilet, installing oven in the ground and alteration of the roof in the house would be indicative of malefic.

Remedies

1. Wear silver.
2. Offer 400 gm coriander or almonds, or both in flowing water.

Rahu in 5th House

5th house belongs to Sun, which signifies male offspring. If Rahu is benefic native will be rich, wise, enjoy good health. He would enjoy good income and good progress. The native would be a devout or philosopher. If Rahu is malefic it leads to abortions. After the birth of a son, wife's health will suffer for twelve years. If Jupiter is also in 5th housefather of native will be in trouble.

Remedies

1. Keep an elephant made of silver.
2. Abstain from wine, non-vegetarianism and adultery.
3. Remarry your wife.

Rahu in 6th House (Exalted)

This house is influenced by Mercury or Ketu. Here Rahu is exalted and gives very good results. The native will be free of all botheration or troubles. The native will spend money on clothes. The native will be intelligent and victorious. When Rahu is malefic he will harm his brothers or friends. When mercury or Mars is in 12th house Rahu gives bad result. The native suffers from various ailments or loss of wealth. Sneezing while going to work would give bad results.

Remedies

1. Keep a black dog.
2. Keep a lead nail in your pocket.

3. Never harm ones brothers/sisters.

Rahu in 7th House

Native will be rich, but wife would suffer. He would be victorious over his enemies. If the marriage takes place before twenty one years, it would be inauspicious. He would have good relations with the government. But if he engages in business connected with Rahu, like electrical equipment's, then he will have losses. Native would suffer from headache and if Mercury, Venus or Ketu is in 11th house, then sister, wife or son would destroy the native.

Remedies

1. Never marry before 21st year of age.
2. Offer six coconuts in river.

Rahu in 8th House

8th house is concerned with Saturn and Mars. So Rahu in this house gives malefic effect. The native would spend money uselessly on court cases. Family life would be adversely affected. If Mars is benefice and is placed in 1st or 8th house or Saturn (benefic) is placed in 8th house, the native will be very rich.

Remedies

1. Keep a square piece of silver.
2. While sleeping Saunf should be keep under the pillow.
3. Do not work in electricity or power department.

Rahu in 9th House

9th house is influenced by Jupiter. If the native has good relation with ones brothers and sisters it is fruitful; else it would adversely affect the native. If the native is not religious minded then his progeny would be useless for him. Professions influenced by Saturn would be profitable.

If Jupiter is in 5th or 11th house then it is useless. If Rahu is inauspicious in 9th house then chances of begetting a son are less, especially if native files court cases against one's blood relation. Rahu is in 9th and 1st house is empty then health could be adversely affected and one gets insulted and mental problems, especially from older.

Remedies

1. Use Tilak of saffron daily.
2. Wear gold.
3. Always keep a dog (it saves ones progeny).
4. Have good relations with your in-laws.

Rahu in 10th House

Keeping one's head uncovered gives the effect of a debilitated Rahu in 10th house. The good or bad result of Rahu would depend upon Saturn's position. If Saturn is auspicious then native would be brave, long-lived and rich and get respect from all quarters. If Rahu in 10th house is with Moon it gives Raja Yoga. The native is lucky for one's father. If Rahu in 10th house is malefic then it would adversely affect ones mother or native's health would also be bad. If Moon is alone in 4th house then native's eyes are adversely affected. He suffers from headaches and there is loss of wealth, because of a dark complexioned person.

Remedies

1. Use blue or black cap.
2. Cover one's head.
3. Offer 4kg. Or 400 Gms of 'khand' in a temple, or in flowing water.
4. Feed blind people.

Rahu in 11th House

11th house is influenced by both Saturn and Jupiter. Native could be rich as long as his father is alive. Alternatively, establishing things of Jupiter would help. Native has wicked friends. He gets money from mean people. After the death of one's father he should wear gold in the neck. If Mars is malefic for a native with Rahu in 11th at time of his birth, there is everything in his house, but everything gets destroyed later. If Rahu in 11th house is malefic then the native has bad relations with his father or he may even kill him. Planet in 2nd house would act as enemy. If Jupiter/Saturn is in 3rd or 11th house then wear iron on the body and drink water in a silver glass. If ketu is in 5th house then Ketu gives bad results. There may be diseases of ear, spine, urinary problems etc. There may be losses associated with business concerned with Ketu.

Remedies

1. Wear iron. Use silver glass for drinking water.
2. Never take any electric equipment as a gift.

3. Do not keep blue sapphire, ivory or toys in the shape of an elephant.

Rahu in 12th House

12th house belongs to Jupiter. It signifies bedroom. Rahu here gives mental troubles, insomnia. It also leads to excessive expenditure on sisters and daughters. If Rahu is with its enemies then it becomes next to impossible to make ends meet, despite hard labour. It also leads to false allegations. One may even go to the extreme of contemplating suicide. One has mental worries. Telling lies, deceiving others etc. may make Rahu even more malefic. If somebody sneezes at the start of any new work if gives malefic effect. There may be theft, diseases or false allegations. If mars is with Rahu here, then it gives good results.

Remedies

1. Take your meals in the kitchen itself.
2. Keep Saunf and khand under the pillow for good night's sleep.

MICROSCOPY OF TRANSITING PLANETS SIMPLIFIED VOLUME-5

CHAPTER FIFTY

TRANSIT OF DRAGON'S TAIL

FROM OTHER PLANETS

Transit of Planet Dragon's Tail from First House of Natal Moon

This transit represents hopefulness, good will, and increased influence. The following are their transit effects as per your Moon Sign. Given here are the general effects as given in the astrology. However they can vary quite a bit based on your individual horoscope.

Transit of Dragon's Tail in the 1st house from Natal Moon

You can experience obsessive desires to uncover secrets, and levels of suspicion run high, as you may be living in fear that significant people in your life are not as attached to you as you are to them. Financially also this could prove to be a tricky time for some of you. Expenses may soar and saving money could be difficult for you. However, avoid taking any kind of loans during this time. Stay away from activities that might defame you in society. Health may suffer some setbacks especially during the fading moon period. You may be especially sociable, tolerant, and generous. Confidence comes from a stronger sense of who you are and the principles you represent. Maintain your calm of mind, as you are likely to be agitated, restless and develop mental affliction. You may even suffer from diseases related to your head. Avoid creating any unpleasant atmosphere at home and avoid arguments with your family members. You are also likely to get involved in fights with your family members during this time.

Transit of Dragon's Tail in the 2nd house from Natal Moon

You may resort to trickery, manipulation, or other such means to keep others dependent on you, or you could experience this through others and experience dominating or controlling behaviours in people close to you. This mostly signifies loss of wealth for you. Your expenses are likely to soar and there could also be a theft in your house. However, you must avoid taking loans during this period. During the period of Moon's waning, you may suffer from physical as well as mental ailments. Take care of your eyes as well. Try to stay away from probable fire accidents during this particular time. If married, you may get involved in a conflict with your spouse.

Transit of Dragon's Tail in the 3rd house from Natal Moon

This brings in happiness financial gains, progress prosperity and successful completion of your work in the projects handled by you. This is the time when you may expect. You would also be able to influence others at work or in the society. You can also expect to get the necessary cooperation of your colleagues and seniors at work. If this position occurs in waning period your business would require some extra attention. There are indications that it could be a good and satisfying period which would bring name and fame and respect for you in the society.

Learners and academic students would get opportunity to excel in their studies and quite a few would be getting additional mathematical knowledge during this transit. You may need to go on a voyage as this period brings in travel in its transit schedule. The direction would be towards the north eastern direction and if the travel plan happens to fall during the non-waxing or so called waning period of the moon, you may move ahead wandering the mountain areas and would also encounter some negative spirits.

Transit of Dragon's Tail in the 4th house from Natal Moon

Not a great day to make plans or decisions. It could be hard to figure out the right move. You may feel frustrated as to where you are headed in life just now. This denotes some troubled times for you. At work, you may have to put in extra effort to see success in your projects. Financially this may not be regarded as a smooth period. However, you must not opt for heavy loans during this time. Avoid any disputes or deals related to your landed property as you may lose the same. Your health would require proper attention as you may become susceptible to diseases. Stay out of the heat if possible during this time. Mentally you may feel restless and lacklustre constantly.

You may feel vague restlessness and discontent with life as it is. Consciously avoid the company of bad people as they might encourage you to indulge in unlawful deeds. You may also lose due to this bad company. Though travelling is on the cards, avoid travelling as much as possible as you may meet with an accident, which may destroy your vehicle as well. The period when the moon is fading you may go on a journey towards the mountains, which may not bring in the desired result. You may also have to take part in the funeral rituals of someone close.

Transit of Dragon's Tail in the 5th house from Natal Moon

You possess strong presence and generally feel confident about who you are and how others are receiving you now. This brings in significant ups and downs into your life. There could be, on one hand, unusual gain of money and excessive expenditure on the other. You may find it hard to stop unnecessary expenses especially if it is a period of the waning moon. These expenditures could be because of your children's mental agony. However, some of you may also expect sudden gain of money during this time. Avoid taking any loan at this time.

You may experience opposition to the way you present yourself. Someone could challenge your sense of identity. During the time of the waxing moon, you may have to go through a rough phase worrying about the health of your children. Do not neglect any physical complaint of your child, as it could also become life risking one. Death of a family member or relative may also happen during this time. Avoid being caught in tricky situations with your relatives. Maintain a cordial relationship with your family and relatives, as there is a chance of them becoming your enemies. Keep your spirits high as due to unsuccessful or suspended endeavours, you are likely to suffer from deep mental anguish during this particular phase.

Transit of Dragon's Tail in the 6th house from Natal Moon

There may be some friction and adjustments needed. It is your choice whether you want to compromise or go solo, but including the other makes for a fuller picture. This denotes good times for you. If you are into business, you are likely to progress in the same and you may also consider improving the same. Those who are involved in agriculture and cattle rearing may expect considerable profit in their respective field of work. Financially you would be sound. You may also gain from lending money to others. Moreover, you would also be able to influence the people from whom you may also expect profit. You are also likely to defeat your opponents and gain over them.

However, your health may need your focused attention during this time. You tend to feel that your personality lacks any vitality. An authority figure could be hard to connect with now. Attend to any physical complaint immediately as you are likely to develop diseases of chronic nature. At home, you may enjoy great times entertaining and being pampered. Some auspicious event like a marriage may commence at your residence or you may even go on family picnics. You would be at peace with yourself and your surroundings during this time.

Transit of Dragon's Tail in the 7th house from Natal Moon.

This mostly brings in personal sufferings for you. You possess strong presence and generally feel confident about who you are and how others are receiving you now. Your health may require utmost care, as you are likely to suffer from many diseases primarily related to the stomach. You may also feel lacklustre and fatigued. Mentally also you may feel sick and agonized. Keep an eye on your expenses, as you are likely to spend your money on useless heads. Avoid borrowing at any cost. If you are into agricultural production, keep an eye on your products, as there could be a theft of the same.

Maintain proper code of conduct and avoid getting involved in any argument with your spouse. You may lack any real sense of yourself today, or be unable to communicate or convey your ideas. Any fight with your spouse may make your spouse leave you during this time. Establish a cordial relationship with your relatives who may become your enemies if not attended to correctly. Avoid all kinds of disputes and litigations during this time. You would also need to hold on to your reputation as it could be hampered and you may be defamed in the society. Travel is also on the cards.

Transit of Dragon's Tail in the 8th house from Natal Moon

This mostly signifies physical suffering for you. Feeling slighted, overlooked, or misunderstood could lead you to seek out attention now. Take care of your health during this time and avoid risking your life in every way possible. You are susceptible to developing various diseases during this time. Fever, body pain and diseases of the reproductive systems may make you experience pain during this phase. Mentally you may feel drained out.

You could have problems relating to superiors, and your vitality may be on the low side. A happening in your place of residence may bring in grief during this time. Watch out your expenses and save for the unforeseen expenses. Try and keep yourself away from illicit practices, which may lead to prosecution. You may also be defamed in the society due to your own misdeeds. However, during the waxing moon, some of you may expect some good time and may also experience a new more zestful life. Your interest in food, and spiritual activities is also likely to rise during this time.

Transit of Dragon's Tail in the 9th house from Natal Moon

During this period, Ketu will move through your ninth house from the Moon. Everything seems to be working together, and you may find yourself expressive and able to communicate well. This signifies, apart from other effects, few minor physical complications and development of mental qualms. Your finances would require careful handling, as most of you are likely to invest your hard earned money in lottery and other speculations. Hold tight to your finances, as you may have to embrace poverty during this particular phase. Most of you are also likely to get involved in some illicit activities, which is unacceptable in your religion.

You possess strong presence and generally feel confident about who you are and how others are receiving you now. There could be a mutual lack of appreciation. Differences in values or ways of expressing affection in your personal relationships are made very noticeable to you now. During the waning moon period, some of you may experience loss due to enemies or rivals in your trade.

Transit of Dragon's Tail in the 10th house from Natal Moon

You may experience opposition to the way you present yourself. Someone could challenge your sense of identity. This brings in mixed results which also depend on the waxing and waning of the moon. During the waxing moon period, your income may rise with the help of some otherwise depraved people. You may also expect to progress in your field of work and gain further monetary gain during this time. However, during the waning moon period, most of you may face loss of money as well as material riches due to some wrong company. You are also likely to suffer from mental agony, which could also be due to loss in trade or lack of progress in your field of work.

Expect significant encounters, meeting individuals who are or will be important players, at least for the moment. Generally, this position of Ketu signifies an increase in your enemy and health problem of your parents. There could also be some function at your place of residence during this period. Some of you may also experience sudden rise in profit in your field of work. You may also look forward to a rise in position in your profession, which would bring in more responsibility as well as respect to you.

Transit of Dragon's Tail in the 11th house from Natal Moon

A vital period with much energy and lots of action. You may feel very focused and even a bit radiant. During this period, Ketu will move through your eleventh house from the Moon. This generally signifies attainment of wealth and acquisition of landed property. This is also a good time to accomplish your ambitions. You are likely to start some new project that would require a big investment promising you the same or more profit in return. There could also be certain sudden gain of money for most of you. At home, your children of marriageable age may find their perfect match and decide on marriage.

This transit sometimes brings recognition for a personal achievement. Whether or not this occurs, you radiate strength and have increased personal presence now. During the time when the moon grows in size, some of you may have the opportunity to meet some spiritual guru. . This period may also bring you good fortune and exotic dairy food. However, if this position of Ketu happens to fall during the waning period of moon, you are likely to develop a feeling of lack lustre and sickness in your mind. This period may also see you developing interest in agriculture. Your enmity with your own family may arise and you may also incur loss in business during this period.

Transit of Dragon's Tail in the 12th house from Natal Moon

Everything seems to be working together, and you may find yourself expressive and able to communicate well. This signifies a bumpy time for you. Your health would require extra attention during this time as you are likely to develop certain bile related diseases. You are also likely to develop piles during this period. Health of your spouse may also become a matter of concern. Due to physical ailments of the couple, conjugal life may also suffer. You should watch that you don't come on too strong today and attract conflict with others. Feeling slighted, overlooked, or misunderstood could lead you to seek out attention now.

Take care of your finances and keep an eye on your expenditures. Avoid taking any loan during this particular time. Keep yourself away from all kinds of litigations as the judgment may go against you and you may even be imprisoned. You are also likely to face humiliation and defamation during this phase. Try and develop a good rapport with your near and dear ones to retain their support towards you. However, some of you may experience happiness and comfort due to the waning moon if applicable. Though inflow of money would be limited; some of you may also expect to travel to foreign land during this period of time.

MICROSCOPY OF TRANSITING PLANETS SIMPLIFIED VOLUME-5

CHAPTER FIFTY ONE

TRANSITING KETU

Planets in Different HOUSES DRAGON'S TAIL (KETU)

In the first house. – Emaciated figure, weak constitution, much perspiration, weak-hearted, slender, piles, and sexual indulgence, diplomatic.

Second house. – Bad speaker, quiet, quick in perception, peevish, hard-hearted, thrifty and economical.

Third house. – Adventurous, strong, artistic, wealthy, popular.

Fourth house. – Quarrelsome, licentious, weak, fear of poisons.

Fifth house. – Liberal, loss of children, sinful, immoral if afflicted.

Sixth house. – Fond of adultery, good conversationalist, licentious, venereal complaints, learned.

Seventh house. – Passionate, sinful, connections with widows, sickly wife.

Eighth house. – Senseless, obscure, dull, sanguine complexion, piles and similar troubles.

Ninth house. – Short-sighted, sinful, untruthful, thrifty, many children, good wife.

Tenth house. – Fertile brain, happy, religious, pilgrimages to sacred rivers and places, fond of scriptures.

Eleventh house. – Humorous, witty, licentious, intelligent, wealthy.

Twelfth house. – Capricious, unsettled mind, foreign residence, attracted to servile classes, much travelling, licentious, spiritual knowledge

MICROSCOPY OF TRANSITING PLANETS SIMPLIFIED VOLUME-5

CHAPTER FIFTY TWO

REMEDIES OF PLANETS

Effects and Remedies

KETU (DRAGON'S TAIL)

Ketu represents son, grandson, ear, spine etc. 6th house is considered to be its SOLID HOUSE It gives its exalted effect when in 5th, 9th or 12th house and its debilitated effect in 6th and 8th house. Dawn is its time and it represents Sunday. Ketu represents the opposite node of Ketu, in the tail of the serpent. Its colours are black and white. Venus and Rahu are its friends, whereas Moon and Mars are its enemies. Forty-two years is the age of Ketu. Ketu is also considered to be the bed. So the bed given by in-laws after marriage is considered to be auspicious for the birth of a son and as long as that bed is in the house, the effect of Ketu can never be inauspicious.

Ketu in 1st House

If Ketu is auspicious or benefic in this house, the native will be laborious, rich and happy, but will always be concerned and troubled because of his progeny. He may fear frequent transfers or travels, but ultimately it would always be postponed.

Whenever Ketu comes in 1st house in Varsha Kundli there may be birth of a son or nephew. There may also be a long journey. The native with Ketu in 1st house will always be beneficial for his father and/or guru and causes exaltation of Sun.

If ketu in 1st house is malefic, the native would suffer from headache. His wife would have health problems and would have worries concerning kids. If 2nd and 7th houses are empty then Mercury and Venus would also give bad results. There would be travels, transfers with no gain. If Saturn is malefic it would destroy father and guru.

If Sun is in 7th or 8th house then after the birth of a grandson the health would suffer. No alms should be given in morning and evening.

Remedies

1. Feed jaggery (gur) to monkeys.
2. Apply saffron as Tilak.
3. If offspring is troubled then donate a black and white Blanket to temple.

Ketu in 2nd House

2nd house is affected by Moon, which is an enemy of Ketu. If Ketu in 2nd house is benefice then one gets paternal property. One has to travel a lot and his travels are fruitful. Venus gives good results, irrespective of its position. Moon would give bad results. If Sun is in 12th house then one starts earning his livelihood after twenty-four years and is happy. If Jupiter is exalted along with Ketu in 2nd house, then income would be in lacs of rupees. If Ketu in 2nd house is malefic, then one has to travel to dry areas. One cannot rest at one place and would be wandering from place to place. Income may be good, but so would be the expenditure. Thus net gain would be negligible. If there is Moon or Mars in 8th house then native's life would be short and he would have serious problem at the age of sixteen or twenty years. If 8th house is empty then Ketu would give malefic results.

Remedies

1. Apply turmeric or saffron as tilak.
2. One should not be of loose character.
3. If one religiously visits temples and bows his head there
 then Ketu in 2nd house would give good results.

Ketu in 3rd House

3rd house is affected by Mercury and Mars, both enemies of Ketu. Number 3 would have an important role in the life of the native. If Ketu in 3rd house were benefic then his children would be good. The native would be god fearing and a gentleman. If Ketu is in 3rd house and Mars is in 12th then the native has a son before 24th year of age. The son would be good for wealth and longevity of the native. The native with Ketu in 3rd house usually gets a job, which entails long travels.

If Ketu in 3rd house is malefic then native loses money in litigation. He gets separated from his wife/sisters-in-law. If such a native lives in a house with its main gate facing south, he will have serious problems regarding children. Such a native cannot say no to anything and so will always have worries. He will have troubles from his brothers and will have to travel uselessly.

Remedies

1. Use saffron as tilak.
2. Wear gold.
3. Offer jaggery, rice in flowing water.

Ketu in 4th house

4th house belongs to Moon, which is an enemy of Ketu. If Ketu is benefic in 4th house then the native is god fearing and lucky for his father and guru. Son is born to such a native only after getting the blessings of one's guru. The son born lives long. Such a native leaves all his decisions to God. If moon is in 3rd or 4th house the result is benefic. Such a native is a good adviser and will never have shortage of money. If Ketu is malefic in this house then the native is unhealthy, his mother is troubled, there is loss of happiness. One may suffer from diabetes. A son is born after thirty six years of age. Such a native has more daughters than sons.

Remedies

1. Keep a dog.
2. Wear silver for peace of mind.
3. Offer yellow things in flowing water.

Ketu in 5th House

5th house belongs to Sun. It is also affected by Jupiter. If Jupiter, Sun or Moon is in 4th, 6th or 12th house then one's financial condition will be excellent and the native will have five sons. Ketu becomes benefic by itself after twenty four years of age. If Ketu in 5th house is malefic then the native suffers from asthma. Ketu gives malefic results till five years of age. Sons will not survive.

Livelihood starts after twenty four years of age. The native is unlucky for ones sons.

Remedies

1. Donate milk and sugar.
2. The remedies of Jupiter would be useful.

Ketu in 6th House

6th house belongs to Mercury. Ketu in 6th house is considered debilitated. This is 'Pucca' house of Ketu. Here again the effect of Ketu depends upon the nature of Jupiter. It gives good result regarding son. The native is a good adviser.

If Jupiter is benefic then the native has a long life and his mother is happy and the life is peaceful. If any two of the male planets viz Sun, Jupiter, Mars are in good position then Ketu is benefic.

If Ketu is malefic in 6th house then maternal uncle suffers. The native has to suffer due to useless travels. People turn into enemies without any reason. The native suffers from skin diseases. If Moon is in 2nd house then mother suffers and even the native's old age is troubled.

Remedies

1. Wear golden ring in the finger of left hand.
2. Drink milk with saffron and wear gold in the ear.
3. Heat up a rod of gold and then dip it in milk. Then drink it. It would restore mental peace, increase longevity and is good for sons.
4. Keep a dog.

Ketu in 7th House

7th house belongs to Mercury and Venus. If Ketu in 7th house is benefice then the native gets the wealth of forty years in twenty-four years of age. The wealth increases in proportion to the children one has. The native's enemies are frightened of the native. If one has the help of Mercury, Jupiter or Venus then the native is never disappointed.

If Ketu in 7th house is malefic then the native is usually ill, makes false promises and is troubled by enemies till thirty-four years of age. If there is more than one planet in Lagna then ones children are destroyed. If one abuses then the native is destroyed. If Ketu is with Mercury then after thirty-four years of age the native's enemies are destroyed by themselves.

Remedies

1. Never make a false promise, be proud, or abusive.
2. Use saffron as Tilak.
3. In case of serious trouble use the remedies of Jupiter.

Ketu in 8th house

8th house belongs to Mars, which is an enemy of Ketu. If Ketu in 8th house is benefic then the native begets a son at thirty-four years of age, or after the marriage of ones sister or daughter. If Jupiter or Mars are not in 6th and 12th house then Ketu does not give malefic results. Similar effect is there when Moon is in 2nd house. If Ketu in 8th house is malefic then the native's wife has ill health. Son will not be born, or may die. The native may suffer from diabetes or urinary problem. If Saturn or Mars are in 7th then the native is unlucky. In case of malefic Ketu in 8th house the native's character determines the health of his wife. After twenty-six years of age the family life suffers.

Remedies

1. Keep a dog.
2. Donate a black and white blanket in any temple.
3. Worship lord Ganesha.
4. Wear gold in the ear.
5. Use saffron as tilak.

Ketu in 9th House

9th house belongs to Jupiter, which favours Ketu. Ketu in 9th house is considered to be exalted. Such a native is obedient and lucky. It increases ones wealth. If Ketu is benefic then one earns wealth through ones own labour. There will be progress but no transfer. If one keeps gold brick in his house then wealth comes. The son of such a native is able to guess the future. One spends a big part of his life in foreign land. One has at least three sons and if 2nd house is auspicious then Ketu gives excellent results. If Moon is auspicious then the native helps his mother's family. If Ketu in 9th house is malefic then the native suffers from urinary problems, pain in back, and problem in legs. The native's sons keep on dying.

Remedies

1. Keep a dog.
2. Establish a rectangular piece of gold in the house.
3. Wear gold in the ear.
4. Respect elders, especially father- in- law.

Ketu in 10th house.

10th house belongs to Saturn. The effect of Ketu here depends upon the nature of Saturn. If Ketu is benefice here then the native is lucky, concerned about himself and opportunist. His father dies early. If Saturn is in 6th then one is a famous player. If one keeps on forgiving his brothers for their misdeeds the native will go on progressing. If the character of native is good then he earns a lot of wealth. If Ketu in 10th house is malefic then one suffers from urinary and ear problems. The native has pain in bones. The domestic life is full of worries and troubled if Saturn is in 4th house. Three sons would die.

Remedies

1. Keep silver pot full of honey in the house.
2. Keep a dog, especially after forty-eight years of age.
3. Avoid adultery.
4. Use the remedies of Moon and Jupiter.

Ketu in 11th House

Here Ketu is considered very good. It gives wealth. This house is affected by Jupiter and Saturn. If Ketu is benefic here and Saturn is in 3rd house, it gives enormous wealth. The wealth earned by the native is more than his paternal wealth, but one tends to worry about his future. If Mercury is in 3rd it leads to Raj Yoga. If Ketu is malefic here then the native has problem in his abdomen. The more he worries about future, more troubled he is. Grandmother or mother of the native suffers, if Saturn is also malefic. Then there would be no benefit from son or house.

Remedies

1. Keep black dog.
2. Wear an onyx or emerald.

Ketu in 12th House

Here Ketu is considered to be exalted. The native is wealthy, achieves a big position and spends on good works. If Rahu is in 6th house, along with Mercury, then the effect is even better. One has all the benefits and luxuries of life. If Ketu in 12th house is malefic then one buys land from an issueless person and the native becomes issueless himself. If one kills dogs Ketu gives malefic results. If 2nd house has Moon, Venus or Mars, Ketu gives malefic results.

Remedies

1. Worship Lord Ganesha.
2. Do not have a loose character.
3. Keep a dog.
4. Saunf and khand under the pillow for good night's sleep.

………THE END………..

OUR OTHER PUBLICATIONS

1. "MICROSCOPY OF ASTROLOGY"

2. "MICROSCOPY OF NUMEROLOGY"

3. "MICROSCOPY OF REMEDIES"

4. "MICROSCOPY OF HAPPY LIVING"

5 ."MICROSCOPY OF TRANSITING PLANETS VOL-1

6 ."MICROSCOPY OF TRANSITING PLANETS VOL-2

7 ."MICROSCOPY OF TRANSITING PLANETS VOL-3

8 ."MICROSCOPY OF TRANSITING PLANETS VOL-4

9 " MICROSCOPY OF TRANSITING PLANETS VOL-5

ORDERS FOR BOOKS CAN BE PLACED AT:

orders.india@partridgepublishing.com

channelsales@authorsolutions.com

HTTP://WWW.AMAZON.COM

HTTP://WWW.AMAZON.IN

HTTP://WWW.FLIPKART.COM

http://www.barnesandnoble.com

http://www.notionpress.com/store

AND AT OUR CONTACT ADDRESS:

PLEASE SEND YOUR QUERIES TO:

BALDEV BHATIA

CONSULTANT-

NUMEROLOGY-ASTROLOGY

C-63, FIRST FLOOR MALVIYA NAGAR

NEW DELHI-110017 INDIA

EMAIL: baldevbhatia@yahoo.com

TEL NO 91 9810075249

TEL NO 91 11 26686856

TEL NO 91 7503280786

TEL NO 91 7702735880

MOST SOUGHT WEB SITES:

HTTP://WWW.ASTROLOGYBB.COM

HTTP://WWW.BBASTROLOGY.COM

HTTP://WWW.BALDEVBHATIA.COM

HTTP://WWW.BALDEVBHATIA.US

HTTP://WWW.BALDEVBHATIA.ORG

HTTP://WWW.BALDEVBHATIA.INFO

HTTP://WWW.BALDEVBHATIA.NET

HTTP://WWW.BALDEVBHATIA.BIZ

HTTP://WWW.BALDEVBHATIA.IN

HTTP://WWW.MICROSCOPYOFASTROLOGY.COM

HTTP://WWW.MICROSCOPYOFTRANSITINGPLANETS.COM

SPECIAL NOTE

FROM THE AUTHOR "BALDEV BHATIA"

THANK YOU FOR READING MY BOOK

MY SINCERE PRAYERS

FOR ALL MY READERS

"GOD BLESS YOU ALL"

"ANY ONE WHO READS AND KEEPS THIS BOOK AS HOLY MANUSCRIPT, GOD IS SURE TO BLESS HIM, WITH ALL THE PEACE, HAPPINESS, WEALTH, HEALTH AND PROSPERITY OF THIS UNIVERSE"

.................HAPPY READING...................